La Familia

A family working to grow corn in Sancayani, Bolivia

La Familia

An International Love Story

Mary Martin

Mano a Mano International • St. Paul, Minnesota • 2016

On the Cover
The dedication of a Mano a Mano clinic in Chiro K'asa, Bolivia.
U.S. volunteers and donors including several Rotarians
took part in the community celebration.

Illustration Sources
All illustrations are from the collection of the Velásquez family, by Margi
Singher and Bob Lundgren, or from Mano a Mano.
All are used by permission.

Developmental Editing
Mary Ann Nord, Minneapolis

Editing, Design, Production
E. B. Green Editorial, St. Paul, Minnesota

Indexing
Patricia Green, Homer, Alaska

Printing and Binding
BooksOnDemand.com, Stoughton, Wisconsin

© 2016 by Mano a Mano International
925 Pierce Butler Route
St. Paul, MN 55104
(651) 457-3141
manoamano@manoamano.org
All rights reserved.

Library of Congress Control Number: 2015920174
ISBN: 978-0-578-17421-1
Manufactured in the United States of America
10 9 8 7 6 5 4 3 2 1

Mano a Mano USA is known variously as Mano a Mano,
Mano a Mano International, or Mano Mano International Partners.
All proceeds from the sale of this book go directly to
Mano a Mano International.

To Fred

Hand in hand—the United States and Bolivia

Contents

Preface	viii
Introduction	3
Part I: Roots	
1. At Hacienda Candelaria	7
2. Beyond the Hacienda	25
3. From Minnesota	39
Part II: Connecting	
4. Cochabamba and St. Paul	59
5. International Family	81
Part III: Realizing the Dream	
6. A Small Group . . .	107
7. Serendipity	139
Part IV: Sister Organizations	
8. Beyond Clinics	169
9. Apoyo Aéreo	179
10. Nuevo Mundo	199
Part V: Water Is Life	
11. Atajados for Omereque	219
12. Four Men on a Mountain	229
Part VI: Twenty Years	
13. In Good Hands	245
14. The Work Continues	261
Afterword: Hacienda Revisited	277
Appendix A: The Mano a Mano Model	287
Appendix B: Mano a Mano Sister Organizations	288
Notes	289
Glossary	292
Index	295
About the Author	300

Preface

I am grateful to my husband, Fred Smith, for walking patiently and lovingly beside me through the long trek to completion of this book. With nearly equal gratitude, I thank Joan and Segundo Velásquez, admired companions who have shared with me their story of Mano a Mano through the years.

When Joan and I were in graduate school, we often lunched at El Amanecer, a Mexican restaurant on the West Side of St. Paul, Minnesota. The name and place of the restaurant has changed several times, but our lunches continue. We talk about our mutual obsession with issues of race and culture and our complicated personal lives—marriage, divorce, children, and grandchildren.

Very early our conversation veered southward to Latin America, a part of the world to which we both are drawn. The cross-cultural story of the Bolivian family Joan married into became even more intriguing as Mano a Mano emerged. After hearing a particularly good tale of U.S./Bolivian cultural complication and resolution within the Velásquez family and/or Mano a Mano, I often said, "We have got to tell this story!"

I sensed something unique in the international Velásquez family, in the bicultural relationship of Joan and Segundo, and in the collective ethos of Bolivia. It is a complex phenomenon, deserving examination and understanding.

Joan began work on a textbook on the policy and organizational structure of Mano a Mano as a replicable model of development; Beaver's Pond Press published that fine work—*Gaining Ground: A Blueprint for Community-Based International Development*—in 2014. But we kept talking about the story behind the organization, agreeing that the deeply personal and culturally rich story of the Bolivian and U.S. Velásquezes and their Quechua sisters and brothers must be shared.

After I retired from teaching, I missed doing qualitative research and I decided this was a story I wanted to understand and tell. I would approach it the way I have always conducted research—by listening to people, by immersion. Beginning in 2010, I interviewed individuals from Bolivia and the United States and interacted with many groups in both countries—from the members of the board of directors of Mano a Mano Apoyo Aéreo to the Mano a Mano staff and government officials, to more than 50 Quechua leaders and residents of Punata about their need for water. In the United States I attended Mano a Mano meetings, volunteer celebrations, and galas. I read innumerable written and electronic Mano a Mano documents and talked informally with staff members and volunteers.

There is no way to measure what I have learned from my encounters in St. Paul, such as when Mano a Mano volunteers mourned the loss of one of their favorite benefactors in Joan and Segundo's backyard. Or from those in Cochabamba and larger Bolivia, where the Velásquez family and members of the Mano a Mano staff embraced me and shared meals at the family table, in a tiny mountain village, and in the back seat of an SUV, with Segundo's mother, Inés, holding my hand. Neither is it possible to count the hours I have interviewed Joan

Preface

and Segundo, together and separately in their home, in restaurants, over the phone, and at our cabin in the north woods.

I have completed this story with the help of many—those willing to talk with me, those allowing me to sit in their meetings and events, those reading my story and providing helpful suggestions—in addition to my husband Fred, my friend and colleague Marilyn Vigil, and again Segundo and Joan.

My editors were invaluable: Mary Ann Nord made suggestions that enabled me to move from my early, inchoate efforts to make sense of what I had learned during several years of listening and writing. Then there was Ellen Green, patiently cleaning and clearing up the manuscript in straightforward but remarkable ways. Thanks to her editing and consultation, I have come to like the telling of the story again.

As to the mechanics of this work, I have changed a few personal names as well as the name of the hospital/clinic that José Velásquez once led. Also, I have come to recognize Mano a Mano as a trilingual, tri-cultural organization that necessarily speaks Quechua, Spanish, and English. Retaining much of the Spanish nomenclature and a bit of Quechua in this book is an admittedly inadequate, but to me important, way of honoring its multicultural, multinational nature. Thus, the first time a Spanish or Quechua word is used, its translation to English follows. The glossary enables readers to find the translation of any Spanish word they encounter after its first use.

I want the readers of this book to know that people thousands of miles apart can work together to bring some little balance to the disturbingly huge differences among us. I am convinced as I follow Mano a Mano's evolution that the resources of the materially wealthy United States, made available to Bolivians working with one another, increase their capacity to develop solutions to the fundamental inequities in their health and well-being.

La Familia

Joan Swanson White in Cochabamba, Bolivia, 1967

Introduction

One day in the fall of 1967, Segundo Velásquez watched a tiny, fair-skinned young woman struggle to carry a tin bucket, full of water, down a dirt road on the outskirts of Cochabamba, Bolivia. Like any well-mannered young man, he caught up with the woman and, though she was a stranger, took her heavy bucket.

For the slender Segundo to intervene when someone needed help was typical. But for Joan Swanson White to accept such help was not. With quiet but fierce self-sufficiency, the young woman from the United States struggled with the effects of childhood polio, pushing herself beyond capacity. One of her arms was nearly useless. Segundo assessed the situation and moved in to help.

That first brief encounter over a bucket of water was the beginning of a deep and lasting connection, a chance meeting that grew into a complex, shared struggle to bring U.S. resources to bear on the profound needs of rural Bolivia.

Their story is one of challenges beginning in childhood, intercultural pitfalls, and ultimately the creation of grassroots international partnership at its best.

I

Roots

Epifanio Velásquez married Inés Irusta at Candelaria, 1945.

1

At Hacienda Candelaria

1911–1956

As a youngster, Segundo Velásquez lived at Hacienda Candelaria, where he was born in 1951. He was the third child and second son of Epifanio and Inés Irusta Velásquez, who first lived and worked in the second and then in the third patio of the big Bolivian *hacienda* (land holding), in the center of a wide valley in rural Cochabamba. Fields of corn, alfalfa, and wheat spread to the distant mountains. Open pastures of grazing cattle extended from a big barn with modern farm machinery parked alongside.

A tall narrow building nearby housed the doves that the *patrona* (female owner) of the hacienda favored for dinner. A small stone chapel stood close to a formal wall; flowering branches spilled over it to the ground. The chapel, wall, and house were painted a soft rosy beige. A wooden door stood beside an ornate gate in the wall, each opening onto the patio with a huge olive tree in the center of a lush garden.

Hacienda Candelaria was typical of the many structured institutions created by the Spaniards after their 16th-century conquest of much of Latin America. The hacienda had flourished for hundreds of years through the use of indigenous *pongueaje* (indentured servants) working under contracts often resulting in lifelong servitude. Pongueaje still counted among the dozens of *trabajadores* (workers) at the hacienda when Segundo was a youngster. Some worked in the fields alongside salaried peasants using new mechanical processes. Some worked within the walls of the colonial-style hacienda, within the walls of the three adjoining spaces that characterized its hierarchal structure.

The "first patio," with tree and gardens, was the home of Patrona Elena Urey, the *hacendada* (female owner of the hacienda) who had taken control of the hacienda for the Urey family after her parents' deaths. Twenty wide steps rose from the first-floor patio to the private upper rooms of the hacendados. Patrona Urey could lean over the railing of the *balcón* (balcony) and look through the gray-green leaves of the spreading olive tree to the formal garden below. Hers was a calm and contained view, seldom shared by anyone outside her family. The Ureys rarely ventured beyond their lush patio.

Opposite the formal entrance to the hacienda was an unobtrusive wooden door, opening onto a second patio. The hacendados rarely passed through it, but it was a mysterious and exciting place for the Velásquez children. Occasionally Segundo tagged along with his older siblings, Ivo and Cati, as they slipped past their mother's *pollera* (traditional skirts) and through the wooden doorway to play in the first patio. Inés went back and forth between the patios to serve the hacendados. The three curious children never got far before hearing their mother's voice—*"Niños, fuera de aqui!* [Children, out of here!]"— shooing them back to the second patio.

To pass from the first patio to the second was to enter a different world. On one side of the door was a bare, unadorned space; no trees or flowers were planted there. The only building other than several storehouses was a small, freestanding adobe house with a single door and no window, the first home of Segundo's parents after they married in 1948. Theirs were the hacienda's preferred peasant family, the one meeting the personal needs of the hacendados.

The Velásquezes also had free access to a rougher entrance to the third patio, on the far side of the second. This door was wide enough for trucks and wagons to bring supplies into the storerooms in the second patio. It also opened onto the third patio, as plain as the second but less orderly. Segundo and Ivo found many playmates there. Their friends' parents were the trabajadores, Candelaria's less preferred field and house servants, many of them pongueaje. None of the children running around the second and third patios was aware of a world beyond the three distinct spaces within Candelaria. They had little exposure to the harsh life of poverty or the unrelenting work that characterized the lives of many of their Quechua relatives in the valley.

The Velásquez family was in a middle place—its status was clearly below that of the Urey hacendados in the first patio but above that of the peasants in the third. The adults of the family were not among the overseers or managers typically standing between the workers and the patrón. Neither were they pongueaje. Epifanio Velásquez worked in the fields and was the hacienda's carpenter, but his wife, Inés, placed the family solidly in the middle. Her considerable household skills tied her to the hacienda. She also had a deep though unacknowledged connection to the Urey family.

Acensia: The Unacknowledged Connection
Forty years before Segundo's birth, his beloved *mamanchaj* (grandmother) Acensia Irusta, his mother's mother, was the first of the family to step through Hacienda Candelaria's gate. During her teens, Acensia had lived in Laguna Sulti, a tiny village two miles from Candelaria. An "illegitimate" child herself, Acensia gave birth to a daughter, Juanita, without knowing the child's father. She had been accosted in the dark while living as a maid with relatives who sold *chicha*, a homebrew made from fermented corn.

Acensia's relatives sent her away from their chicheria when she became pregnant. She found menial jobs, providing just enough money to pay for a room and food to enable her to nurse her baby. Little Juanita was several months old when Acensia learned in the market what all of Laguna Sulti was talking about. The wife of Patrón Urey of Hacienda Candelaria had died in childbirth.

The patrón called his newborn Alonzo. Little Alonzo had survived his mother's death but needed milk. The patrón decreed that a wet nurse be found. Candelaria's *capataz* (overseer) knew of a single nursing mother named Acensia living alone in the village. He found her in her tiny room in Laguna Sulti and pressed her to come to Candelaria: "Patrón Urey insists that you come!"

Denying the patrón, the most powerful person in the valley, was not easy. And Acensia had no solid way to earn a living for herself and her baby. So she bargained with the capataz: "If the patrón gives me enough corn to barter for what I need for my baby and myself, I will come to Candelaria to nurse his baby."

Alonzo was a hungry infant, and soon Acensia was going from Laguna Sulti to the hacienda several times a day. The widowed patrón, Rosendo Urey, was pleased with her, and after a few weeks he said, "You are coming many times a day. You and your child should come to live at Candelaria. That way it will be easier for you to nurse both your baby and Alonzo." Acensia knew she probably would be taking care of the newborn baby and other Urey children, but her life in Laguna Sulti was hard. And she worried for her baby Juanita when she was gone. She agreed to move to Candelaria.

Acensia nursed the motherless Alonzo along with her own child as she tried to keep track of the older Urey children. Soon after she settled into her life in the hacienda, the patrón took advantage of her presence there. Acensia continued her work at Candelaria until she gave birth to the patrón's son, whom she called Luciano. Now she had three babies: Juanita, Alonzo, and Luciano.

One day when Luciano was only weeks old, Acensia sat nursing him in the hacienda *cocina* (kitchen) as Juanita and Alonzo played around her pollera. An old pongueaje women sitting beside them whispered, "You know this will not be your only child by the patrón. He will *cargarte con hijos* [burden you with more children] if you stay here."

Realizing that well could be the case, Acensia made a plan to leave Candelaria. She was reluctant to leave the Urey children, especially Alonzo, whom she had been nursing for a year. Still, she bundled up her own two and snuck away. She traveled the hundred miles to Uyuni, where some relatives found her a place to live with Juanita and Luciano. Again she struggled to feed herself and Juanita—and now Luciano too.

Back at the hacienda, Alonzo—the patrón's baby—died. The whole hacienda watched as the patrón grieved his loss. Even the villagers knew of his despondence: His wife had died while giving birth, and now the child was dead too. The woman who had nursed the patrón's son and cared for all his children was gone, and he wanted her back.

When the patrón learned that Acensia had fled to Uyuni with Juanita and Luciano, he sent his capataz to demand her return. With trepidation, Acensia heard the capataz's words: "If you don't bring the patrón's child back, he will come on his horse to get both the baby and you. He will tie your hair to the strappings of his horse and drag you to Calendaria."

Acensia understood that Patrón Urey was a powerful man. She feared he would do exactly as the capataz had said. She gathered up Juanita and Luciano and returned to the hacienda to bargain with the patrón at Candelaria. She insisted that the patrón allow Juanita, as well as their son, Luciano, to live with her in the second patio. He agreed.

Acensia found the hacienda in turmoil and so took on the care of the patrón and his children. Slowly she began to move between the third and first patios, caring for her offspring and the older Urey children. As foretold by the old pongueaje in the cocina, the patrón continued to use her for his own purposes. When she realized she was pregnant again, she decided to await the birth of her child at the hacienda but to draw no attention to herself. She remained in the second patio with

Acensia Irusta—Mamanchaj—in her later years

her three small children. She was afraid of the patrón's response should she flee again. And she was captive to her responsibility for Juanita, Luciano, and the child she was carrying.

Acensia gave birth to a girl she called Inés—then ran away to Laguna Sulti. The patrón came to Laguna to visit Luciano and Inés, but Acensia refused to be present while he was there. Not long afterwards, Patrón Urey committed suicide. Acensia was as shocked as everyone in Candelaria. The man who had earlier insisted on her return—and the reasons he chose to die by his own hand—were buried in a small plot next to the little chapel beside the wall around Candelaria.

Acensia Irusta finally was free of the patrón, but in Laguna Sulti she struggled to build a life for her son, Luciano, and her daughters, Juanita and Inés. They were poor, but Acensia bartered her cooking skills with the wealthy for the potatoes and corn she needed for food. Daughter Juanita was soon old enough to help her mother in the cocina, and Acensia started a garden that earned enough money to pay the rent. Inés, Acensia's child by the dead patrón, grew into a strong, competent girl able to tend her own sheep at age 12.

After years of selling his labor to farmers in the area, Luciano was able to buy a cow. Eventually he was conscripted for military service. He went off to war, leaving the cow for his mother and sisters with instructions to buy a tiny house. He even arranged a loan from a neighbor to make the purchase possible. Luciano never returned—he was wounded in the war and died from an infection. Acensia and her daughters grieved his loss.

The little family struggled to pay back the neighbor who held the loan on their house. They used most of the cow's milk at home but managed to make a little cheese for sale and barter. Inés and Juanita brought their products to the market, where Inés was attracted to the women who sold the *blusas bordadas* (embroidered blouses) they made. Recognizing that she could embroider in the evenings to augment their income, she seized the opportunity, trading cheese for fabric, needles, and thread. She watched the women at the market at their work and asked their advice. Eventually she became an accomplished seamstress.

Juanita—the oldest of Acensia's girls—was the first to leave their tiny adobe house. She married Juandelo Montaño, a young man who also lived in Laguna Sulti. The young couple lived next door to her mother and sister and so was in touch with Acensia and Inés every day. Through much hard work, the mother and daughter finally paid off the loan on their house.

Returning to Candelaria

After Juanita's marriage, Acensia began to worry about the future of her youngest daughter. She realized that given her staunch independence and tendency to go her own way, Inés was unlikely to make an early marriage as her more amenable older sister had done. Acensia wondered whether they should go back to Hacienda Candelaria, where Inés was conceived and born. Despite its beauty, she did not relish going back to a place that had been so harsh.

But Acensia was looking for ways to ease Inés into an adulthood less harsh than her own. She had never regretted leaving Candelaria, but she couldn't think of a better alternative for Inés than what might be available there. She had just learned that Elena Urey, the oldest daughter of the dead patrón, was returning to Candelaria. Perhaps Inés could look for opportunity with the new patrona. Despite Inés's lack of interest, Acensia insisted they walk to the hacienda: "It is time for you to meet your father's family."

So mother and daughter walked the dusty road from Laguna Sulti to Candelaria. The 14-year-old Inés stood slightly behind Acensia as she rang the bell at the wooden door beside the wide gate to Candelaria's first patio. Like her mother, Inés wore a wide, flat-brimmed, white hat, a sweater over the white blouse she had made herself, and a dark skirt that came just below her knees. Mother and daughter each had worked her dark hair into two braids woven with narrow ribbons down her back. Each had a colorful sash at her waist. Acensia, in her mid-thirties, was a striking woman with high cheekbones and fine features. Her daughter's youthful beauty surpassed even Acensia's good looks. Still, the patrona looked at the two peasant women at the hacienda's front door and wondered at their impertinence in presenting themselves there.

Dressed in tailored European clothes and makeup, Patrona Elena Urey did note the attractive simplicity of the women before her. Acensia, still standing with her daughter outside the open gate, began to tell Elena about their connection to her dead father. She introduced the girl at her side as Inés, Elena's half-sister, the daughter of Patrón Urey.

Looking closely at the young Inés, Elena saw that her skin was far lighter than that of her mother, Acensia, and that her face showed more than a hint of the Ureys' European features. She led the pair to sit with her on a bench beneath the olive tree in the first patio. The gray leaves and huge white flowers of the ancient, twisted tree shaded them from the bright sunlight.

Acensia spoke. She reminded Elena Urey that after her mother had died in childbirth, she—Acensia—had come to care for her and her siblings: "Patrona, it was I who brought Luciano, your father's son and my first child, into this life. You must remember how you played with Luciano—and Juanita, his big sister. And don't you recall carrying this one," she pointed to Inés, "on your hip?"

She told Elena that Luciano had died and that she had given birth to another child, also fathered by the patrón: "And here she is." She reminded Elena again and again that Inés was her half-sister. The two peasant women told her more about their shared past. Elena sat with them, listening without comment. When Acensia stopped talking, the three women remained seated in silence on the bench.

Inés looked around the patio in the stillness. She saw the twisted trunk of the old olive tree, flowers she had not seen before, the soft hues of the house and the walls. She remembered all the things her mother had told her about Candelaria, how they had lived in this beautiful place when she was a youngster, but she had no memory of it.

Elena abruptly broke the silence, turning to the young Inés with questions: "What can you do? Are you a good worker? Can you cook?"

Inés nodded silently to each one.

"Can you sew?"

Touching her blouse, Inés answered, "Yes, I made this."

Elena looked closely at the blusa, fingering the seams, assessing the quality of the young woman's handiwork. Acensia broke in to elaborate on her daughter's gifts, saying she sold her blusas at the market, that she tended the sheep, made cheese, did her chores with serious efficiency.

There was another long silence as the patrona thought about her response to the lovely young woman said to be her sister. When she finally spoke, Elena said nothing to Acensia and Inés about their connection to the Urey family. But she did ask Inés to come to Calendaria each day as her *compañera* (female companion).

Inés looked about her and said, "Yes, I will come."

So every day Inés walked the two miles to Candelaria, and in the afternoons she and Elena sewed together. As they sewed they talked—or rather Elena spoke and Inés listened. Inés learned that Elena had been sent off to school in Argentina. After her father's death, she had lived with the Grillo family related to her mother, in Oruro. The Grillos' oldest son, César, one of Elena's cousins, became a successful miner, and Elena went to work for him. Elena often talked about "Señor Grillo" to Inés, about how unhappy he was in his marriage. Over time, Inés came to understand that César Grillo was Elena's lover. Inés was well aware of his regular visits, alone, to Candelaria. And though Elena owned the land, her lover took on much of the role of patrón.

Inés thrived as Elena's discreet and loyal compañera, and she took on more and more responsibilities at Candelaria, becoming invaluable to Elena. Eventually Inés moved into the little adobe house in the second patio, where Acensia had lived 16 years earlier. Elena assigned a pongueaje to Inés as her responsibilities expanded.

This put Inés right in the middle rank of Candelaria. Inés continued to sew with Elena. She also began to supervise many of the house workers and to order and organize supplies. She oversaw the work of the cocina and learned the special recipe for preparing doves that Elena, like her mother before her, was especially fond of.

Though Inés was central to the workings of Candelaria, her deepest connection was with her Quechua heritage. She regularly visited her mother, Acensia, in the adobe house in Laguna Sulti. She continued to dress in traditional garb, though Elena urged her to dress in the European clothes that she herself preferred. Mother and daughter went together to the market in Punata to shop and be with their friends. Inés sold some of the blusas bordadas she had made as she sat with Elena.

Eventually Epifanio Velásquez, a young Quechua man from her village, noticed the beautiful Inés and began to court her. She returned the affection of the strong, hardworking man. As the owner of a small brick-and-tile business, his father was one of the few successful Quechua businessmen in the village. He and his wife had chosen a young woman of good reputation to be Epifanio's bride, but he was set on marrying Inés.

Epifanio admired Inés for her beauty and quiet assertiveness, and he was used to resisting his parents' wishes. When he was a child, they had considered education a useless endeavor and refused to send him to school. He wanted to go to school so much that he persuaded one of his aunts to pay his registration fee in Laguna Sulti, and he managed to attend for three months before his mother found out and withdrew him from the school.

There was little affection between Epifanio Velásquez and his parents. He told Inés how seldom they attended to him, how they drank and partied, often for days at a time. That he had gone to school for three months without their noticing convinced him that they were not interested in his welfare. So when they objected to his marrying Inés because of her illegitimacy and that of her mother, Acensia, Epifanio simply ignored them. But Epifanio's resistance left him without the money to marry Inés or to begin a life with her.

When Patrona Elena learned that Inés was unhappy about Epifanio's family's rejection of her, she summoned Epifanio to Candelaria so as to determine the sincerity of his intentions. Epifanio insisted he would marry Inés. He acknowledged his parents' disapproval, that they would not pay for a wedding. Yet he declared his love for Inés and said he would do anything, borrow the money if necessary, to marry her.

Elena responded, "No. You will not spend a boliviano [a unit of money worth about 15 cents]. We will take care of that." She had a chapel on her hacienda and the money to trump Epifanio's parents.

In 1945 Inés Irusta and Epifanio Velásquez married in the little chapel alongside the main house of Candelaria. Filigreed paper streamers decorated the chapel. Flowers from the first patio graced both the bride and the altar. Elena sent for her wealthy lover from Oruro to take part in the celebration, and she provided for an extravagant wedding fiesta with truckloads of food delivered for the event. Family lore attributes her generosity to her otherwise unacknowledged recognition of Inés as a blood relative.

After the wedding, Epifanio shared the adobe house in the second patio of the hacienda with Inés. Three children were born, one after the other. The first boy was Ivo; next came a daughter, Catalina, or Cati. That the third child—but second son—was named Segundo is testimony to the highly gendered nature of Bolivian rank. The second child, a girl, held a place of lesser importance.

When Inés became pregnant for the fourth time, Elena arranged for Ivo, Cati, and Segundo's baptism and became their *madrina* (godmother). She had two adobe rooms built for Inés and Epifanio and their growing family in the third patio. Epifanio worked in the fields and did carpentry work and other tasks for the patrona. Inés's responsibilities increased until her touch reached almost every aspect of hacienda life.

Revolution in Candelaria

The early years of Epifanio and Inés's marriage coincided with a revolution in Bolivia that reached into their immediate surrounds. From the 1930s the free, indigenous people in rural Bolivia—those who were not pongueaje—began to challenge agricultural elites such as Patrona Elena Urey of Candelaria.[1]

Many of the free villagers were Quechua, as were Epifanio Velásquez and Inés's mother, Acensia. And though Inés was technically half European, she lived and saw herself as Quechua. The Quechua were (and are) a people who retained (and have retained) their own language and culture over centuries of political oppression and instability. They are deeply communal, living by the traditional Andean *ayllu* system of collective decision-making.

The Quechua are accustomed to coming together with their geographic neighbors to discuss and act on mutual issues. Their elected leaders expect and receive the nearly universal participation of members of the community when they are needed. The Quechua acted from their ayllu tradition when they chose to join with other indigenous groups such as the Aymara in the peasant movement of the early 1950s. They also came together with the labor unions, some military officers, and some college students in revolt against the government. This was one of the nearly continuous revolts against the government that the country has endured for hundreds of years.

By virtue of their presence at the hacienda and their status within it, Epifanio and Inés Velásquez were very much in the middle of a genuine uprising, unwitting participants in the Agrarian, or Bolivian Revolution of 1952. The growing unrest, so much of it focused on the elite of the haciendas, so frightened Patrona Elena Urey that she fled Candelaria for the safety of Cochabamba City.

Life at the hacienda continued as usual with the assumptions that the patrona's absence was temporary and that the Velásquezes would continue their central role at Candelaria. They were not the managers of the operating farm or just workers in the house: Epifanio was making regular trips to nearby San Benito to pick up supplies. Inés continued overseeing most things. She regularly filled trucks with food and Elena's belongings to send to Cochabamba, and Elena depended on Inés to see that the resources of Candelaria enabled her to live in comfort in the city.

So Epifanio Velásquez and the other Candelaria workers continued to maintain the fields as the unrest in Bolivia went on. In the meantime the government honored the countrywide protests with new laws specifying the removal of the hacendados and the confiscation of weapons they might possess.

One day, looking up from his work in the field, Epifanio saw a cloud of dust rise beyond the hacienda. Some say it was the dust of hundreds of men, some say of thousands, rushing toward Candelaria. Epifanio worried that the crowd was part of the peasant movement against the haciendas. He ran to the main house afraid for his pregnant wife and children, concerned that things would get out of hand. He was right. He found men breaking down the gate and filling the first patio. They began to drag furniture from the formal rooms on the first floor.

Epifanio saw Inés with Segundo, their youngest, hanging onto his mother's ankles while his older brother and sister hovered at the bottom of the stairs to the second floor. Epifanio had never been especially critical of the hacendados he lived with and worked for; he was offended by the anger and destruction in front of him. It never occurred to him to join the protest.

Epifanio jumped to the third step and called out: "Compañeros, the new law says you are supposed to be checking for weapons. Breaking down doors and stealing are not checking for weapons." He was concerned for the windows—as the hacienda's carpenter, he would have to repair them.

Someone in the crowd called out, "Compañeros, we have just rid ourselves of one patrón. It looks like we now have another. What should we do with him?"

Another replied, "Let him wait. We'll cut off both of his hands and feet." These men were Quechua, Epifanio's father's neighbors. But they were also members of the *junta vecinal* (community council) that Epifanio had questioned.

Inés, seven-months pregnant and standing nearby, suddenly went into labor. The children began to cry and pull at her pollera.

Another leader spoke up: "Compañeros, this is Compañero Epifanio, and he is one of us. Let us form scouting parties of threes and fours to inspect Candelaria for weapons. Let us not destroy."

And so it was. Some of the men conducted an orderly inspection. Others dispersed. And José—the fourth child and third Velásquez son—was born two months before his time.

The revolution ended the viability of Bolivia's hacienda economic system. Many hacendados were killed or run off their property. But unlike thousands of other haciendas in Bolivia, Elena Urey's was not destroyed by the peasants or split up by the laws resulting from the revolution. Inés and Epifanio, like the rest of the Candelaria workers, respected her for her enlightened treatment of the trabajadores, as did the government, which established that this particular hacienda had not abused its workers. Its efforts to mechanize crop production were seen as advantageous rather than exploitative.

So the government allowed Candelaria to survive, though not to function as a power in the community. Patrona Elena was not affected because she had already abandoned Candelaria for her home in Cochabamba. She remained in contact with the Velásquezes, who continued to live in the two adobe houses in the third patio.

In fact, Elena distributed Candelaria land to some of her trabajadores. She recognized Inés's mother, Acensia Irusta, and gave her 15 acres for having cared for the Urey children after their mother died. Acensia, and eventually Epifanio and Inés, benefited from the largess of their hacendados.

Acensia asked Epifanio and Inés to farm her portion of the land. This, combined with a parcel that Epifanio had bought previously, gave the family a limited source of income. But the Velásquezes no longer worked for Candelaria. There was no one to tell Epifanio to repair the damage that the protesters did in the first patio; there was nothing left for Inés to manage. Inés and Epifanio no longer went through Candelaria every night, checking each room and hallway to see that all the lights were out. They no longer went to Elena's rooms to see that she was content before they retreated from the first patio, turned off the light over the entry door, and walked to the third patio to sleep. There was no one left in the first and second patios. For the first time, the Velásquezes could concentrate on themselves and their children.

The Velásquezes had a bit of land, but they were very poor. The family lived in the adobe houses in the third patio of the eerily quiet Candelaria for four more years because it had no income elsewhere. But it was able to cultivate its little bit of land.

Ivo was nine years old when the Velásquezes began to farm on their own; Segundo was four. Cati, between the boys, was six years old and a steady help to her mother with baby José. Ivo and Cati went to school in Punata, which required a walk of several miles. Epifanio and his sons walked each day to farm their acres, previously part of the hacienda.

With a strange malady affecting Epifanio's muscles, especially in response to the repetitive movements of farm work, he much appreciated the help of his sons. He relied on both boys, Ivo completing many tasks usually reserved for grown men. Segundo, at age five, was also a willing helper. He didn't know that no child his age typically was expected to accomplish the things he did. He did know he could barely reach the harness of the ox as his father managed the plow behind him. The little boy directed the huge animal to the exact place of the next furrow and kept the ox from getting away.

Segundo spent a great deal of time watching the other animals of the farm, too, so that they did not run off or get into the fields and trample or eat the produce. He and Ivo particularly kept watch over the lima beans that grew along both sides of the river running through the family land. They gathered big, smooth lima beans when they were ripe and often built a small fire under a black pot to cook and eat them as they watched the animals together by the side of the river. Eating the just-cooked limas was one part of the long day they relished.

Because of their father's erratic but chronic illness, Ivo and Segundo learned earlier than most about finding ways to enjoy themselves during days of hard, sometimes unrelenting, labor.

Candelaria changed during these years. *La policía* (the police) locked up the main house in the first patio as well as the adobe house and storerooms in the second. They left the third one open so that the Velásquezes could continue to live there.

Inés and Epifanio benefited from their many years with the Urey family. Epifanio's work in the fields was more humane than it would have been at another hacienda, and he learned much about modern machinery. Inés gained a great deal more experience at Candelaria than she would have with her mother in Laguna Sulti. And the parcel of land from Elena was invaluable in feeding their family.

But living at Candelaria isolated the family from schools and markets. Ivo and then Cati walked miles to school in Punata, one of the two market towns visited by the Velásquez family. There was no school for the younger siblings nearby. For the sake of their children, Inés and Epifanio decided to leave the hacienda.

Epifanio and Inés, surrounded by their eight children, in Cochabamba: (back) Segundo, José, Ivo, Cati, (front) Rubén, César, Blanca, Margui

2

Beyond the Hacienda

1956–1965

In 1956 the Velásquez family moved to Laguna Sulti, where both Inés and Epifanio had grown up. Making their life independent of the hacienda, they moved into a house behind the senior Velásquezes' home and down the road from Inés's mother, Acensia, and their *Tia* (Aunt) Juanita. They put Segundo in the small school in the village, while Ivo and Cati continued in Punata.

The family's home was in the midst of a grove of towering eucalypti. Epifanio sold some of their land on the hacienda so as to buy a parcel outside Laguna Sulti. Struggling to increase the income of his growing family, he and his sons shuttled between two parcels of land, one near their home, the other at the hacienda. Inés gave birth to Margarita (Margui), their second daughter and fifth child. Ivo and Segundo continued to do more work than most boys their ages because of their father's health.

The two boys walked the two miles to their land to harvest the alfalfa grown there for their animals. Ivo and Segundo each used small hoes with curved, edged blades to cut handfuls of alfalfa; they threw the handfuls aside for later bundling and moved on. As they did this work through the winter, the boys' hands became cold and raw. Ivo

Beyond the Hacienda

typically did much of the heavier work. Segundo also helped his father with watering the Laguna Sulti fields.

The Velásquezes, like all their neighbors, lived in adobe structures clustered within walking distance of their fields. The residents shared the water flowing from the mountains through a canal to their fields. The Laguna Sulti irrigation *sindicato* (community union based on occupation) made sure the village farmers shared the water equitably and kept the channel clear. Each community had its irrigation sindicato to manage its unique *usos y costumbres* (customary practices). These practices were mutually agreed upon, voluntary, and not imposed by anyone outside the community.[1] The sindicato included all who owned land in the community, and it allocated water by specifying the time when the channel was opened into a field each day.

Epifanio also flooded his fields in the dark to take advantage of the free water that flowed by all night long. Segundo got up with his father during the night, as he had on their hacienda land. He carried the lantern to provide light so his father could be sure the water was properly distributed.

In addition to distributing irrigation water, the sindicato organized the process of keeping the channel clean. Certain days were set aside for cleaning. Each villager was responsible for keeping three or four meters of channel clear, depending on how big his fields were and how much water he needed. Each farmer was expected to remove soil and debris from the bottom of the river channel, far deeper than the men were tall. Throwing shovels of soil to the top of the channel was difficult.

Ivo and Segundo built a ledge on each side of the channel so that their father could throw his shovel of debris onto it. The boys, now ages eight and five, shoved the debris to the side of the channel to make room for the next shovelful. When the channel was open and water rushed through, Segundo's older brother could see that some sections were not thoroughly cleaned or not dug as deep as others. This caused overflow and waste when the water ran fast.

26

The eight-year-old Ivo was concerned about this inefficiency and about the fairness of a system allowing someone to waste water valuable to others. He asked the sindicato leader, "Why is that part of the channel not cleaned? Where is the villager who is supposed to clear it? What will happen to him?"

The leader said to him, "There will be severe consequences. That *campesino* [peasant] may not get water for some time, maybe never." Ivo learned that the usos y costumbres of the irrigation sindicato depended on the vigilance of the community.

So the Velásquez family experienced the advantages and limitations of participatory communal living in its Quechua village. The farmers knew they could not farm at all without the organization the sindicato provided—a farmer could not harness the water from the mountains alone. But Epifanio and Inés resented the infringement on their life by the protesters of the 1952 revolution. They sometimes missed the orderly, efficient system of the hacienda they had left behind.

That Inés and Epifanio could neither read nor write became more of an issue as their children reached school age. Epifanio had not returned to school after the three months his aunt maneuvered for him. Inés had never gone to school at all. Epifanio told Inés and the children two stories about opportunities lost because of his lack of education.

First, as a young man having finished his obligatory year of military service, Epifanio had gone to the city to find work. He was hired as a manual laborer with hundreds of other men, to build a road to the planned monument to the *heroinas de Cochabamba* (brave women of Cochabamba). The young men all stood at the bottom of the high hill where the road was supposed to go, waiting with their picks and shovels to begin the digging. Epifanio watched the engineer-in-charge trying to figure out the best route.

After a few hours of impatient waiting, Epifanio began to think, and soon he figured out a solution to the problem. He came away from the crowd of workers with his pick and started laying out markers showing the width and incline as well as where the turns should be. He left small piles of dirt outlining his vision of the road to the top of the hill.

The boss noticed Epifanio's work, looked at it, liked it, and said, "That is what we will do." He noticed that Epifanio was able to do what his engineer could not and called him into his office to talk about a promotion. He thanked him for his contribution and asked him in Quechua, "Can you write in Spanish?"

Epifanio said he could not.

The boss asked, "Can you speak Spanish?"

Epifanio said he was not proficient.

And despite his contribution to the project, Epifanio lost the opportunity for advancement.

In the second case, Epifanio, after finishing his work as a manual laborer on the road to the monument, took a job with a railroad company. Soon he was helping another engineer, pointing out ways to do the job more efficiently. Again his boss noticed his ability and offered him a better job. Again it required the reading and writing of Spanish. Epifanio lost another opportunity.

Inés and Epifanio hoped that living in Laguna Sulti would give their younger children a good start on the education that neither of them had. They scraped together enough money from selling their produce to send the older children to school in the bigger town of Punata. Segundo continued in Laguna Sulti.

In a short time, the Velásquezes became disappointed in the quality of the village school. Just as there was a sindicato for managing the water, there was one to oversee the village school, and its leader ignored the concerns of the young parents. News of their discontent traveled quickly through Laguna Sulti, and many wondered about the family from the old hacienda.

The family found the intimacy and interdependence of tiny Laguna Sulti frustrating. Inés and Epifanio were in contact with Madrina

Elena Urey, who still lived in Cochabamba and still took an interest in the Velásquez children. She encouraged the parents to send their older children to a school in Cochabamba and promised to help with uniforms and books.

In the meantime, complaints of the Velásquezes to the leaders of the school sindicato stressed their rapport with the Laguna Sulti community. These struggles, combined with the family's difficult relationship with Epifanio's parents and siblings, caused the young parents to rethink their decision to settle there permanently. They were pulled to the opportunities for better education for the children in Cochabamba as well as to its potential for privacy and independence.

So Segundo's parents sold their two parcels of land and moved to Cochabamba. There they bought a lot at the city's edge. Segundo, by this time seven years old, was the only one to stay in the village with Mamanchaj—so as to finish the school year.

But even with Mamanchaj and Tia Juanita, Segundo felt left out, like a bystander in the excitement of the move. He watched his parents and Ivo get into the front seat of their rented truck, with Cati, José, Margui, and by this time two more—daughter Blanca and son Rubén—piled in the back on top of a load of corn. Segundo had helped to load the corn from their last harvest and pack up the cocina for his mother, but still they left him behind.

Segundo soon felt resentful about being left with few personal belongings. He had no shoes, only *abarcas* (sandals made of used tires). He wanted a pair of real shoes for school and immediately began scrounging for shoes around Mamanchaj's little adobe house, his home for several months. His search took him through the village and into the surrounding fields. He finally managed to find some shoes that fit him well enough, though one was black and the other brown.

Segundo knew his classmates would laugh at him, especially when his big brother was not there to protect him. So he took the burn from the bottom of Mamanchaj's pots and made the brown shoe black. Still he was bereft. He had always been embedded in the security of his immediate family, and now he was alone.

Finally Home

The Velásquezes rented a small house next to the lot they had bought in Canata, a *barrio* (neighborhood) on the edge of Cochabamba City. Segundo's father immediately drew on his skills as a carpenter. He found a job as a bridge builder and began constructing a one-room adobe house on his new land. Soon after the family's move to the city, Epifanio happened upon an evangelical preacher in the streets near the barrio. As a younger man he had come to the city to work and been deeply moved by just such a sermon. This time he waited to talk with the preacher, who happened to be from Unión Cristiana Evangélica (UCE), a Protestant denomination quickly taking root in Bolivia.[2]

Epifanio was one of many Quechua people to move to the city and find support in a small, egalitarian church community. He identified with the church's special commitment to serve indigenous people, its rejection of alcohol, and its emphasis on moral character. He began attending the evangelical church, demonstrating an independence from the Catholic culture and hierarchy as well as from Laguna Sulti.

Meanwhile, Inés and the children continued their weekly participation in the Catholic mass at a nearby parish. As Epifanio continued his involvement with the evangelicals, he flourished in that tightly knit Cochabamba community.

The Velásquez family lived for more than 20 years in the tiny house that Epifanio built in Canata. He expanded the house as family income allowed. In the early years the family had little money left after school fees and necessities. All slept inside the single room, cooked in an open-air cocina under a thatched roof, and did most of their day-to-day living in the roofless patio. As their financial means improved, they added a bedroom. An enclosed cocina with counters and a sink followed. Later an additional bedroom housed the five boys. When Ivo was to be married, two rooms were added on the perimeter of the lot for the wedded couple.

Then came a dining room. Epifanio built a huge table, big enough to seat his whole family. He sat at the head, strong after his visits with a *curandero* (traditional male healer), who with the help of much chicha had cured him of his debilitating muscle pain. Inés was supposed to sit at the empty spot at the end of the table but rarely did so during the preparation and serving of meals.

Epifanio typically directed the few words he uttered during a meal to Ivo, the oldest, who usually sat next to him. The handsome Ivo listened carefully to his father's directions for proceeding on the current family project, speaking only to clarify the details of the tasks, so that he could direct his brothers in their responsibilities.

The other children placed themselves around the table in no special order. Cati, the oldest girl and the liveliest, was up and down helping her mother. Margarita joined her as a helper. Segundo, the third child and second boy, who by this time had long rejoined the family, sat within earshot of Ivo and his father, ready to act when his role became clear. Segundo sometimes missed the details of his tasks because of the hearing difficulties that plagued him as a small child. José, the fourth child, always one to concentrate on his studies, was likely to come to the table with a book.

The younger children, Blanca, Rubén, and César (the only one born after the move to the barrio), found spots around the table to await their mother's delicious food. Blanca helped the older girls clear the table after the meal. Washing up after a meal was a challenge in the several years before their outdoor cocina had running water. Even later came the final touch of a bathroom with plumbing in the patio.

Inés, who had learned all about flower gardens at Candelaria, was not able to make a single thing grow in the burned earth when they first moved into the house in the city. The lot was relatively cheap for a reason: a kiln formerly located on the property had damaged the soil.

Beyond the Hacienda

Almost immediately, Epifanio began what became a 20-year effort to improve the soil so that Inés could bring a garden to their home. He and the boys dug a trench along the perimeter of the lot and used the dirt to make *adobes* (mud bricks) for their new home and the wall surrounding the house and patio. He persuaded garbage collectors to fill the trench with trash and builders to drop their excess dirt there. The children, oblivious to their father's ingenuity in providing a garden for their mother, played in the trench and considered a rubber tire buried in the trash their greatest find. Eventually the trench disappeared amid fertile soil, and Inés had a lovely garden.

As the Velásquezes settled into their new home, it became obvious that Epifanio's pay from building roads and bridges was not sufficient for their needs. Epifanio worried about finding other ways to feed his family. He learned that a nearby neighbor was selling a small machine for making colonial roof tiles, and he decided to buy it. Soon the entire family joined him in learning the mechanical intricacies necessary to turn out 113 tiles a day. Each child had a particular task. Some mixed the cement and sand; some loaded the machine that formed the tiles. Ivo specialized in polishing the formed tiles before others removed them from the machine and placed them on a rack to dry. Finally, they soaked the tiles for a prescribed time and put on a layer of paint.

The children worked on the tiles whenever they weren't in school. Every morning Epifanio continued making tiles with his machine, and the children went off to their various schools, returning to help again. Tile making was the first Velásquez enterprise, and it was dirty, hard, labor-intensive work. But the many Velásquezes were willing and able to put in the effort, and the business was a success. Soon Epifanio and his sons added on another covered space in the courtyard for producing tiles. The business enabled the family to pay for the significant tuition and supplies of the children's private schools.

After a few years of making tiles, the Velásquezes had enough money to buy a small, flatbed cattle truck. At first they used it to pick up materials for making and delivering the tiles. And they used it to drive Inés and the children to Sunday mass during their early Canata years. Soon they were using it to transport cargo to and from the market for themselves and others. They also hauled cattle and anything else that people wanted moved.

Still, there were times when the truck sat idle, which bothered Epifanio's sense of efficiency. He noticed how difficult it was for his family and their neighbors in the barrio to get enough clean water. There was no public water source for those who had come from the countryside, for those who, like the Velásquez family, had to make a life on the edge of the big city. Epifanio saw the opportunity for another business. He typified the "innovation, flexibility, and risk taking" that business scholar Graham Tipple has found in home-based entrepreneurs across the globe.[3]

Epifanio decided they would build a tank on the flatbed, fill it with water, and sell the water to their neighbors. The Velásquezes quickly found buyers for the crystal-clear water they got from a spring in the mountains and delivered it door to door from the back of the truck.

Epifanio did not want to limit the truck's use to hauling water, so he and his sons built a device enabling them to easily put the tank on and off the truck. When Segundo was a teenager, he joined his brothers in lifting the tank off the ground with the long poles it was sitting on. They all pushed it onto the truck, and one of them secured it, temporarily, to the flatbed.

The Velásquezes soon tired of waiting in line for hours with other entrepreneurs to draw water into their truck. To avoid the long lines of water haulers, the brothers began fetching water in the middle of the night. Acquiring water in the dark worked well in the early years in the barrio partly because, compared to others, most of the members of the Velásquez family needed minimal sleep.

Soon Epifanio Velásquez saw another way to improve his water business. He decided to build a cement pool on the family lot, where he could store water. The pool allowed the family to fill truckloads when the waiting time for water was short, thus allowing more trips and more water in less time. It was a joke in Canata that the family was building a swimming pool. But the Velásquez children understood their father's plan. They hauled truckloads of water from the spring to the tank at night and were off early in the morning to deliver it to their customers.

Inés had her own way to augment the family income. Twice a week she strapped her brightly colored burden cloth, bulging with cow fat, onto her back. She bought the fat from a butcher in Cochabamba and carried it to sell at nearby market towns. On Tuesdays she took a bus or rode on the family truck to Punata, on Sundays to Cliza. She set up a *puesto* (open marketplace or stand) and set her little scale on it. She cut off a one-or-two-pound hunk of fat, put it on the scale, weighing it against a small stone used as a measure of weight. It was worth two or three pesos, but most people chose to barter. She bartered and sold the fat to as many as a hundred people in one day.

Inés traded the cow fat for eggs or a ball of cheese or bunches of peas or potatoes. For the people who came from the mountains to the market, the cow fat was the only kind of meat they could afford. For the Velásquez family, the bartering process was the primary source of *comestibles* (groceries). When the cow fat was sold, Inés laid her burden cloth on the ground and put the comestibles and the scale on it. She wrapped it together, put it on her back, and took the bus back to Cochabamba to cook for her family.

Every member of the Velásquez family worked hard to make a success of their several businesses—their puesto and their tile-making and water-hauling businesses. But Epifanio and Inés never allowed work to interfere with their children's education. Epifanio especially wanted each of them to gain the skills he had lacked as a young man.

By this time Epifanio had taught himself to read, and he read the daily newspaper voraciously. He was unrelenting in urging his children

A much later sketch of Inés in her kitchen in Canata

on academically. Each completed elementary school and moved on to one of the high schools in Cochabamba. Ivo, Cati, and José went to the high school Yugoslavia, a favorite of Madrina Elena. Segundo attended high school at night so that he could work during the day. Margui and Blanca attended the public schools.

Segundo had an educational disadvantage unique in his family. He was told as a child that his parents could not use their money to educate him beyond high school. They were confronted with the harsh choices that parents with many children and little money too often face. Segundo had chronic ear infections as a child, and his parents had spent a disproportionate amount of their meager resources to care for him when they first moved to Canata—all they could spare.

It wasn't that Segundo's parents ignored his future. Inés was still a Catholic at that time, and she decided her second son was to become a priest. The church would pay for the education of a young man with that goal. Segundo, having already developed a strong sense of self, rejected that option. He told his parents, "I am always looking for opportunities, but this is not the one I want."

Segundo's search for opportunity led him to choose evening high school. He was driven to learn new things but also wanted to add to his family's income. He worked for a while making pants, earning a bit of money but learning nothing new. He was especially interested in things mechanical. He believed from watching his father that if he had a hammer and a screwdriver, he could do anything.

One Urey relative noticed Segundo's mechanical skill and passion for mechanical things in high school. He heard there was a nearby racecar driver who needed help with his vehicles and arranged an interview for Segundo as the second helper. The driver's nephew was the first. Segundo knew the racecar driver spoke only Spanish, not Quechua. Segundo was conversant in the Spanish he had used through his 12 years of schooling.

But Segundo also knew he was most articulate and comfortable in the Quechua language spoken in his home. To prepare for his interview, he walked up and down the streets by the racecar driver's garage, repeating in his mind the way he would present himself in Spanish. The interview went well, and Segundo became the driver's second helper, eager to learn the intricacies of racecar mechanics.

Segundo was thrilled when his new boss gave him the task of cleaning a gearbox that the driver was to reassemble. Segundo saw this as a great opportunity—the gearbox was complex, and he wanted to know how to take it apart and put it back together. He cleaned it as fast as he could with all his might. He hoped he could watch the driver reassemble it before lunch.

By lunchtime, Segundo was done cleaning the gearbox, but his boss didn't seem interested in putting it back together. So Segundo raced home on his bike, gobbled down his lunch, and rushed back to work early, hoping to learn the secrets of the gearbox. By this time, the driver had put it together in Segundo's absence. Segundo was deeply disappointed and worried that his boss would never share his knowledge. To make things worse, Segundo did not feel comfortable in the job. He felt the driver and his nephew looked down on him for his peasant ancestry. Did he really belong there?

At one point Segundo's boss accused him of stealing a tool. Segundo protested and went home to tell his parents. Inés returned to the racecar driver's garage with Segundo and vouched for her son's honesty. She offered the racecar driver the gift of a chicken that she carried in her apron. Such a gift was the typical response to an appeal for resolution in a conflict in the barrio. Inés's interest was not only to prove Segundo's honesty but also to preserve her family's relationship with the racecar driver, who was a member of their community.[4]

The driver took the chicken but continued to accuse Segundo of thievery. Segundo soon quit the job, regretting both that he did not have the driver's trust and that the driver had refused to share his knowledge of mechanics. Segundo viewed the experience as an example of class discrimination and jealousy. But he didn't let the unpleasantness diminish his commitment to learn or to earn more money for his family. He was ever alert to opportunity.

Arnold Swanson married Stella Scholten in 1936.

3

From Minnesota

1930–1967

Long before Segundo and Joan were born, her father, Arnold Swanson, was a teenager watching his Swedish father lose the family farm during the Great Depression of the 1930s. The farm, near Valley Springs, South Dakota, was just west of the Minnesota border, a part of seemingly unending acres of lush farmland. Arnold watched the trauma his family experienced when the sheriff came to the home place with orders to sell off the farm machinery the next week to honor a bank debt.

Recognizing the injustice of the situation, neighboring farmers came quietly in the night and secretly took some of the Swanson's most needed machinery, which had been scheduled for auction the next day. Risking the consequences, they hid the machinery in their own barns to return it to Arnold's father after the auction. Nevertheless, everyone knew that the Swanson family's money eventually would go to the bank and that the Swansons would lose their farm.

From then on, Arnold's family of Swedish immigrants lived in a state of economic fragility requiring unwavering frugality. Arnold and his sister, Margaret, inherited the Swanson love for the land and a disciplined austerity. But no matter how hard they worked their rented

From Minnesota

farms or how carefully they managed their money, Arnold and Margaret could never afford to buy farms of their own.

When Arnold married Stella Scholten in 1936, their families likely scrambled to afford a proper wedding. The newlyweds went home to Arnold's rented farm near Valley Springs.

Many Swansons and Scholtens lived nearby, and nearly every Sunday afternoon the families gathered, drawing perhaps 40 aunts, uncles, and cousins together for a backyard picnic or other get-together. In 1941 Stella and Arnold's first child, Joan, was born. They delighted in including her in the family gatherings.

The Swansons and the Scholtens, like most families in the United States at that time, were aware of the new polio epidemic. They had heard that children should not be together in big cities, where they were more apt to catch the disease. But Valley Springs was a small town with fewer than a thousand people. Most of them were spread around surrounding farms. Besides, no one they knew had ever had polio. So they felt safe.

One Sunday in 1943, Arnold, Stella, Margaret Swanson Scholten (she married Stella's brother Mike) and their children failed to appear at the weekly picnic. The aunts and uncles soon learned that two-year-old Joan and two of Margaret's boys were in the hospital with polio. After a few weeks Margaret's boys came home from the hospital, almost back to normal. But two-year-old Joan was totally paralyzed; she had to be in an iron lung even to breathe.

Joan's doctors recommended that she go to St. Mary's Hospital in Rochester, Minnesota, for further treatment. But Rochester was more than 200 miles from Valley Springs, too far for a toddler to be from her parents. The young couple decided that Stella would go to be with Joan in Rochester while Arnold stayed in Valley Springs on the farm.

Stella found a job in the hospital kitchen, and Joan worked every day with the therapists in Rochester to relearn the use of her damaged muscles. Slowly she learned to sit up, then to stand, and finally to walk.

Cousins (back row) Marlys, Jackie, Shirley, Mildred, Sophie, Geneva, Billie Jean, (front row) Arla, Marilyn, and Joan

Every evening Stella came to her daughter's room to share supper and spend the evening. Through the course of her treatment, Joan came to understand what was required of her to complete the basic tasks of life. It was nearly a year before the family reunited in Valley Springs.

On the Farm in Hills
Everyone in Valley Springs knew that Arnold wanted to rent a farm with better soil. One of his cousins told him about such a farm for rent a few miles over the state border with Minnesota. It was just outside Hills, a small but thriving town of 600 people. Stella, Arnold, and Joan moved to the farm west of Hills in 1945, when Joan was four years old.

The family's new home was a modest and classic midwestern farmhouse. Arnold put the Swanson name on the mailbox standing beside the metal gate, where the long, narrow, dirt driveway met the road. A small orchard with well-tended trees and flowers encircled the small, two-story house. An open area with a vegetable garden stood between the house and the outbuildings—a silo, a barn, fenced-in sheds, areas for the animals and chickens, then fields as far as the eye could see. A few of those fields were part of Arnold's rented farm. Arnold planted alfalfa, oats, corn, and soybeans, alternating the crops to preserve the rich earth. A huge cottonwood tree stood beside the outhouse just beyond the back door.

Joan had difficulty walking. Going through that door to use the outhouse was a continuing challenge, and she often needed help. She knew her parents were sometimes overwhelmed in responding to her many needs. She got pneumonia frequently, and once she overheard a doctor saying she "might not make it this time." But she did recover, time and time again.

As Joan's parents struggled to sustain her health, they also strained to make a go of the farm. One morning while it was still dark, Arnold Swanson pulled on his bib overalls as he watched his wife, Stella, tie her apron over her housedress. As he headed through the living room to the kitchen to the back door, he heard Joan moving about in her bedroom upstairs.

After using the outhouse, Arnold glanced into the barn and saw that the chickens were safely roosting. He stopped awhile as he watched the cattle bunched together in the field beyond. He thought about his sheep in the far pasture, relieved that he could soon get the flock ready to sell. He figured the proceeds from that sale would get them through the next six months. But now the sheep needed water and food, and he sent the dog to bring them in.

The dog returned alone, barking and jumping up on his master. Arnold walked swiftly through the deep grass, his overalls dampening from the morning dew. The dog circled him frantically. Arnold began to climb over the fence to the upper pasture, then stopped and stood stunned. His sheep were spread bleeding and dead across the field, chunks of flesh gouged from their rumps.

Arnold stepped into the field and walked from carcass to carcass counting, "One, two, three . . ." until he found every one of his 21 sheep dead. He turned around, then rushed to the house and in through the front door. He saw Stella coming from the kitchen. He put his arms around her, his head on her shoulder, and sobbed. "The wild dogs in the night. The sheep. All dead."

Joan was lying on an old hospital cart in the living room, waiting for her mother to fix breakfast. She looked up and saw something she had never seen before—her father in tears. She heard him say through his sobs, "I don't know how we are going to eat, how we are going to live." That was when she began to grasp that her family lived on an economic edge.

In September 1947, just as the leaves were beginning to turn gold and red, the five-year-old Joan was ready to go to school. Her mother helped her walk past the garden that was beginning to fade and down the dirt road to the metal gate. Joan caught the school bus to start first grade. She was ready.

Joan delighted in joining cousins, Sunday school friends, and new students she didn't know. As she had already taught herself to read, she found school easy. She did exceedingly well in her schoolwork and in making new friends. She was especially attached to Dianne Nelson, whose farming parents were close friends of Arnold and Stella.

One day when Joan was in first grade, her mother took her to the Hills drugstore. Stella set Joan on the floor as she talked with a friend behind the counter. Joan was just six; she could walk but not very well. She sat beside a magazine rack and began to explore the words and pictures around her. She sounded out the words in a headline—"The Horrors of Having a Handicapped Child"—and quickly turned the magazine over. Joan said nothing to her mother about those words, but she knew that her doctors referred to her as "handicapped." Did that mean it was a horror for her parents to have her as their child? And what exactly was a horror? It must be something scary.

Joan knew her mother did many things for her that her aunts did not do for her cousins. She knew those cousins were helping their parents with chores by the time they were six years old. And she knew she

From Minnesota

couldn't do any of those tasks—running to fetch something, feeding the chickens, gathering eggs, or running after a younger child. Joan couldn't run. Still, Joan's mother found ways for her to feel useful, and Joan knew she was a help. She folded the laundry, sometimes doing almost all of it herself. She knew she could sit quietly when her mother was preoccupied and that she was getting better at cleaning carrots and peeling potatoes.

But Joan was increasingly aware of her "differentness." She knew no other "only" children, and she had heard people talking about how spoiled only children were. She didn't want to be known as spoiled, so she began pestering her parents for a little brother or sister. More than once she heard her mother talking to her father about having another child or adopting one.

Arnold invariably responded with some variant of "If we have another child, how would we take care of Joan?" or "With what we do for this child, how would another fit in?"

When Joan was a fourth grader at Hills Elementary, a nurse came to the farmhouse to talk to Arnold and Stella about Joan's health. She was from the Gillette Children's Hospital in St. Paul, Minnesota, and she was visiting rural communities in an effort to find children with disabilities who might benefit from treatment. Following up on a comment from the school superintendent, she learned that Joan had developed severe curvature of the spine. That was a frequent side effect of polio, and the superintendent thought the nurse might be able to provide some help for Joan.

Joan's parents knew it was getting harder for Joan to breathe and walk comfortably, and sometimes she mentioned a pain in her back. They remembered that the Rochester doctors had not been hopeful that she would fully recover her mobility. The nurse told the Swansons that there had been progress since Joan contracted polio and that they might want to try a new treatment method.

Stella and Arnold were reluctant. St. Paul was as far away as Rochester, and they well remembered the hardship all three of them endured during Joan's year of rehabilitation at St. Mary's Hospital. They saw Joan happy at her school and with her friends. Despite these reservations, the Swansons decided to go to St. Paul—perhaps there was something that could make Joan's life better.

In and Out of Gillette
The Swansons made the 230-mile drive to St. Paul for their appointment with physician John H. Moe. They were unaware that this soft-spoken, middle-aged man was already famous for his work with soldiers who had spinal injuries. He told Arnold and Stella that he could help Joan straighten her spine through a combination of casting, surgery, and bed rest.

Trusting the physician, the Swansons brought Joan to Gillette for the spine program. She was put in a full body cast, the first of several over the course of the next five years. She shared a small room with five other children. Their room opened onto another one with 20 children, in beds lined up on either side of a wide opening. Joan, who loved being with other children, found herself in a family of kids. She was especially empathetic with the two children in her room who had cerebral palsy. She saw that in addition to not being able to walk, they had trouble speaking and sometimes thinking. She was grateful her limitations were much less severe.

Joan thrived in the community of kids at Gillette but found her first Christmas there difficult. The hospital worked hard to create a nice holiday for the children who couldn't go home. Each child received three or four gifts—dolls, trucks, games. In addition, Arnold came into the ward with his arms full of presents for Joan, saying, " I think half of the families in Hills sent you a present."

As Joan opened one gift another, she began to feel sick and then sicker, until finally she vomited. A nurse rushed in laughing, saying that Joan had eaten too much Christmas candy. "No," her mother said, "She knows that no one should have this many gifts, that no one should have more than they need."

Joan was in and out of casts and in and out of Gillette. She first came home to the farm encased in a huge body cast with only her arms and one leg free. The curvature in her spine gradually straightened, and she underwent new, less confining treatments. But some of them brought unexpected results, and the curvature worsened.

Believing it would become even worse should he wait, Dr. Moe performed a full-back spinal fusion despite Joan's young age, After surgery, a new cast was built around her. Arnold and Stella were told she would require years of bed rest. They worried about that prospect but were delighted that she would be able to be at home.

Back at the farm, Arnold wondered how he could entertain his daughter, who missed her old classmates in Hills. She couldn't walk or sit up during this phase of the treatment, and she was expected to lie on her side much of the day. He and Stella found an old hospital gurney, and on nice days they rolled it out to the backyard, where Joan could watch her mother work in the garden.

Arnold knew that his ten-year old daughter needed more. One evening while sitting under the under the old cottonwood, he noticed the pleasant sound of leaves rustling in the breeze. He brought Joan out on the gurney to enjoy the evening with him and suddenly had an idea: "A swing! I will build her a swing."

He tied a heavy rock to the end of a thick rope and managed to throw it high enough to reach a sturdy branch. Finally, with two strong ropes secured to the branch, he fashioned a broad seat between them just long enough and low enough for Joan to lie on it with her toes touching the ground. She spent hours perfecting her technique of pushing, until she went so high that her parents had to urge her to slow down.

The casts that eventually enabled Joan to walk required constant adjustment. At one point she began to vomit after eating, and Stella took her to the local family doctor, who said Joan was outgrowing her cast. He sent her back to St. Paul for a new one. Noting Joan's growth spurt, Dr. Moe gave her a new and bigger cast equipped with a hole they came to call a "window" for her stomach. He told Stella they would have to return periodically to accommodate Joan's growth.

Eventually a smaller cast was designed to give the by-this-time-12-year-old Joan the freedom to walk. The family went to Gillette, where a technician built the new cast around her. When they were done, the nurse brought Stella into the room to help get Joan dressed to go home to Hills. Stella saw no window in the smaller cast and looked for someone to tell. She found the social worker responsible for Joan and told her of her concern. The social worker insisted it was impossible to do anything then—it was the end of the workday, everyone had gone home, and the Swansons would have to come back another day.

Stella reminded the social worker that they lived 230 miles away and couldn't come back. Arnold, who by then had come looking for Joan and her mother, saw Stella speaking to the social worker. The social worker said Joan should have told the doctors about the window when they were applying the cast. Joan and her father cowered a bit when they saw Stella put her hands to her hips. That meant she wasn't finished.

"Well, I do not think it is up to my 12-year-old daughter to tell you people how to practice medicine. And I am going to stay right here until someone comes and cuts a hole in that cast." Technicians came to put the window in the cast, and Joan continued in her confidence that no matter what, with her parents nearby, she would be all right. She also saw the value of a mother who would speak up in her behalf.

Despite their unrealized dream of owning a farm, their continuing struggle to make ends meet, and their concern about their daughter's health, the Swansons built a solid life for their only child. They were deeply connected to the little town of Hills after moving there in 1945. It had a school building that held all 12 grades, which Joan attended when she was well enough. Most people's lives centered around that school and one of the three churches in the town.

The Swansons were active members of Bethlehem Lutheran Church. Joan had as many as 30 cousins to play with when the families had their Sunday picnics. She sat at the edge of the yard when she couldn't run and play with the others and figured out how to fit in. She didn't accept isolation from her cousins, and she became adept at attracting them to her by telling them stories and listening carefully to theirs. She excelled in the art of being a friend.

Dianne Nelson (now Van Goor), Joan's best friend to this day, speaks of their enduring connection. Dianne and Joan's parents shared a commitment to playing cards, farming, their Lutheran church, and politics. And they shared their daughters with each other. The two little girls were inseparable from first grade on.

Dianne missed Joan during the five years she was out of school for fusion surgery and subsequent hospitalizations. Though Joan was tutored at home when she wasn't at Gillette Hospital, Dianne stayed close. She often spent the night with the Swansons, who had scrimped to buy a television set when a station in Sioux Falls, South Dakota, began to broadcast. They thought it would be a nice diversion for Joan who was so often confined. Dianne came to Joan's place to watch *The Ed Sullivan Show* on most Sundays.

Dianne talked about spending whole weekends with the Swansons: "When I stayed overnight, her mom carried her up these steep stairs in the farm and put her in a twin bed upstairs. I crawled into the bed with her, and that is how we slept. And that cast was enormous. We giggled and giggled because she tried to roll over, and I would fall out of bed. It was during those years that we molded into one.

"After she had her casts, Joan had to relearn to walk three different times. Her folks called me on the phone to tell me she was ready to walk. Mom and Daddy dropped me off at the house. The Swansons had a back entry. It came down one step, and then you had to walk about

Joan on the farm at age 14

ten feet to the outside door. Arnold stood at that door and opened it for me. Then Stella helped Joanie down that step, and Joanie walked to me. So I was the first person who got to see her walk. It wasn't easy."

Joan learned to walk after each of the cast episodes. After the third cast and a lot of rehabilitation work, her step was firm. She returned to school and took on the full range of academic activities the small-town school could provide. Joan and Dianne's mothers were heavily involved in all their activities. Dianne's mother made the matching checked calico dresses that the girls wore when they performed at musical competitions. Stella was active as an adult leader in 4-H. Both mothers supported whatever their girls were involved in.

Growing up in a small town, Joan came to know a range of social and economic classes among the 600 people there. She knew some families at the church who lived in nicer homes and drove brand-new cars, and she knew a few who lived in broken-down homes, whose children looked different from her and her friends.

Joan also knew her parents spent a lot of time talking and worrying about money. She never forgot about the tears her father had shed over the loss of income from his sheep. As she grew older, she wondered how her parents had survived that loss of six months' income. She was careful to make few requests for things that would disrupt what she understood to be a tight budget. She recognized that her family was more frugal than most.

Joan also saw that her parents were somehow different from many of the folks in Hills. Her parents (along with their immediate neighbors, the Swedish Thorin "boys," who lived well into their nineties) were two of six Democrats in the entire township, Her mother served on the Rock County Welfare Board and participated in statewide welfare board activities. Her father counted votes at elections and came home afterwards to celebrate or bemoan the results with Dianne's parents, over a traditional oyster stew. Politics were central to the Swansons, and their take on the world was progressive.

Joan was a good listener to her friend Dianne, who was more physically active and gregarious. Joan's capacity to emphasize their similarities and relish their differences began a pattern of reciprocity and compassion that followed through her life. Dianne was a fast runner, but Joan was bit better at schoolwork. Dianne saw Joan as generous and intelligent. In high school Dianne worried over her homework and came to the Swansons' at night when she needed Joan to help work her through a math problem. According to Dianne, Joan got her through algebra. When they were younger, Joan had more physical limits. Dianne saw that Joan needed help sometimes, and that she could give it to her. She was good at that.

As the two girls grew older, Joan was able to help Dianne, and their

friendship became truly reciprocal. Their parents fostered the friendship—if one girl got a new doll, the other soon found one among the
gifts for her birthday or under the Christmas tree. They grew up in
tandem in the security of their families' intimacy and the support of
a small, homogeneous community. They were good students—Joan
graduated as valedictorian of her class, and Dianne was the salutatori-
an. When it was time to go off to college, they were ready.

Making Her Life
Joan and Dianne graduated from Hills High School in 1959. Dianne
went to Augustana, a small Lutheran college in nearby Sioux Falls. Joan
went the 230 miles to Macalester College in St. Paul, where she had
spent many months of her childhood at Gillette Children's Hospital.
Now the high-school graduate was healthy and eager for an intellectu-
ally demanding life.

Macalester was broadening its student body by actively recruiting
international students, and Joan relished the diversity she found there.
Macalester had been flying the United Nations flag on its campus every
day as an outward symbol of its international commitment. Its emphasis on international affairs appealed to Joan's childhood wish to be a
missionary and molded that inclination beyond religion.

Joan lived in the college dorm for two years and then moved off
campus. Resonating with the profession's respect for the worth and
dignity of all human beings, she became a student in the preparatory
social work program. She economized by renting a room at the home
of her sociology professor. Her mother's commitment to public welfare
and her own experience with poverty and a major disability clearly
influenced her aspirations.

Joan's last year at Macalester was eventful. She met her future husband, David White, and her family moved off the farm that had always meant home to her. Finally, after 20 years of working his rented
acreage, Arnold Swanson realized he was never going to make enough

money to buy a farm. He took a job with the U.S. Department of Agriculture in nearby Luverne, Minnesota, and he and Stella bought a small house in Hills.

Joan was saddened by the move, knowing of her father's passion for the land and his fundamental sense of loss in not succeeding to undo the family failure as independent farmers. She had inherited his pride of place, of ownership. She knew the purchase of a small house in Hills did not fill that need. But like her parents, Joan knew how to make do. And she chose to emphasize in her mind that Stella was planning a garden for the new house and Arnold seemed relieved to be on to a life removed from the seasonal demands of farming.

Joan had her own life decisions to make. Her boyfriend was eager to marry. Joan was less interested and said, "I have things to do. My high-school class thought I should be a missionary in Africa. But the missionary thing has slipped away since I started thinking about things differently."

The public-policy material of Joan's sociology and social work studies had broadened her view of personal and social change. Her new way of looking to the future moved her to apply for a graduate social work program at Western Reserve (now Case Western) University in Cleveland, Ohio, and she was accepted. She went off to get her master's degree in social work while David returned to Macalester, to graduate at the end of the next school year.

Joan and David remained a couple while Joan went to Western Reserve, seeing each other sporadically in Cleveland, St. Paul, and St. Louis. Joan was attracted to the liveliness she found in his family's home. He was the oldest of 13 children: Joan loved the energy she found there, and the family welcomed her calming presence. Coming from a small, low-keyed family, she relished the contrast.

Just as she had learned to build friendships with her more active cousins, Joan made connections through listening and empathizing with the voluble Whites, and she decided to become a part of the huge family. She and David married in Hills on the last day 1964. Joan's old friend Dianne was the bridesmaid. Joan's Aunt Margaret described the New Year's Eve ceremony at Bethlehem Lutheran Church as "a very simple and beautiful wedding."

After they finished their degrees, the two took a four-month driving trip to Central America. When asked about that journey, Joan said, "It was fun, and it was miserable. It was when we really got to know each other." Their deep differences of style and temperament began to emerge as a challenge for them both.

When the couple returned to St. Paul, David started graduate school and Joan began her career as a family social worker in the Ramsey County Welfare Department. Her colleague Gloria MacRae admired and was a bit in awe of Joan's tenacity and thoroughness: "She was always there at 7:30 in the morning, before the rest of us got there around 8:00. I kept saying to her that she had to take some time off, that she had to have a coffee break. So then we went for coffee. Then I said that she had to take time to have lunch, and so we had lunch. We had dinner together every Monday when David was at a class at the U." Joan was making another close and lasting friend.

During the time Joan worked in that first job for the county, her husband came home one day with an application for the two of them to join the Peace Corps, a surprise to Joan. When she told Gloria that they would be leaving, Gloria saw it as a "loss because we had been so close, even though it was only a year."

The couple had been worrying over the probability of David being drafted into the conflict in Vietnam. He was eligible for the draft because they had no children. Joan was well aware that having a child was not an option for her physically. And like so many of their contemporaries, neither Joan nor David supported the war. They saw the Peace Corps as an altruistic, desirable alternative to military service. In addition, Joan was still the same person who had contemplated becoming a missionary in another land. Her Macalester experience had re-directed her interest in the religious life and nourished her international and altruistic inclinations. She was immediately pulled into the idea of the Peace Corps, and the couple began the application process with a genuine desire for acceptance. Joan read a book about a woman who was one of the first Peace Corps volunteers to work in Latin America, resonating with her experience there.

But Joan was intimidated by the sheer physicality of the Peace Corps training she read about. She knew she would never be able to fulfill the physical demands the writer described.

Though Joan was afraid of the physical challenges she would certainly face, she was deeply attracted to the idea of the Peace Corps. She had several conversations with staff members and filled out innumerable forms. When it came time to complete the required physical examination, she went to her regular doctor, who refused to sign the required form. He felt strongly that her polio-related limitations were too great for her to go to an unspecified foreign country with a new and untested program: "The Peace Corps may be a great idea, but it's not for you."

Joan rejected his opinion and undertook a tenacious and systematic journey toward her goal of becoming a Peace Corps volunteer. She went to another physician, only to receive the same negative assessment. Nevertheless, she was convinced that the Peace Corps was something she wanted and would be able to do.

As a social worker, Joan had many contacts in the healthcare system, and she looked around for a doctor who wouldn't examine her too closely, one practicing in a busy place, who might typically be in a rush. The busy doctor she found never really looked at her, but he did fill out the form and return it to her. She sent it off to Washington, D.C. She also completed a medical history in which she could not avoid acknowledging that she had polio as a child. Then she received a request from the Peace Corps for a pulmonary function test.

Joan had never taken this test before, but she believed a negative result could jeopardize her acceptance into the program. She learned she must go into an airtight chamber and demonstrate that she could breathe more deeply than she thought she actually could. When she took the test, she quietly left the door unsealed to increase the amount of air in the room—and she passed, once again disallowing the impact of her childhood polio to limit her opportunity. Authorized to join the Peace Corps, the couple left St. Paul for a ten-week training program near Seattle.

By June 1967 Joan and David White were on their way to their two-year Peace Corps tour in Bolivia. They were assigned to the Uyuni mining area in the southern *altiplano* (plateau). The primarily indigenous population tolerated the harsh climate and the altitude of 13,000 feet. The couple landed in La Paz, Bolivia, for a week of orientation before moving on to Uyuni.

Joan approached the mountainous La Paz with some trepidation. Her struggle to get into the Peace Corps made her more wary of the impact of polio on her body than she had been in the past. She was afraid she wouldn't be able to breathe so was relieved when she felt good coming off the plane. But by the time she got to the hotel, the air seemed depleted, and she found it increasingly difficult to breathe. She did not realize that the muscles below her lungs were so damaged they couldn't pull air into her lungs at that altitude.

When Joan almost stopped breathing, the Peace Corps physician was called to the hotel. Her breathlessness brought her back to those years when she was a child, recovering from bouts with pneumonia, struggling to catch every breath. The doctor brought a portable oxygen tank to the hotel and examined Joan. He insisted that she use the cumbersome device until she was in a lower altitude.

Joan, David, and their Peace Corps companions then learned that they could not go to their assignments in Uyuni because of a bloody revolt in the mines. People were killed in the uprising, which was far worse than the typical resistance and disruption across Bolivia. Joan

From Minnesota

continued her use of the cumbersome oxygen tank as they waited for a decision from the Peace Corps about their future there.

The unsettled band of Peace Corps volunteers spent a month in the hotel waiting for word about their situation. The director of the program finally decided they could not go to the Uyuni mines because the unrest there had not abated. Everyone was disappointed—all of the training had focused on the people of the mines. There was an alternative to going home, however: "If you can find volunteer work somewhere else in the country, we will support your stay in Bolivia. Otherwise the Peace Corps will fly you home."

Returning to the United States wasn't an option for any of the young people eager to be of service, and they began to assess places other than the mining communities in which to begin their work. Finding somewhere with a more manageable altitude was a serious consideration for Joan and David. A few of the young people in the group went to small villages in other parts of the country. Joan and David learned through informal Peace Corps connections of opportunities in a barrio outside Cochabamba, known for its beauty and climate. At an altitude of 8,000 feet, the city was far lower than La Paz. A few others joined the couple in Cochabamba, which became their home for the next two years.

II

Connecting

Children greeting Joan at the gate of the daycare center she started in Cochabamba

4

Cochabamba and St. Paul

1967–1975

In 1967 when Joan and David White arrived at a barrio on the outskirts of Cochabamba, Segundo Velásquez was one of the first people they met. Without introducing himself, Segundo had grabbed a heavy bucket of water from Joan, relieving her of an unmanageable burden.

Segundo was walking down that particular street because he had heard there was a *gringo* (Anglo from North America) who was teaching auto-mechanics at no charge to young men of the barrio. Segundo was looking for this opportunity to learn about motors when he was distracted by Joan's need.

As he followed Joan, carrying her bucket, Segundo told her he was looking for a Señor David White, the gringo with motors. She laughed and told him that David was her husband. She asked him to follow her down the road into the enclosed patio, where a young blond man was bent over one of the many old motors he had scavenged from the Peace Corps and set up on benches and stands under a thatched roof.

Segundo set the tin pail at the door of the house and introduced himself to David. The two men were soon into detailed exploration of the motors. This was Segundo's first lesson in the mechanics David taught him. The *voluntario del Cuerpo de Paz* (Peace Corps volunteer) had scrounged the broken motors to attract people like Segundo.

Just as David White created his own Peace Corps job, Joan Swanson created hers. She heard about three priests from Iowa who wanted a volunteer for their new and needy Parroquia San Rafael (San Raphael Parish). Coming from Hills, Minnesota, which had three Protestant churches, Joan had never before had contact with Catholics. She came home from her first meeting with them and told David, "They are wonderful."

The priests did not have a specific program for a Peace Corps volunteer to undertake. But they knew of the unlimited need of people in a newly populated barrio with no running water, no city streets, no stores. The priests helped Joan find a place for her and David to live. Then they left her to her own devices.

Joan had learned of Saul Alinsky's strategy of community organizing when she was studying for her master's degree in social work. She remembered his admonition to start by getting to know another's point of view.[1] She took his words to heart and applied his tactic of meeting one-on-one with the people she hoped to move to action. As a social worker, she knew she had to get to know the community before she did anything else. She needed to know who her neighbors were, what they were like, and what they wanted.

Joan went to every single house in the poorest area of the parish, halfway up the foot of a mountainside. She was surprised at how willing all the women were to talk with her. She consistently introduced herself as a U.S. Peace Corps volunteer, but most of the women she connected with didn't really know what that meant. They accepted her as she was. They saw her as a representative of the parroquia, and no matter what she said, they thought she was a nun. One day, as she walked with a few of the women through the barrio, she asked them about the sign on nearly every house announcing that it was a *casa Católica* (Catholic house).

"Those signs are there to keep away evangelical church members who go door to door trying to convert us," they told her.

Joan was not an evangelical Christian, but she *was* a Protestant in a Catholic-dominated culture. She began to see that this could be a barrier to her work, but she was grateful to have the unquestioning support of the priests of Parroquia San Rafael. She did not deny her Protestantism, but in her typical quiet manner, she simply did not draw attention to the differences between her and the women of the barrio. The people she met when she knocked at their doors seemed exclusively Catholic. She also noticed that there were few men. She learned that they were away working at the mines or otherwise in and out of their households.

Every one of the mostly single mothers told her about a little girl who had recently burned to death. Joan was shaken as she told David about these conversations: "It was a five-year-old girl they all knew. The mother, with an infant on her back and a toddler in hand, went to the market to sell vegetables. It was her only source of income. You can take one or two children to the market, but taking three is really, really hard. And five-year-olds are often left alone.

"When she left for the market, the mother locked the door to protect the child she had to leave inside. The women think the little girl tried to make dinner by starting an *anafe* [Bunsen burner] with kerosene—you know, the kind that you pump and light with a match, something I never can do. And here was a five-year-old trying to do it!

"The women think her dress caught on fire. She was screaming. The neighbors could hear her. The door was locked. Before they could get to her, she was dead."

After Joan had visited nearly a hundred of the makeshift houses, she returned to the priests. She told them that the women she talked with agreed they needed a safe place for their children when they went to the market to sell their wares. Joan wanted to start a daycare center with them.

Cochabamba and St. Paul

The priests provided a room in an unfinished building for a center, and Joan applied diligence and quiet assertiveness to acquiring resources for the project. She got food from the U.S Alliance for Progress, convinced a local group of wealthy Bolivians connected to the alliance to provide a grant of $500, and enlisted her equally determined mother in Hills, Minnesota, in the fundraising effort. In Hills, Stella Swanson raised money through bake sales and come-as-you-are breakfasts.

Joan soon had enough furniture, supplies, and money for the salaries of a cook and a *niñera* (childcare worker) for three months. She went across the barrio to work with the 50 youngsters who came to the new daycare center, while David taught a growing group of aspiring mechanics in their front yard.

Segundo Velásquez, the son of a Quechua farmer-turned-tile-and-water-entrepreneur, was among the first of David White's many students, one intent on increasing his already considerable knowledge of how to make all manner of things work. David was intrigued with Segundo, impressed not only by his technical skills but also by his energy and active intelligence. He said he had never seen anybody who comprehended mechanical things the way Segundo did.

Segundo, already seeing broad advantage in a life beyond the barrio, also became a student in the English-language class Joan had started. Joan saw this protégé of David's as a good young man, but she had little to do with him outside the classroom. She considered him "David's person."

Segundo attached himself to David, following him about, trying to be of help, and the two became nearly constant companions. Segundo soon noticed he was not the only one gravitating to David, who had rigged up his bicycle to a carry a toddler. His occasional traveling companion was Natividad, whom everyone called Nati. She was the daughter of Flora, a woman who rented a room in the house where David and Joan lived. Nati had attached herself to both of them, and she soon began attending the daycare center.

Cochabamba Challenges

As Joan oversaw the center and worked with the children, she continued to look for the $80 the center needed each month to keep it afloat. She beat on doors through the neighborhoods of Cochabamba. She went to the *alcalde's* (mayor's) office on the Plaza Principal and told him the story of the San Rafael daycare center and its needs. With gracious politeness he told her that in a month there would be money from the *gobierno* (federal government), for which the center was eligible.

In exactly one month Joan came back to him, and he said, "Oh, Señorita, you must have misunderstood. There is no money." Sitting across from his the desk, Joan recalled the Peace Corps training in which she had passed a test to establish her fluency in Spanish. She knew she had not misunderstood the alcalde. She did not tell him of the depth of her Spanish fluency but said, "Señor, you are a *mentiroso* [liar] and a *ladron* [thief]. I know that the money is there, and I expect some of it for my daycare center." And she left.

The next day a truck arrived at the center full of food products. Joan made good use of the truckload while she quietly accepted that she would get nothing more from the alcalde.

Having little success with the government in her search for resources, Joan decided to approach another institution of power in Bolivia— the Catholic Church. She took a bus from her barrio to the Plaza Principal, where a big church stood. She was looking for the archbishop of Cochabamba. First directed to an old building, she was then sent to a formal reception room filled with indigenous people dressed in poor Quechua clothing.

The people waited in silence. Their dark clothes made the broad white hats of some of the women especially noticeable. A fair-skinned man in a black, floor-length dress with many small buttons sat at a desk. He took Joan's name and wrote it in a book. Eventually a door opened, and all eyes turned to an older man in long robes wearing a tall white hat that made him seem immense. The tiny American Protestant wondered how his splendor affected the waiting Quechua people, most of them as small as she.

Joan was uncomfortable when she heard her name called before the many who had been waiting before her, but she walked slowly to the archbishop. He stuck out his right hand, and she shook it. She noticed his frown of irritation as she followed him into his office.

The archbishop sat behind a huge desk, facing her as she told him about the mothers and children of San Rafael, a story she had presented many times in her efforts to raise money. The archbishop listened impassively, then ushered her out the door, saying he would see what he could do.

As the door closed behind him, Joan sat with the others quietly waiting their turns. She knew there was something she needed to learn about the process of talking with an archbishop. A bit later, the door opened again, and a new name was called. A Quechua couple walked up to the archbishop standing in the doorway. First they knelt before him, putting their foreheads to the floor, then they kissed the big ring on his hand before rising to their feet.

Joan understood that she had not given the archbishop the proper respect. If she *had* known, she thought, she would have found the ritual of kneeling and kissing his ring too foreign and demeaning to undertake. Also, she realized with humor, had she knelt, she would not have had the strength to get up off the floor. Unlike the alcalde, who had at least made a token response to Joan's request, the archbishop did nothing for the women and children of San Rafael.

Working and living with their *vecinos* (neighbors) in the daycare program and the mechanics classes was comfortable and satisfying for Joan and David. Some of their neighbors wondered why they lived in a modest house such as their own and why they lived frugally. These neighbors never quite grasped that the voluntarios del Cuerpo de Paz were expected to live much as the people they served. Joan and David's stipend reflected the Bolivians' meager incomes.

The couple received a very different welcome when venturing onto the university campus backing right against their barrio. Frequently, when they walked in that direction, students screamed and yelled, "Go home!" Joan and David were gringos and *Yanquis* (Yankees or North Americans). They did not miss the irony—they felt a political kinship with the students. In addition to their commitment to improve life for the poor in Bolivia, they were serving in the Peace Corps partially in resistance to David's being drafted into the U.S. military misadventure in Vietnam.

This was a tumultuous political time in Bolivia and in the western hemisphere. Bolivia had an elected but military president, and many protested his authority. That the Cuban-sponsored revolutionary Che Guevara was in the Bolivian jungle as part of the resistance to the military government complicated matters. Cochabamba was often in a state of siege. People were coming from outlying towns to support the president, who was born and had lived in the rural areas and who spoke Quechua. Demonstrations in the Plaza Principal included large numbers of people, some carrying coffins labeled "Uncle Sam."[2]

David and Joan stayed clear of the upheaval, but they got to know several Bolivian students in a nearby café, and they were able to convince them that they weren't CIA agents. The couple eventually made friends with some of them. Edgar Paz, a medical student, was one they came to know well. One evening when they went to the café, he wasn't there, and they soon learned he had been killed in a demonstration.

This personal loss brought the political situation in Bolivia into vivid consciousness but did not deter them from their work in the barrio. Joan and David were glad that the United States was admired there. People like Segundo Velásquez and his family had none of the political leanings of their lost friend.

Segundo heard tales of Joan's meetings with the alcalde and the archbishop and the couple's university friends. He admired Joan's calm assertiveness and her willingness and ability to move on from disappointment like the loss of her friend Edgar. He saw that she was unwilling to accept that she must rely only on the support of the three priests and the small payment that each mother made to leave her children at the center. She raised the money needed by nearly continual fundraising, as did her mother in Hills.

Joan maintained her relationship with little Natividad, and Segundo watched her tenderness with the girl. He noted Joan's tenacity in laboring up and down the hills and paths of the barrio with Nati in hand. He had already acquired a friend and mentor in David, and he was delighted to come to know and respect Joan. As Segundo became closer to David, he learned that the couple was considering bringing Natividad to the United States when they returned home.

As Joan and Natividad's mother, Flora, came to know one another, Flora revealed that she would like to have her daughter live with Joan and David in the United States. Segundo, sensing opportunity, mentioned to David that he too was interested in living there. David told Joan it might be a good thing for Segundo to live with them in St. Paul.

Joan reminded David of their conversations about taking Natividad to the United States. But Flora had some doubts about sending her child away. And no matter how much Joan promised to keep Nati in contact with her, Flora remained unconvinced. Also, Joan was learning of nearly insurmountable barriers to obtaining a visa for the child. She had come to love Natividad, and she was deeply disappointed, but she finally accepted that she would have to say good-bye to her.

And it was fine with Joan for Segundo to return with them to St. Paul. David gave additional English lessons to Segundo in hope that by the time he got to St. Paul, he would have some fluency.

Leaving Bolivia
When Segundo brought up going with the Peace Corps volunteers to the United States, his parents were unsettled. The place was foreign to them and so far away from Bolivia. This was the third time they'd had

to respond to the prospect of one of their children going beyond the family circle.

The first was when the Velásquez family moved from the hacienda to Laguna Sulti. Madrina Elena Urey of Candelaria, who lived in Cochabamba, had pushed Inés and Epifanio to send the older children to school in the city. Cochabamba was another world to parents who rarely ventured beyond Laguna Sulti and San Benito. They shared Elena's belief that the best education was to be found in a big city. But rather than send Ivo and Cati away, they decided that the whole family would move on to new opportunity. So they left Laguna Sulti for Canata, on the edge of Cochabamba.

The second time Epifanio and Inés were faced with balancing wishes for their children against their commitment to keep the family together involved José, Segundo's younger brother. The headmaster of the Yugoslavian school that three of the children attended invited José to further his education in Yugoslavia. The headmaster saw José's high intelligence, diligence, and gregariousness and felt that he would be enriched by a European education. He offered José a full scholarship, but after much discussion José's parents decided he could not accept the invitation. They were not willing to send him so far away without being able to follow him to Yugoslavia. His deep disappointment did not outweigh Inés and Epifanio's desire to keep their children nearby.

So Segundo was not surprised to meet his parents' almost total resistance to his plan. His challenge to the family's togetherness was profound; he made little headway with his argument. Segundo was older than the others had been when his parents considered their departure; he was more apt to settle far from home. He wanted to go off to a foreign place and likely would never return. They thought they would never see him again. Further, the family adhered to the tradition of giving such an opportunity to an older, if not the firstborn, child.

Finally, Ivo intervened for his brother Segundo. He reminded

Segundo at age 19, in Minnesota

his father that he, the oldest child, did not want to go to the United States, and that the second child, Cati, had not been invited. Ivo contended with persuasion and compassion that Segundo was next in line. And so Segundo's parents decided to bless Segundo in his adventure.

Segundo was relieved when his father finally said, "If you get the opportunity to go to the United States, then you may tell David White that your parents are interested in helping you to do that." Epifanio and Inés gave Segundo some of their hard-earned savings for his airfare. When David and Joan's two-year tour in Bolivia ended, Segundo traveled with them to the United States.

A New World
The transition from Bolivia to the United States was difficult for both Joan and Segundo. Two years earlier, when Joan stepped off the plane in Cochabamba, she was relieved to find she could breathe without oxygen after her month of difficulty in La Paz. But though she had worked successfully in the relatively low altitude of Cochabamba, her body had been stressed in the city that was still much higher than the Minnesota prairie she had grown up on. Furthermore, she found that

leaving the daycare center and traveling to the United States via Peru was exhausting.

At one point during their journey home, Joan, David, and Segundo had a layover in Lima, Peru. Joan collapsed into a bed in a hotel in Lima. She was eager to see her parents, who were planning to meet the three of them for a tour of Mexico, but she felt fragile and wondered whether she had the energy to get on another plane in the morning.

Segundo looked at the frail woman on the bed and knew he must watch over her in his new life in America. After a night's sleep, Joan recovered to the extent that she was able to board the plane with David and Segundo and reunite with Stella and Arnold in Mexico City.

The difficulty in Segundo's transition from his homeland was different from Joan's physical challenge but nonetheless unsettling. Arnold and Stella met the threesome at the Mexico City airport in a two-toned blue Ford LTD. Joan's parents rarely made such extravagant purchases, but Arnold was proud of his car and of the practicality of his choice. He pointed out the trunk to Joan, announcing that it was big enough to carry a crate of fresh eggs.

Segundo was fresh from his first experience in an airplane, his first experience in a new country, and now he was riding along with Joan's parents. They were the first people he had ever known who spoke neither of his languages, Quechua and Spanish. Segundo felt lost. His head was spinning. He thought, "I know I am in Mexico. I know I am on earth, but I am floating. I guess this is what Joan and David call 'shock de cultura.' After all, I am going to a place where people tell me that the streets are paved with gold and money grows on trees."

The trip north from Mexico City was a blur for Segundo, sitting with David and Joan in the back seat of Arnold Swanson's car. Stella shared the front with Arnold. Once they crossed the border between Mexico and the United States, Segundo found himself in motels and restaurants that were modest by U.S. standards but luxurious to a teenager from the barrio. He was astonished at the amount of money spent.

Cochabamba and St. Paul

Arnold, a baseball fan, stopped in Houston, Texas. He wanted to see the first dome-covered multipurpose stadium in the country and to show this architectural feat to Segundo. He went to the ticket office to buy the dollar-per-person tickets to view the Astrodome. Segundo said to Joan quietly in Spanish, "I don't need to see the stadium. That's too much money to spend to see a building. Imagine what could be done with a dollar in Bolivia."

When Joan translated Segundo's concern about the expense, Arnold turned to Segundo and gave him a dollar bill. The others entered the stadium, leaving Segundo behind. Later, in the car, Segundo spread the bill on his lap and told the group, "A campesino would have to work for a whole day to earn this dollar. I am going to send it to my mother." Stella took him to a post office in Houston to get an international mailer and helped him send the dollar to Bolivia.

This was neither the first nor the last time Segundo forewent something for himself so as to extend the meager income of his Bolivian family. The letters that began to arrive weekly from Cochabamba when he settled in St. Paul were constant reminders of the vast difference between the comforts of his life and the continuing financial struggle of his relatives.

When Joan and David returned to St. Paul in 1969 after their two-year absence, the two rented an apartment big enough to accommodate Segundo as well. He was disappointed to find neither streets of gold nor trees filled with money near the modest apartment. But he soon recognized his new world as one of opportunity.

Searching for a program to help Segundo improve his English, David enrolled him in classes at St. Paul Central High School. He knew that having a diploma from a high school in the United States would improve Segundo's financial opportunity. And Segundo knew that fluency in English and a good education could bring him what he wanted most—a good job that would provide him enough money to bring his whole family to live in the United States.

Meanwhile, Joan's parents embraced Segundo. After arriving in St. Paul, he left almost immediately for Hills to spend the summer with the Swansons. Joan felt that the best way to improve Segundo's English quickly was to have him live in a house in a town where no one spoke Spanish. The Swansons readily agreed, and Segundo left the busyness of St. Paul for the relative tranquility of Hills. This resulted not only in a big improvement to his English but also in cementing a bond with the Swansons. By the time he moved back to the St. Paul apartment in the fall, Segundo was referring to the Swansons as Mom and Dad, just as Joan and David did. His U.S. "parents" had smoothly integrated Segundo into their extended family, their church, and their town.

In the fall Arnold and Stella brought Segundo back to St. Paul to continue his high-school education. Segundo wanted to get a job, and Arnold, supporting the idea, took Segundo to University Avenue, where all the St. Paul car dealerships were. They found a job opening at Midway Ford, and Segundo applied for it. When he was offered the job, Arnold helped him bargain a good salary. Segundo worked one night a week and every Saturday as a helper, sweeping and cleaning.

When Segundo received his first paycheck, Joan assumed he would contribute to their household. With David in graduate school and her job as a county social worker their sole support, money was tight. But Segundo didn't even offer to help. When Joan asked him about it, he said he had sent the cash to his mother, just as he had the dollar from the foregone Astrodome tour. At first displeased, Joan then agreed, at least for the time being, to his sending nearly every penny he earned to his family in Bolivia.

Segundo exchanged weekly letters with the Velásquezes in Cochabamba. He also got to know the Whites; several of David's adult siblings lived nearby. David's parents lived several hundred miles away in St. Louis, but the couple's ties with them were strong. Joan was delighted to be surrounded by so many Whites and Swansons. Segundo was pleased at how comfortable he felt in the mix. It seemed only natural that the huge extended family welcoming him so warmly would be equally accepting of his family. Segundo frequently reminded his St. Paul family that he intended to apply for visas for his seven siblings as well as for his parents as soon as he became a citizen.

Changes

In 1970, as Segundo was completing high school and dreaming of reunion with his Bolivian family, David delivered devastating news. He told Joan he wanted a separation and that he would be moving out of the apartment. Though their life together had never been truly satisfying to her, the decision stunned her.

In addition to the many changes that now confronted her, Joan was concerned about how Segundo would react to David's departure. She insisted that David be the one to tell him, and he did as she asked. Joan assumed David would take Segundo with him when he moved out: she reminded him that Segundo had no options should David relinquish his responsibility.

David answered, "If Segundo can't make it on his own, he will have to go back to Bolivia," and despite Joan's entreaties, he left without Segundo. Segundo and David's sister Emily White, who had come to live there for a few months, stayed with Joan.

Joan turned for solace to her sister social worker Gloria MacRae, as she always did when big things happened. Joan told Gloria about the unanticipated separation and shared her concern for Segundo. She did not mask her deep disappointment and frustration with David.

"Segundo is lost now that David has left," she told Gloria. "He was Segundo's anchor here. It never occurred to me that Segundo would be living with me without David or that I would be Segundo's anchor. Now I realize I will have to be."

Segundo wrote his family in Bolivia about David's decision. In a return letter, his parents insisted he leave the house immediately: His life was in danger. David would come to kill him for stealing his

72

wife. When Segundo showed Joan the letter, she laughed and then was dismayed.

The Velásquez family's response to the separation added to her growing appreciation of the depth of difference between Bolivian and American sensibilities. It had never occurred to her that anyone would think she and Segundo had an intimate relationship, let alone that David would kill Segundo should that in fact be the case. Segundo asked David to explain the situation, and David quickly wrote to the Bolivian family that Segundo was not the reason for the separation.

Joan settled into life after David by buying a little house on Laurel Avenue. David's sister Mary had taken Emily's place as a member of the household. Joan, Mary, and Segundo moved into their new neighborhood, and the new home Joan created became a centering place for many in the following years. David occasionally visited to eat with the family on Laurel. And though the visits tapered, Joan assumed he would eventually return. But three years after the separation, David initiated a divorce that ended his legal connection with Joan and the family on Laurel.

Segundo was still a student at St. Paul Central in 1970, when his older sister, Cati, grew impatient waiting in Bolivia for him to finish his education, become a citizen, and start the long process of applying for visas for his family. She found a quicker way to get to the United States. A letter from the Velásquezes told Segundo that Cati was in California with a Bolivian man and several other young women. The family had given him money in exchange for his promise to Cati of an education, a job, and a visa.

When Segundo and Joan reached Cati by phone, they learned there was no schooling, no job, no visa. Fearing that she had been caught in a prostitution ring, they wired Cati money for a bus ticket to St. Paul. Cati gathered her few belongings and left California without telling her questionable Bolivian helpers.

Cochabamba and St. Paul

Cati was grateful to be away from the man who had tricked her into coming to North America. But she was also anxious about taking a long bus ride through a strange country. She was relieved to see Joan and Segundo at the St. Paul bus station. Their faces were the first familiar ones she had seen since leaving Bolivia the previous week. Cati was barely more than 20 years old. She spoke almost no English; she was shaken by her recent experience and confused about her future.

Joan immediately moved into the advocacy mode so natural to her. She went to the Immigration and Naturalization Services (INS) office and connected with a red-haired official who was so helpful to Cati that Joan knew she would remember him for the rest of her life. He believed Cati and acted in her behalf. He agreed to investigate the man who lured her to the United States and told Joan that if she could find an educational program that would admit Cati, the INS would give her a student visa.

Cati was interested in studying to be a nurse, and Joan, through her work, had developed a good connection with the nursing program at Midway Hospital in St. Paul. Soon Cati had her student visa and was enrolled in Midway's nursing program. Cati became Mary White's roommate in the house on Laurel, and Segundo and Joan became her English tutors.

As Segundo neared his 1971 graduation from Central High School, his teachers and counselors encouraged him to go on to college. Had he stayed in Bolivia, he would have studied to be the architect he had always hoped to be. But with the determination to bring his family to the United States, he gave up that dream. He looked for a quicker way to becoming credentialed for a job that would bring him a good salary.

Building on the mechanical skills he had been nurturing at a job repairing racecars in St. Paul, Segundo applied to Minneapolis Area Vocational Technical Institute (now Minneapolis Community and Technical College). In Bolivia, aviation was an especially lucrative area, so he was pleased to be accepted into the popular two-year aviation mechanics program. He combined his time studying airplane mechanics with flight training at Anoka Aviation. In 1973 he graduated with his aviation mechanics licenses, acquired his private pilot license, and began a full-time position with S.A.E.F., at Fleming Field in South St. Paul.

Segundo not only repaired and flew airplanes but also bought them. In the years he worked with S.A.E.F. Air Repair, he bought two small planes: a Mooney and a Cessna. Having negotiated the use of the company's facilities and tools after work hours, he often stayed after his eight-hour shift to spend another four hours repairing and improving his planes. He sold one for a significant profit and kept the other for his own use.

A New Relationship

Gradually, Segundo took on more of the traditional male roles in the household on Laurel Avenue. All things mechanical reverted to him, but he also began to share more financial and family decisions with Joan. Joan took a while to see her evolving relationship with Segundo as romantic.

The first hint that their connection was changing occurred in 1974, as they drove together to Montgomery Ward, a huge department store on University Avenue that carried most anything a person might want for the home. Joan and Segundo were on their way to get a part for the washing machine. Segundo was driving, and Joan was in the passenger seat. No one else from the house was with them, as Segundo took care of almost everything for the house. Joan noticed his hand tightening a bit on the stick shift when he started a sentence with, "When you and I are married . . . "

Joan interrupted him with a laugh: "Are you joking?" She really didn't get it. She grasped the seriousness of his intent only when she looked into his eyes. She found the idea of marriage to a man ten years younger than she as "weird." She had known Segundo since he was a youth in Bolivia. He had lived with her in the house for five years as a friend, or brother. As she rode alongside Segundo, she realized that something had changed without her noticing.

Yes, she and Segundo had been doing more things together lately, without the other people in the house. They went canoeing and walking. Sometimes they drove to South Minneapolis to a theater that had cheap movies and good popcorn. She depended more and more on Segundo's opinions and support. But this "married" thing was something she and Segundo must talk about. The already years-long conversation continued as they became a couple, sharing responsibility for the household on Laurel Avenue.

Joan was well aware that almost everything Segundo did was tied to his deep commitment to his family in Bolivia. She understood—her relationship with her own parents was equally important. But there were significant differences. Segundo's family's financial need was great. And as Bolivians, they placed a greater cultural emphasis on family, and the family was huge. It included his parents—Epifanio and Inés—his seven brothers and sisters, and more recently, their children.

The Swanson family numbered only three. Off the farm and with Arnold's government job, her parents were financially secure. Joan and her parents were emotionally supportive of one another, talking frequently on the phone and visiting often. Segundo was inextricably tied to the financial life of his family in Bolivia—he had sent home nearly every cent he made. But he had not been to his homeland since coming to the United States in 1969.

Meanwhile, Segundo's dream for his Bolivian family had evolved beyond improving their life in Bolivia. He wanted them with him in the United States. Both he and Joan saw this as something they wanted to do together. They imagined Segundo's Bolivian family living in St. Paul, and they began planning to make that a reality.

Segundo frequented garage sales and auctions to buy good, inexpensive furniture for a place he hoped to buy for his family, storing the stuff in his garage and attic. He examined properties for sale that might be suitable for family members coming next to St. Paul. Later, he and Joan bought an apartment building in need of repair so that Segundo's father and brothers would have something to work on when they first came to live in St. Paul.

As the couple planned for the Velásquez family to move to the United States, Segundo moved along the road to American citizenship. Working with S.A.E.F. Air Repair, he sent most of his salary to Bolivia. Joan continued working for Ramsey County, devoting her income to the household on Laurel Avenue and saving for a doctoral program. Mary White lived with Joan and Segundo; other Whites stayed with them from time to time. Cati Velásquez, feeling the tug of her mother's wish to have her home, left her hospital job in St. Paul and returned to Bolivia.

Segundo became a citizen in 1974 and thus was able to begin the process of obtaining visas for his many family members. He began to think concretely about bringing them to the United States. His father, who operated from a typically hierarchal view, assumed that Ivo, the oldest brother, would have the first opportunity. But Segundo, less tied to Bolivian tradition, considered which family member would benefit most from a move to the United States, which would best fit into their home. He insisted to his father that his youngest brother, César, be the first—precisely because he was the youngest. Segundo wanted his brother to make the transition when he was younger than he himself had been—Segundo had found the adjustment to a new country difficult, especially in terms of the language.

Ivo told his parents that he agreed with Segundo about César, which helped move them from resistance. And Epifanio and Inés eventually deferred to Segundo. This was the first time since he had pushed for parental approval to move to the United States that Segundo so dramatically inserted himself into the Velásquez family decision-making.

The 11-year-old César came to St. Paul chaperoned by his older

César and Joan during César's first year in Minnesota

brother Ivo. Joan was delighted to be caring for a child, and to have Ivo as well in her household. After a few months Ivo returned to his family in Cochabamba. The household on Laurel at that time included Joan, Segundo, Mary, and César, plus the newly arrived Dan and John White, two of Mary's brothers.

Joan and Segundo on their wedding day, 1978

5

International Family

1976–1993

Though letters provided the only means of communication between the United States and Bolivia, the Velásquez family ties remained strong. César immersed himself in American life, going to school and making friends. When Joan went to the University of Minnesota to study for her doctorate, César was at the bus stop daily to help her carry her books home. But he missed his mother and wrote her faithfully.

As each Velásquez came to the Laurel house, he or she struggled to integrate the ways of the new homeland with those of Bolivia. Segundo's sister Cati had enjoyed the Laurel house as she attended nursing school, worked part time, and little by little set aside some of her earnings. But as the oldest daughter, she became convinced that it was too hard on her mother for her to be away for so long.

Cati returned to Bolivia in 1974. By then the tile and water businesses were sufficiently successful that Epifanio and his sons had been able to add two bedrooms and a living room to the property. Cati, with her savings, bought her mother appliances and a set of living-room furniture. Delighted to have her back, Epifanio treated her as the young, unmarried women she had been when she left four years previously.

Epifanio had always been a strict disciplinarian, especially with his daughters, who he thought needed special protection. Now Cati, finding she could not accept the restriction of going from the house only when accompanied by another member of the family, resisted her father's rules. Her years in the United States had made her too independent to fulfill highly gendered Bolivian expectations. Within months she married, and she became pregnant almost immediately. She and her husband moved into the nearby home of Mamanchaj—Acensia Irusta—and Tia Juanita.

In 1975 Joan and Segundo went to Cochabamba for the first time since they had left in 1969. Now they were a couple, and this was the first time they saw Segundo's parents after the fundamental change in their relationship. One of the first things Joan and Segundo did was visit Cati, who was pregnant and living at Mamanchaj's adobe house.

Segundo, like Cati, had been changed by his five years in the United States in ways he did not realize before his return to Bolivia. He had left as an 18-year-old, and he returned from a typical American middle-class life with Joan.

The Velásquezes still lived in the home place in Canata, now part of a busy, urban community. Ivo and his family lived in rooms across the patio from Epifanio, Inés, and the other children. José was well on his way to becoming a pediatrician. Margui was in college. Blanca and Rubén were in high school. The whole family appreciated the refrigerator that Cati had bought for their mother, especially for the ever-cool pitcher of sugar water their mother boiled and placed there.

The cool sugar water in the new refrigerator was too sweet for Joan, who asked Segundo to ask for a separate pitcher of water, without sugar. He brought this up at the dinner table. José, asserting his role as the primary independent male in the house after his father, denied the request, teasing Segundo that this was not the way things were done in the Velásquez house. Inés quietly put a second, sugarless pitcher of water in the new refrigerator, but for days José went through the house singing the song "Tradition" from *Fiddler on the Roof.* Joan and Segundo understood that they had broken a family tradition.

The sugar-water scenario was a useful reminder that even the introduction of a refrigerator and the temporary visit of a bicultural son and his partner from the United States could disrupt cultural patterns evolved over centuries. The cool sugar water was a welcome addition to the household. But its counter to Joan and Segundo's taste elicited responses symptomatic of the complexities of interdependence in the international Velásquez family. It was no accident that Inés's quiet placement of the second pitcher of water enabled the disparate members of the family to move on.

Joan and Cati had become close in Minnesota, and from the moment of Segundo and Joan's visit to Cati, the two women spent a lot of time together in Bolivia. Cati was especially eager for Joan to visit the cemetery holding the remains of Ivo's first child. Not yet a year of age, he had recently died of an infection. But when the two women walked through the huge stone and metal gate, Cati put one hand on her barely swelling belly and reached out to touch Joan's arm with the other.

"Do you know there is a superstition in Bolivia that if a pregnant woman goes into a cemetery, her baby will die? You don't think that's true, do you?"

Joan was silent for a bit before answering. "I don't really think so. But perhaps there is some type of bacteria in the cemetery that we don't know about. We certainly don't need to go in."

Cati decided that the superstition was just that. She took Joan's arm, and the two women walked into the mausoleum to find the vault holding Ivo's baby's remains.

When Joan and Segundo were near the end of their visit, his parents made a special effort to talk to them privately. Epifanio and Inés knocked on the door of the bedroom that the couple was sharing with Segundo's siblings. They told Segundo and Joan that they hoped the couple would formally adopt César.

Inés sat down beside Joan on the bed and took her hand, addressing her in the Spanish version of her name. "Juanita, now that César will be in America, you will be César's mother. You will take care of him as your son."

Joan realized she had been thinking of César as Segundo's primary responsibility, that any legal tie would involve César and Segundo, not her. She was not ready to decide about marriage to Segundo. But when Inés made it clear that Joan must be the mother César needed while making a life so far from home, Joan accepted that no matter what happened between her and Segundo, she must take care of César as her own child. Joan and Segundo told Inés and Epifanio they would begin the process of adopting César.

Satisfied with their decision, Epifanio turned to Segundo, asking him when a wedding would take place. Politely excusing herself, Joan made it clear she would not be part of this conversation. She left the room, and in minutes Segundo and his parents emerged. Segundo had established that he and Joan were not planning marriage in the near future. The couple returned to St. Paul with a relationship more defined by Joan's commitment to parent César but less defined than Inés and Epifanio had hoped.

In the 1970s, international phone service was limited. But several weeks after Joan and Segundo returned to St. Paul from Bolivia, they received a phone call from a short-wave radio operator in South Carolina with a devastating message from Ivo, who had been trying to reach them for days.

In the seventh month of her pregnancy, Cati had died. She had complained to her mother of stomach pain, and they went together to a clinic in the city. The doctor told Inés that the baby was about to be born and she should go home for baby clothes. When Inés got to the house, she found José, who had stopped by from medical school. They rushed back to the clinic with the new clothes.

The doctor barred the way when Inés tried to go into the examining room where she had left Cati. He pulled José aside, whispering, *"Hijo, ven* [son, come]. Your sister is dead." Inés heard the words and rushed into the room. Cati was lying there with an IV tube in her arm, the doctor mumbling that she had had a heart attack.

José, about to become a physician himself, was shocked that his healthy sister, who had selected the most respected private clinic in Cochabamba to care for her during her pregnancy, was now dead.

Joan and Segundo reeled from the news of Cati's death just as they were becoming increasingly concerned about Joan's pervasive weakness and new difficulty in navigating the stairs. Segundo's sensitivity to her fragility had not waned from the time he assisted her with the bucket of water on the dirt road of the barrio many years before. He insisted they see her doctor.

Joan and Segundo learned that her new symptoms were part of the only newly understood postpolio syndrome. People, like Joan, who had polio in the 1940s, were beginning to show symptoms of fatigue and muscle deterioration 30 years later. The seriousness of the syndrome was related to the severity of the childhood episode. Joan had been totally paralyzed as a child, and her version of the syndrome was severe.

Minimizing the centrality of the diagnosis of postpolio syndrome, Joan tried, with some success, to conserve her energies while moving on in her life with Segundo. In 1977 Segundo had moved to a good position in the sheet-metal shop at Northwest Airlines (NWA). In 1978 he and Joan bought a new house and married, much to the delight of both sets of parents.

Since their trip to Cochabamba in 1975 Joan and Segundo had known they would marry. Busy with family and work, however, they gave little thought to when their wedding might be. Then, in 1978, Joan was invited to speak about her research at a national conference. This triggered a plan to take advantage of the NWA flight passes she could receive if she were married to Segundo. With a free pass, she could use her travel budget to cover the cost for a member of her staff to attend the conference as well. So Joan and Segundo chose February 4, 1978, shortly before the conference, for their wedding date.

They were married in the chapel at Macalester College, Joan's alma mater. Joan remembers: "We chose Mac because it was very inexpensive, and we purchased nothing new to wear for the occasion. I happened to have a long, mostly white dress, bought a couple of years earlier and worn several times. Segundo wore slacks and a jacket from his closet. My mother was the only person who bought something new. She always welcomed a chance to dress up."

With only a few guests, the wedding was small. A friend played the harpsichord, and longtime colleague Don Bump, also a Presbyterian minister, presided. Mary White, Joan's former sister-in-law, was the bridesmaid, and 14-year-old César Velásquez, whom Joan and Segundo were raising, was the best man. They wrote their own vows and exchanged inexpensive puzzle rings, each a chain of interlocking circles.

Before the wedding ceremony, the rings fell apart—first one, then the other. The harpsichordist played an extra 20 minutes while guests struggled to reassemble them. When one ring fell apart a second time, the attendants worked hard to stifle their laughter. According to Joan, "Their response reflected the informality of our wedding and much of the rest of our lives."

After the wedding, Joan and Segundo received guests in the dining room of the Midway Motor Inn on University Avenue. Joan had planned a KFC picnic in the room below the chapel, but their friend Gloria MacRae insisted that was going far: "You can't have KFC for your wedding reception." They had a sit-down luncheon instead.

On his next trip to Bolivia, Segundo replaced the puzzle rings with simple gold bands. After 37 years, he still jokes that Joan married him only for his passes.

Margui and Rubén came from Cochabamba to live with the newlyweds to improve their English and attend vocational classes. And Joan completed her doctorate with a sophisticated dissertation on the efficacy of milieu therapy in the treatment of those who are chronically mentally ill. Her new position at Ramsey County increased her salary and responsibilities.

As the research director of Community Human Services, Joan designed and implemented an innovative evaluation system for use in all the county's service agencies. She worked assertively and calmly through the complex intergovernmental maze of county, state, and federal bureaucracies, becoming invaluable to the executive director of her agency. She wrote grants and proposals to fund the agency's work with a remarkable level of success.

Joan frequently went up Kellogg Boulevard along the Mississippi River from her agency to City Hall. That was where her employer, the Ramsey County Board of Commissioners, conducted its business. She made frequent presentations and recommendations to the commissioners. One day when she came home in the casual clothes that she typically wore to work, Segundo asked her about her day. She started describing a problem with the report she had presented to the board that morning.

Segundo, noticing her outfit, just a step up from blue jeans, smiled and said, "Joan, now that you are spending so much time at county board meetings, I think you might want to think about the clothes you are wearing."

She responded that she was always neat and clean, but Segundo interrupted: "I think they expect a more professional look. Joan, let's go down to Petite Sophisticate."

Reluctantly accepting the unsuitability of her typical work clothes for government meetings, she accompanied Segundo to a shop specializing in clothes for people as small as she.

At the store, Joan felt more and more uncomfortable with each flattering outfit she tried on. She quickly bought three suits. By then she was thoroughly ill. When she got home, she vomited, flashing back

Joan in 1980

to her first Christmas at Gillette Children's Hospital. She recalled her mother saying, "No one should have more than they need."

Joan could hardly overcome her Swanson frugality and empathy for those who had less. But she dutifully donned one of the suits on the days she might be attending a commissioners' meeting. She reminded herself that even though she was the owner of three "extravagant" outfits, she was arguing for those who did in fact have less. She thought her mother would approve.

Ancianos

The Velásquez family was in continual flux. Margui returned to Bolivia, having found Minnesota winters too cold. Segundo's trips between Cochabamba and St. Paul increased as he advanced at Northwest Airlines, receiving more vacation time and free airline passes.

On returning to the United States, Segundo always reported to Joan about his parents' increasing age. He was convinced they deserved a more comfortable, safe, and clean home to live in for the rest of their lives. In 1980 Joan and Segundo first brought Inés and Epifanio to live in their home for several months.

The *ancianos* (elders) then came every year. They delighted in watching their sons César and Rubén flourish in their new home. Everyone at the U.S. end relished the time spent with Inés and Epifanio during their annual visit. The parents tried hard to be useful. Epifanio cleaned the snow off the cars every morning before they went to work; Inés pleased everyone at the table, cooking all of Segundo's favorite meals.

Despite everyone's hopes that the senior Velásquezes would move to St. Paul, Joan and Segundo eventually got the sense that Epifanio and Inés were not really comfortable there. Language had always been an issue for them. Inés spoke only Quechua, in a part of Bolivia where most of the people she knew were bilingual. Epifanio was fluent in both Spanish and Quechua, but neither one spoke English. This hampered and isolated them when they were in St. Paul.

One day when both Joan and Segundo were working, his parents took a walk through the neighborhood to a corner store to buy milk.

Epifanio spoke to the woman behind the counter: "Leche?"

She didn't understand, even after he repeated the word several times: "Leche! Leche! Leche!"

The clerk shook her head again.

Looking at her intently, the old man lifted both hands into the gesture of milking a cow, pulling up on and down on imaginary udders. He raised his voice: "Le-che?"

With still no response, Epifanio rushed toward the clerk, putting his hands to his head and his fingers to show he was a cow with horns, repeating "Le-che, le-che." The clerk walked away from the counter and did not return. Epifanio went outside and told Inés in Quechua that there was no milk.

"How can that be? There has to be milk. Give me the money," Inés said holding out her hand. With a five-dollar bill in hand, Inés walked into the store. The clerk came to the counter and saw a very small woman with braided, beribboned white hair, wearing a long dark skirt, a white blouse, and a colorful sash.

Inés looked directly at the woman and said clearly, "Milk-o?" and put the money on the counter. The clerk gave her a quart of milk and the change, which Inés took outside to her husband.

Epifanio told Joan and Segundo the comical story when they got home from work that evening to great laughter. Everyone in the family knew Inés had an amazing ability to communicate. That gift had blossomed in the bilingual Spanish/Quechua world that the elders were part of in Bolivia. Inés had negotiated the purchase of the milk, but she and Epifanio never felt comfortable in the English-speaking world.

The milk-o story convinced Joan and Segundo that expecting the ancianos to adapt to life in the United States was unrealistic. They would have to learn English, an overwhelming task at their age.

Inés was also concerned about the health of her older sister, Juanita, and unhappy about leaving her grandchildren. Upon receiving a letter from her second daughter, Margui, with the news that she was expecting, Inés announced that she had to go home. She had lost her daughter Cati during a pregnancy, and she wanted to be with Margui during her time. Inés and Epifanio went home early from that last visit, thrilled that they would be present for the delivery of Margui's first child.

The increasing number of births, of grandchildren and their events, made the arrangement of trips for the United States for the ancianos all but impossible. Joan and Segundo slowly dropped their dream of having Epifanio and Inés live with them and began thinking seriously of ways to give them a more comfortable life in their homeland.

Before Segundo's next trip to Bolivia, he and Joan talked about offering to pay for building a new house for his parents in Cochabamba.

Segundo had just been promoted to a managerial role at NWA, entailing significant supervisory and administrative responsibility as well as greater flexibility and a higher income. Nevertheless concerned that the plan to build a house in Bolivia would require a major commitment, the two examined their finances.

Segundo typically devoted his whole salary to his Bolivian family; the promotion gave him more to work with. And Joan had managed to build up some savings, so they concluded that they could offer to buy a piece of property, at least, for the ancianos.

At the end of Segundo's first family meal on his next trip, he asked his mother to sit down at the table. Typically she would have moved on to meal cleanup without joining them at all. Now she sat beside Epifanio as Segundo told them that he and Joan would like them to think about moving out of their house.

"The house is not aging especially well, and you are not really safe in Canata," he said. "Dad, you know that the dust from the dirt streets all about you is aggravating your eyes."

Epifanio and Inés were silent, seemingly uninterested.

Segundo continued: "You will have to decide where you want to live—in the city, the barrio, or the *campo* [countryside]."

The silence continued for a few minutes.

Then Segundo asked his parents what they thought about the idea.

Epifanio said, "Yes, it would be good. But everyone is gone and married, and we are getting older. We can't live alone in a new house."

Segundo told his father that this was a new issue to consider and that he needed to talk with Joan about it. Everyone knew that with the now-more-direct phone connection between Bolivia and the United States, Segundo called Joan every evening. The family conversation ended in anticipation of Joan's response.

Joan and Segundo decided to offer to build a house that was big enough to include the family of one of Segundo's siblings as well as their parents. After hearing that offer the next morning, Epifanio ac-

International Family

cepted it. The whole family got involved in the general idea and covered many possibilities in long conversations around Inés's table.

When it was time for Segundo to go home a few days later, he left with a plan for the house that was a bit more amorphous than he had hoped. All he knew for sure was that they would build a smallish house for two families, probably in the city of Cochabamba. He left with the tacit understanding that Ivo, his oldest brother, would make this happen. Ivo had construction experience, and Segundo trusted him.

A few weeks later, Segundo got a call not from Ivo but from his father, with a serious question about the house big enough for two families: "How will I choose among the four children who live in Bolivia? How can I choose one and none of the others?"

This called for another conversation with Joan. Segundo called his father back and said, "We will build some sort of structure that will accommodate each of the children who live in Bolivia."

"That will be all right," Epifanio said. "But what about your Tia Juanita?"

Segundo replied, "Of course. We'll add a bedroom for my tia."

With the scope and cost of the project rising with each conversation, Segundo and Joan hoped this was the last major change.

Epifanio, not one to make frequent long-distance calls, was on the phone to St. Paul within a few days: "Segundo, I don't think this plan will work. I have seven living children, but three of you live in the United States. How are you all going to feel if the *herencia* [inheritance] goes only to those who live in Bolivia? It isn't right. All my children must have una herencia."

After several conversations, Epifanio finally accepted Segundo's insistence that the children living in the United States did not want to live in Bolivia, that they needed to make space only for Ivo, José, Margui, and Blanca. Joan and Segundo agreed that the only way to improve the ancianos' living situation and also address Epifanio's concern for his children was to build something big enough that he could see as a potential home for at least four of his children and their families. The project had clearly grown beyond their initial intent. But after more conversations with Epifanio and Ivo, Joan and Segundo told Epifanio they would build an apartment building that eventually would have space for everyone. Epifanio was satisfied.

Within weeks, Ivo called Segundo to say, "We have found the perfect spot. It is right in the middle of the city, and the price is right."

Segundo told Ivo he would gather his and Joan's savings, fly to Cochabamba, and buy the lot. Stunned by the rapidity of their decisions and actions, Joan pointed out that they were about to spend everything they had on a piece of land that neither of them had ever seen: "And how can we possibly pay for the construction of a whole apartment building?" She slowly accepted that they could manage the cost though they had just bought a modest house on the edge of St. Paul.

More important, Joan recognized Segundo's opportunity to give his parents a life as comfortable as the one he, Joan, Rubén, and César had. It was a different way of life from theirs, but it would fulfill his parents' dreams for their last years. An extended family living in one apartment building was as Bolivian as their own calm nuclear household was American.

Epifanio's Herencia

Joan drove an intensely happy Segundo to board a plane for Bolivia to buy the lot for his parents' apartment. Ironically, the new property was a few blocks from the historic Convento de Santa Teresa, which epitomized the hierarchal structures the Velásquezes had seen eroding since their years at Candelaria. Segundo quickly completed the purchase in Cochabamba and returned a few days later, leaving the project in the hands of Ivo, who remained in conversation about the project with everyone in the Bolivian-based family. He also arranged for enough cash to fund the *obra gruesa* (framed but unfinished structure) of the building.

International Family

Despite their recent move to Mendota Heights, Joan and Segundo were able to finance the beginning construction in Bolivia that summer. Frequent progress reports from Bolivia described an apartment building growing ever bigger, far beyond anything they had imagined.

Having far less tolerance for ambiguity than Segundo, Joan left the continuing negotiations to him. The innumerable arguments about the apartment were unpleasant by Joan's standard but manageable for Segundo. Everyone in the family—his parents and brothers and sisters—had ideas about what was essential, things neither Joan nor Segundo had considered.

At one point in the construction process, the U.S. Velásquezes realized that the Bolivian Velásquezes were building an apartment not just for their parents but also for the future. The plan included a big communal space on the roof as well as individual apartments. Some of the Bolivian family's choices seemed extravagant to Joan and Segundo, who had meant to build a simple, clean, safe place for the ancianos to use immediately.

Somewhat exasperated, Joan told Segundo, "The Bolivian family is thinking 125 years in the future. By then we will all be dead."

The two came to appreciate that this was exactly what the family was doing—establishing a place around Epifanio and Inés that would be home to Velásquezes for generations.

Constructing an apartment building full of children and grandchildren was the best possible way to meet Joan and Segundo's goal of providing a place where the ancianos would be safe and comfortable. There would be none of the dust of their home in the barrio, no threat to their safety, none of the deterioration of their old building. They would be cared for constantly and lovingly by their children and grandchildren. And they would go into their last years with Epifanio accepting the generosity of his son in a way that honored him as head of the family, able to bequeath una herencia while he was still alive.

Joan and Segundo had given up their dream of Epifanio and Inés

94

Inés and Blanca in the ancianos' new apartment kitchen

living with them in the United States when they realized that their idea of what was good wasn't acceptable to the ancianos. Now they realized that their focus on the ancianos alone was inconsistent with the meaning of family to the Bolivian Velásquezes. Joan and Segundo gave up their tendency toward frugal efficiency and allowed the design of their assistance to unfold along a Bolivian path.

The movement of Inés and Epifanio into the apartment was more complex than anyone had anticipated. The financial arrangements to make the apartment project work were intricate. Joan and Segundo's careful money management enabled them to take on the building project for their parents, but it quickly grew beyond their resources.

In 1986, one year after construction had begun, Inés, Epifanio, and Tia Juanita moved into the first-floor apartment. Inés was caring for her ailing sister just when she and Epifanio needed more and more help themselves. But none of their children and grandchildren was there to care for them. The Bolivian families couldn't afford to complete the apartments they had hoped for and planned to live in, nor could Joan and Segundo fund them all. Epifanio's dream of an apartment for him and Inés surrounded by family was far from realized.

In 1987 no Velásquezes occupied the five vacant and unfinished floors above Inés and Epifanio's place on the first. Joan and Segundo worked with the family to develop a plan for bringing the whole family into the building. Each sibling was to occupy one floor. Ivo agreed to accept a salary to oversee construction. Segundo and Joan borrowed the money needed to complete two apartments on each floor—one for the family to live in and the other, adjacent space to provide it with rental-property income.

In this process, the Velásquez families demonstrated something important to their future—the capacity to transcend economic and cultural differences, to stay and work together for a common purpose. They worked together with remarkable tenacity, creativity, energy, and combined resources to create una herencia for the Velásquezes in Bolivia. Their success stood on the financing and planning of Joan and Segundo, the technical and personal leadership of Ivo, and the commitment of José, Margui, Blanca, and Ivo to manage the building.

Joan and Segundo came away from the project much more aware of the cultural differences between the U.S. and Bolivian Velásquezes. Perhaps more important was that everyone could see that with discussion, argument, generosity, and compromise, the Bolivian and American Velásquezes were capable of amazing accomplishment.

Dreams beyond Family
Over the years the apartment building at the intersection of Junin and Ecuador became the center of the international family. Every Velásquez but Joan, Rubén, and César has lived there at one time or another.

The entrance to the building is a metal door opening to a high staircase. On the steps of each of the six floors are earthen pots full of green plants reaching toward the long windows at the landings.

The long table that was the center of the adobe house the children grew up in was moved early to the new apartment on the first floor. When Epifanio built that table in the 1960s, he lay on it to ensure its proper length. The table, like everything else he built, had to be of multipurpose use. It was long enough not only to seat all the members of his big family but also for bodies at least as long as his to be laid out for review after death. He knew he would one day grace it himself.

Because Inés and Epifanio found the first-floor apartment too cold, the family decided to install an elevator and complete the apartment on the warmer fifth floor, so the ancianos could live there. Since José, Segundo's younger brother, had become a physician, he and the family decided that the first floor was the perfect place for him to see patients. After Inés and Epifanio moved to the fifth floor, José accepted patients in a new office on the first.

Though Segundo continued to live in St. Paul, he had a small apartment and office on the sixth floor of the family building in Bolivia. He traveled to Cochabamba at least twice a year on the free passes he received as an employee of NWA. His suitcases invariably bulged with items that one or another family member wanted but could not get in Cochabamba.

When Segundo was in Bolivia, he distributed the clothes, medicine, and books—whatever he was able to stuff into his bags. Then he went down one floor to eat with his mother or down two floors to eat with his sister Blanca, who lived there with her husband and five sons.

In the 1980s José became the director of the nonprofit Centro Médico, which operated a hospital with a big outpatient clinic on the outskirts of Cochabamba. As Segundo distributed gifts from the United States, his conversations with José often turned to the lack of even the most basic medical supplies and instruments for Centro Médico's patients, typically poor Quechua families new to the city.

International Family

As in most developing countries, José's patients had to pay not only the doctor but also for the supplies and medicine required for their treatment. The brothers talked of their sister Cati, who may well have died because of the lack of a piece of medical equipment or the simple unavailability of gloves or microscope, items routinely absent from many Bolivian clinics and hospitals.

As Segundo took this in, his concern for his family expanded to something broader. He began to think about what he could do to make things better for the many poor and ill Bolivians who might benefit from the affluence of the United States.

"What have I learned in all those classes in management and planning that could be useful?" he wondered.

In the mid-1980s, Segundo had begun completing his college work at Metropolitan State University in St. Paul, taking one course a term toward the liberal arts requirements needed for graduation. Always looking for opportunities to maximize his efforts, he moved his pursuit of single courses into a systematic plan to acquire the managerial skills he needed in his new position at NWA. He did not ignore the question that was becoming part of his persona: "How can I use this knowledge to help my family and my homeland?"

Segundo began thinking in a more focused way about how and what he might learn that would enable him to pass some of the wealth he saw in St. Paul to Cochabamba. He hoped that learning about nonprofit organizations and foundations might be a way to give back to Bolivia.

Turning to the College of Management, Segundo took courses in grant writing, nonprofit management, and business. Carefully working toward what he wanted for himself professionally, he graduated with a bachelor of arts degree with a concentration in nonprofit management. He also moved toward his possible contribution to Bolivia: "How can I use what I'm learning at Metro for the good of my brother's Centro Médico patients?"

Segundo began to ask physician friends for medical supplies that were being discarded. They gave him used, hand-held instruments that had been replaced in the United States with more advanced technology, and some offered easy-to-transport items like gloves and gauze, which he could pack into a suitcase. The gifts were added to the items that Velásquez family members asked Segundo to bring. It was a seemingly simple way to address a problem that mattered to the Bolivian family and that spoke to the revulsion Segundo felt toward wastefulness. He was confident that at some point he would do more.

Change of Direction

Joan had always worked around the complexities of the Velásquez international family despite the demands of her job. She shared Segundo's commitment to buying things the family needed and carrying them in his suitcase when he traveled. She helped Segundo gather and pack the supplies for trips to Cochabamba. She wanted to do more but found that getting herself to work every day took most of her energy.

Several years after Joan accommodated her wardrobe to her job, her postpolio syndrome began to slow her down. She had less and less breathing power. Segundo built a bench covered with Bolivian fabric that matched the Bolivian art on her office walls, so she could lie down and rest between meetings. She began to limit her office hours and work instead at home, lying on her bed next to an oxygen tank. By the early 1990s she was spending only two hours daily in the office.

Joan found it increasingly difficult to work, sitting or standing. The agency director, knowing Joan would accomplish much from her home, accommodated her schedule. Joan and her staff created a highly efficient system for their collaborative work, and soon one or another was visiting the Velásquez home on the Mississippi at least twice a week. They took the results of their consultation with Joan back to the office to carry out their new projects.

This routine seemed an ideal adaptation, and Joan settled into her modified work mode. Still, there were some tasks that only she could do—a final statistical decision, the last touch to a report, a set of recommendations, a crucial policy presentation . . . She was leaving her oxygen and her bed more than she realized.

When Joan went in for a routine physical, the doctor examined her, turned to her with a serious look, and said, "If you continue at your current pace, you will kill yourself. You are underestimating the toll of your work on your body. If you continue to overuse the weakened muscles you have left, you will not be able to breathe. You will not live."

Speechless, Joan listened, then acknowledged to herself how drained she was, how each meeting with her staff exhausted her. She recalled the physical cost of making a recent presentation to the county board. But she struggled with the idea of giving up the ideal job, work in which she used all of her training and talents interacting with people she liked and admired—and in which she had a great deal of fun. She sat in the doctor's office in a muddle.

The doctor continued to push: "You need to leave your work, replenish your energy, and preserve your remaining muscle strength. You are killing yourself."

Joan knew how depleted she was and that she wanted to live. She reluctantly accepted his assessment. Coming home with the recognition that she must take a medical leave, Joan blurted out her news to Segundo. He listened intently, knowing that his wife had been charging through life, often beyond her physical limitations, from the time she was a toddler. He remembered watching her struggle to carry the tin pail of water down a dirt road shortly before they met.

The necessity for medical leave was a limitation Joan could barely accept and one Segundo couldn't figure out a way for her to accommodate. She talked about how much she loved her work. She even admitted that she was eminently successful at it. Joan fell onto the couch exhausted by the trip to the doctor and the immensity of her recent decision.

She looked up at Segundo and asked, "What can I do now? If I quit working, I will never meet another new, interesting person in my life."

Segundo knew better than anyone the depth of the pain that the doctor's pronouncement gave Joan. He understood her commitment to her work and her determination to transcend her medical condition. He had been watching with fear for her life as her health slowly but steadily deteriorated.

Rather than trying to convince Joan she should quit, Segundo smiled, saying, "First you must rest. When you feel better, you can help me figure out how to collect enough medical surplus to give to the Bolivian Centro Médico. But that can wait until later."

Joan did little but eat and sleep in the first three months of the medical leave that her boss immediately but reluctantly agreed she should take. Little by little she recovered from her almost total exhaustion. Staff members came to the house regularly, as they always had, for her ideas and direction. Joan carefully planned each 90-minute meeting as the extent of her activity for the day. She extended her six-months medical leave status three times, ultimately accepting that she could never return to her job. In 1995 she took permanent leave.

When Joan began to receive visits from work colleagues, Segundo decided it was time to enlist her in his desire to improve life for the poor in Bolivia. Joan was adept at analyzing social problems, looking for pragmatic solutions, and effecting them. She knew about the lives of the Bolivians who used the Centro Médico clinic, and she had experience with the complexities of Bolivian organizational structures. Segundo had immersed himself in transferring U.S. resources to Bolivia, which involved concrete problems to which he could apply his education.

"I think we can help them," he said. "I'll do the footwork, and you do the rest. You have always said 'I can do anything from my bed.'"

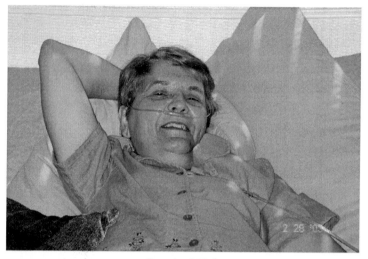

Joan in 1994

Segundo saw clearly that the learning and experience of Joan's ambitious and successful career could further the cause. Sharing the drive and commitment that fueled them both, he knew that as much as Centro Médico needed resources for its patients, Joan needed a way to devote her energy to an altruistic cause.

Joan began to think that supporting this cause would further her husband's dream of giving back to Bolivia, the country he had left as a young man. He could apply the management skills he had acquired in supervising as many as 200 mechanics at NWA at a time.

Segundo and Joan committed mutually to the search for a consistent stream of supplies so that Centro Médico would always have them available for patient care. That Joan was unable to participate in the Bolivian discussions about medical supplies did not keep her from focusing on the needs of the Quechua patients.

Joan and Segundo began to work through the steps necessary to achieving their goals. She recognized that they had to learn which people to approach for the greater amount of surplus supplies that donors in the United States might be able to provide.

Having inherited their parents' talent for frugality, Joan and Segundo took their commitment to the careful use of resources seriously. They explored local hospitals and medical-supply organizations, slowly coming to realize the scale of the waste in the healthcare systems of the United States. Offended by the casualness with which hospitals and manufacturers ignored their wastefulness, they found few existing efforts to redistribute unused supplies. With a deepening awareness of unending Bolivian need, Segundo and Joan made it their mission to find medical supplies and get them into the hands of José Velásquez and his colleagues.

Certain that some organization somewhere must be sending medical items to Bolivia, the poorest nation in South America, Joan called a friend in the planning department of an agency she'd worked with and asked whether he knew of any nonprofit organizations working in Bolivia. That afternoon a list of 90 nonprofit organizations that might take on such a problem found its way to the couple's home.

Joan had been pulled into the medical-supply conversation just as the blessed warm sun of a Minnesota summer pulled her out to the chaise lounge in their backyard overlooking a creek flowing into the river. The next afternoon she was sitting with her longtime friend and former sister-in-law Ann White Foxen when Segundo arrived home from work. He began to talk with Ann about their interest in collecting medical supplies for transport to Bolivia. When Joan mentioned that she had received a list of places to call, Ann volunteered to spend half a day each week with her until they contacted every one of the 90.

Joan and Ann spent several afternoons calling in the sun, to learn that no one was managing a medical-supply project for Bolivia.

III

Realizing the Dream

Segundo, early securing cartons of medical goods for transport to Bolivia

6

A Small Group . . .

1994–2000

In 1993 Joan and Segundo attended a wedding on the St. Croix River just east of St. Paul. They found themselves in the middle of a crowd, knowing no one but their hosts, who were busy with the many guests. On this warm summer day, they sat quietly, enjoying the sun on the river. Segundo suddenly brightened when he saw a tiny girl with pitch-black hair toddling toward them. She could have been the little Natividad, whom Joan had cherished so many years before in Cochabamba, or one of the beloved nephews Segundo saw when he went home to Bolivia.

Glancing across the crowd, Segundo looked for the little one's parents, who he assumed would be South American, maybe even Bolivian. But a slightly gray-haired white woman rushed forward, laughing and sweeping the little girl into her arms. She carried the child to a nearby table, where another white woman, clearly just as attached to the child, took her into her arms. Segundo pointed out the three-some to Joan, and they delighted in watching the members of the little family enjoy each other. Walking over to their table, Segundo introduced himself. He learned that the women were Deb Kotcher

A Small Group . . .

and Deb Bushway, adoptive mothers of the beautiful Isabel. Segundo invited the family to join him and Joan. Soon the two couples were deep in conversation.

They established that Isabel was not from Bolivia but from neighboring Peru and that the mothers were more than pleased to share their rambunctious child with the Velásquezes. The conversation, while frequently interrupted by everyone's mutual enchantment with Isabel, revealed a happy level of complementary interests.

All friends of the hosts, the two couples shared their very different histories with one another. The Debs were interested in adopting a brother or sister for Isabel and talked with Joan and Segundo about possibilities for adoption in Bolivia. As the afternoon went on, it emerged that Blanca, one of Segundo's sisters, was involved in facilitating international adoptions. The two couples parted, agreeing that they would get together again soon. Within weeks, Joan and Segundo went to the Debs' home for dinner and spent a great deal of time enjoying Isabel. After she went to bed, the conversation turned again to the idea of the Debs adopting a second child—perhaps from Bolivia. Segundo had talked with his sister Blanca in Bolivia, who invited the Debs to come there and work out an adoption plan.

Several months later the two couples were in the first stages of planning such a trip. Segundo casually commented, "And of course, when you go to Bolivia you can take some extra suitcases with medical supplies." The medical supplies topic had not been discussed in their many conversations to date. Deb Kotcher was full of questions for Segundo.

"What kind of supplies? Where? Why?" She had gone to Bolivia several years previously to help a friend with connections there create an intensive-care facility in La Paz. She was struck by the uncanny similarity between her experience and Segundo's.

Deb had been a respiratory therapist, and during her earlier trip to Bolivia she had learned first-hand of the challenges of finding unused supplies in the United States and the even greater difficulty of getting the materials to Bolivia. They swapped stories. Segundo talked about the depth of the need for basic medical supplies that his brother experienced in his hospital and clinic. Deb described several resources for surplus supplies in the area that Joan and Segundo were unaware of.

Both Debs shared Joan and Segundo's visceral revulsion to wastefulness. And as the friendship deepened, they noticed and admired Joan and Segundo's frugality and commitment to the careful use of resources. The two couples had come together as strangers at a wedding only to learn quickly that they had far more in common than their delight in an adorable toddler from South America.

The Debs' hope for a brother or sister for Isabel and the Velásquezes' commitment to Segundo's homeland became shared agendas. Joan and Segundo became involved in Isabel's life, participating in family meals and religious events. And thus began a partnership grounded in familial intimacy and a serendipitous merging of gifts and skills.

Deb Kotcher's solid awareness of the intricacies of the medical industry as well as Deb Bushway's organizational sophistication became invaluable in fine-tuning the informal efforts of the U.S. Velásquezes to address their mutual concern about the inadequacy of healthcare in Bolivia. Deb, Deb, and Isabel became collaborators with Joan as she lay abed searching by phone for medical-supply resources. Deb Kotcher accompanied Segundo as he raced around the Twin Cities, scrounging for things that José identified as necessary for the Cochabamba clinic.

Segundo called Deb Kotcher when he learned about a cache of supplies in a closing hospital to ensure he choose useful and safe items. Deb Bushway took on the immediate care of Isabel during these searches. Soon other friends and family members started hearing stories from Joan and Segundo about José's needs and the availability of unused medical supplies in the Twin Cities. A cadre of volunteers emerged.

The Debs became a part of the Velásquez family. Deb Kotcher was beginning to think about hospitals and auctioneers who might contribute supplies for Bolivia. As always, she had practical concerns and

A Small Group . . .

raised the liability issues that might face both the Velásquezes and perhaps future donors of supplies.

One day John Foxen, M.D., came to the Mendota Heights house to pick up his wife, Ann, who had helped Joan contact international organizations during the summer. Dr. Foxen had heard the stories of unused medical supplies and been pulled into the vortex: He brought some equipment that he had decided to replace in his own practice, thinking it might help José. Sure it would be appreciated, Segundo asked Foxen to vouch for the usefulness of the instruments in a small hospital like his brother's in Cochabamba. He was planning a trip to Bolivia and wanted to be sure the things he stuffed into his suitcases would be of help.

One day in the late summer of 1994, John Foxen, Joan, Segundo, and the Debs sat around the dining-room table in Mendota Heights, brainstorming about the needs in Bolivia and the limits of their little group of volunteers to address it. They were almost too tired to listen to Deb Kotcher when she said, "You guys, there are real liability issues about these relationships we are building with hospitals and suppliers. I really think we have to incorporate, become a nonprofit."

John Foxen broke in: "Remember earlier this summer when Joan and Ann made all those phone calls? They learned that no such group exists. Lots of people they talked to thought there needed to be one."

And thus it was that five concerned Americans decided to create a new organization to take on this responsibility. Joan felt well enough to do tasks that could be done from her bed. She investigated the process of incorporation and learned that, at a minimum, the group had to have a board of directors and a name.

On another evening, around the same table, the five agreed that they would become the board, recognizing that they needed a good lawyer to join them. Taking the lead, Joan called Gloria MacRae and asked whether she knew of a good attorney who would be willing to work with them to incorporate an international medical-supply line.

Gloria knew Chris Ver Ploeg, a lawyer from her church, and soon asked for her recommendation. Chris was at a busy point in her life: "Remember, I have four kids, two careers, a new marriage, and a new house. But I am just beginning a sabbatical from law school."

Chris Ver Ploeg was a professor at William Mitchell College of Law and a labor arbitrator. She acknowledged that she had been planning to use her sabbatical as a time to rethink her life. Still, she ended the conversation thinking, "For many years I have been committed to my career and family, but I do still have a social conscience."

A few weeks later Ver Ploeg said to herself, "Okay, my sabbatical is a window in which I could do this. I'm sure it would be a minimal thing." She decided that she would be the lawyer for this infant organization and called Gloria to say, "I'll do it."

Segundo then asked Carlos Mariani, a friend and member of the Minnesota House of Representatives, to join the fledging organization and so lend it the legitimacy of a Latino public official.

The group began in search of a name for the organization-to-be. Deb and Deb brought Isabel to its first meeting. She was two then, and she sat on the floor, singing her most recently learned song. The group wanted a short, catchy name, maybe like the words that Isabel sang again and again: "Twinkle, Twinkle, Little Star." With Isabel singing in the background, Segundo brought the slightly unruly group back to the naming problem. As usual, he spoke with his hands, hitting the top of the table for emphasis.

Segundo described the system: all the supplies traveling from the hands of the U.S. volunteers (hit to table) to the hands of the Bolivian packers and transporters (hit to table) to the hands of the patients in the mountains (hit to table).

"And you see [three hits], it goes from hand, to hand, to hand."

No one is sure who reminded the group that "hand to hand" translates to *mano a mano*, a common phrase in Spanish conversation. But after the meeting Joan moved ahead with incorporation of Mano a

Mano Medical Resources and development of its mission statement. The board wholeheartedly approved these words: "The mission of Mano a Mano Medical Resources is to increase the capacity of Bolivian healthcare providers to care for their impoverished patients."

The 1994 creation and incorporation of Mano a Mano Medical Resources (hereafter Mano a Mano) as a nonprofit organization occurred upon the commitment of a half-dozen people—a hands-on, hardworking board of directors. Joan often reminded herself and her Mano a Mano companions of what cultural anthropologist Margaret Mead had said: "Never doubt that a small group of thoughtful committed citizens can change the world."[1]

Joan did not expect them to change the whole world but rather just a small part of a poor country. She recognized that her personal availability and ability to take on leadership was central to harnessing the energies of the group. And she accepted the nearly full-time role as de facto co-director with Segundo. Joan's skills and availability enabled Mano a Mano to grow with a level of administrative and organizational sophistication that few voluntary programs can claim from infancy.

Joan was frequently the voice and face of Mano a Mano, especially when Segundo was working. As the primary phone and contact person with hospitals and suppliers, she was responsible from her bed for Mano a Mano communication details. She also managed the $3,000 startup budget funded by thousand-dollar contributions from Joan and Segundo Velásquez, and Chris Ver Ploeg.

During the day, Joan was the only one home when the doorbell rang. She put her computer to sleep and turned off her oxygen to answer the door. Invariably the person at the door was a friend or family member needing to know where to put donated medical supplies.

Often the caller was Jerry Sauter, one of the earliest and most loyal friends of Mano a Mano. A retired engineer from Honeywell and a polio survivor like Joan, he had become less mobile and more wheelchair-bound. This did not deter him from becoming Mano a Mano's primary delivery person. He traveled in his station wagon to pick up supplies from a hospital or nursing home or manufacturer and bring them to the Velásquez house.

At first Mano a Mano stored unused supplies in the anteroom between Joan and Segundo's garage and kitchen. After that was full, the boxes piled up at the edges of the kitchen, then down the stairs and into the basement. The Velázquez home soon resembled the family home in Bolivia in the Cochabamba days, when it was not only a place for the Velásquezes to return to after a hard day's work or schooling but also one from which to conduct the family tile and water enterprises. It was especially busy in the evenings and on the weekends, when Segundo and involved friends and family were not working their day jobs.

The Mendota Heights home became the center of a circle of Joan and Segundo's family, friends, and friends of friends, who became an efficient and committed team of volunteers. Both of the Velásquezes were gifted in nurturing their network of many and deep relationships. They tended to share their concerns and activities with family members and friends. When the health needs of Bolivians became a priority, those needs became the focus of their broadly defined, extended family.

There were the many Whites, whom Joan and Segundo considered family long past Joan's divorce from David. Several of his siblings had lived with them over the years, and many of them became involved in the medical-supply work. John Foxen, married to David's sister Ann, was on the Mano a Mano board. Ann Foxen and her sister Mary White were always available to support Joan in whatever she might be doing.

Three former Whites—or "off-Whites," as they called themselves after their divorces, were active volunteers. Joan (White) Velásquez was one; Nancy (White) White became one of the most involved; and Mark Petzoldt, long divorced from one of the White sisters, was one of the earliest, most faithful volunteers. Mark arrived at the Mendota Heights door each Saturday morning to pick up, pack, or deliver whatever might be on its way to Bolivia. Roy White, another volunteer,

A Small Group . . .

came up with one of Joan and Segundo's favorite slogans—"Put surplus into service for better health"—during a family dinner.

Segundo and Joan's passion for Mano a Mano attracted almost everyone they knew into the Bolivian project. In addition to the well-represented Whites, half a dozen of Segundo's NWA coworkers helped with the medical-supply effort. Several of Joan's colleagues from Ramsey County, professional social-work colleagues, and fellow members of Unity Church–Unitarian volunteered as well. Many of those joining in the work began sending their teen and adult children to the Saturday workdays to learn about supporting a cause. Identifying, transporting, unpacking, sorting, repacking, and transporting medical supplies to Bolivia was a time-consuming endeavor. But within a year of incorporation, 50-plus volunteers prepared more than 3,000 pounds of supplies to be sent to Cochabamba.

By late 1995 the volunteers had displaced the two Velásquez cars in their double garage with carefully packed boxes. Not long afterwards, the readied boxes spread from the garage to the far reaches of the property. Segundo and Mark Petzoldt erected three huge tents behind the garage to hold the excess in readiness for transport to Bolivia. The scale of the inventory was outstripping the space to contain it.

When the garage was completely full of supplies, Segundo and Joan put up their first building for Mano a Mano—a big addition to the unused horse barn behind their home. The barn became the place for processing and storing supplies. Asked how the neighbors felt about the tents, the addition, and the volunteers on the nearby property, Joan replied, "Oh, they're great. They come on Saturdays and help us." By 1996, two years after incorporation, more than a hundred volunteers were coming to work on the property on staggered weekends.

A New Partner
Joan and Segundo were adept at pulling anyone who crossed their path into their passion for the work in Bolivia. One day in 1998 Segundo

got a phone message from Dick Wagner, an NWA pilot from Milwaukee. Dick had read about Segundo's Bolivian medical-supply work in *Passages,* an internal NWA magazine that often featured stories about employees engaged in interesting activities. One of the magazine's staff members interviewed Segundo and other NWA employees about the need in Bolivia and their volunteer work with Mano a Mano. By the end of a more-than-hour-long telephone conversation, the men were on a first-name basis.

The two men had a lot in common. Both worked for NWA. Both were pilots—Segundo's flying recreational and Dick's professional. Both were committed to sharing their resources with those who had less. Both were passionate about what makes things work—from the parts inside an airplane to the structure of a volunteer organization.

Dick ran a business that manufactured and distributed parts for general aviation aircraft worldwide. Segundo was especially versed in the mechanical parts that were the basis of Dick's wealth. As a mechanic and later a manager in NWA's technical operations, Segundo worked with similar parts every day.

Unlike most Americans, Dick Wagner was familiar with Bolivia, having both personal and philanthropic relationships there. He was a devout Catholic who was friends with a mission priest in Bolivia. Segundo, often the one to ask the questions in a conversation, wanted to know more about Dick's Bolivian connections. Before he worked his inquiries into their conversation, he learned that Dick was a man full of questions too. He wanted to learn about Mano a Mano, but one conversation was not enough. They agreed to stay in touch.

A few weeks later Dick called and made a date to meet Segundo over lunch. Dick was a congenial man, older than Segundo but equally energetic. After some idle conversation, his questions began: "Who does all the work involved in the medical-supply program? How do you do all this without staff? Who is responsible for the sophisticated Mano a Mano materials you've brought to me?"

Segundo replied, "As the cofounders of Mano a Mano, my wife and I are equal partners."

Dick laughed. "Aha! She is your Bobbie." He explained that his wife, Bobbie, managed the parts business and almost every other aspect of his life.

Chuckling at their mutual luck with their wives, Segundo and Dick arranged to continue the conversations. They talked on the phone and connected by e-mail frequently. Dick decided to support the medical supply program. He made contacts with distributors in the Milwaukee area who had extra supplies that could meet needs in Bolivia.

Joan got a call from Bobbie, saying that she and Dick had rented a truck for all the supplies they had collected and were on their way to Minnesota. Joan was struck by the modesty of their journey. These people who had their own foundation funds were frugal. They were clearly pleased to have a hand in avoiding the waste inherent in the United States' use of medical supplies. Joan also sensed that they liked to be personally involved in their philanthropy.

Bobbie and Dick Wagner arrived at the Mendota Heights house to help Segundo unload the supplies from the truck into the garage. Joan and Segundo followed them to U-Haul to return the empty truck and took them to the airport to fly home to Milwaukee. A friendship that became central to Mano a Mano blossomed.

International Logistics

By 1995 the scale of the medical-supply program had overcome two hurdles in both St. Paul and Cochabamba: Mano a Mano needed far greater capacity than that of Segundo's suitcases to transport supplies from Minnesota to Bolivia. And it needed approval from Bolivian customs to get the supplies into Bolivia.

The board of directors had struggled to find the least expensive response to both hurdles. From the beginning it was a classic "working" board, planning cautiously and finding answers to its questions while the organization was still emerging. Regarding transporting complexities, the board began with this question, "Who, other than Segundo, can help Mano a Mano get this stuff to Bolivia?"

The logistics of delivery to Bolivia were so complex that Mano a Mano had to create many partnerships to assure safe arrival of the medical supplies at their intended destination. Two airline companies, a truck driver at the Miami Airport, the U.S. Air Force Reserves, Catholic Relief Services of Boston, the U.S. Department of Defense, and the U.S. Agency for International Development (USAID) were among those who helped the tiny nonprofit move what came to be more than 200,000 pounds of supplies annually to Bolivia.

By the end of Mano a Mano's first year, Segundo had approached Northwest Airlines with a request for the free transport of Mano a Mano cargo. Because NWA did not fly to Bolivia, it could carry the supplies only as far as Miami. Segundo made an arrangement with Lloyd Aéreo Boliviano (LAB) to fly the supplies from Miami to Cochabamba at 25 percent the standard cost for additional baggage.

Joan and Segundo had already secured a rickety trailer to collect supplies in the Twin Cities. When he had 32 packed and labeled boxes, Segundo strapped them onto the trailer, hauled them to the airport, sent them to Miami via air cargo, and using his NWA pass, boarded a passenger plane for Miami.

When he arrived and discovered that the air-cargo terminal was three miles away, he hailed a taxi and went to pick up his boxes. But he had no way to get them from the cargo terminal to the passenger terminal for his flight to Bolivia. He knew the semis lined up at the cargo docks would not be willing to move this relatively small load for the few miles to the passenger terminal. And he knew that he couldn't do it alone.

Standing there searching for a solution, Segundo spotted a *paisano* (compatriot), a Latino driving a battered cattle truck. He knew this familiar-looking fellow would help, and he did. Together they loaded

A Small Group . . .

the boxes onto the truck and hurried to the passenger terminal. Segundo's paisano helped him unload the boxes on the curb that divided several lanes from the airport. Then, one by one, Segundo moved the boxes across two lanes of traffic to the terminal building and the LAB counter. All of the boxes made it onto the LAB plane to Cochabamba.

While this process solved the problem at hand, Mano a Mano's board recognized that the organization would quickly outgrow that solution. Segundo was able to enter the country with a few suitcases of donations, but bigger shipments would require duty-free status.

While the organization was arranging transportation of supplies from the United States, Mano a Mano people in Cochabamba and St. Paul were negotiating with Bolivian customs for acceptance of the goods into Bolivia. Mano a Mano could not afford the thousands of dollars of duty it might normally pay on hundreds of pounds of medical supplies. It tried many times but failed to get a duty-free declaration for the anticipated donation of supplies, the only affordable solution.

Mano a Mano searched for several months for someone in Bolivia's national government to explain the process of applying for duty-free status. Segundo talked with dozens of officials, each of whom referred him to others. He also asked friends to help Mano a Mano contact an official who could help them—also without success.

Mano a Mano finally accepted that it did not have the direct connections to obtain duty-free entry without bribery. It would have to take a different, legal route—that is, to look for another U.S.-based organization that would extend its agreement to Mano a Mano.

After months of frustrating and unsuccessful negotiation with customs officials, Joan turned to Catholic Relief Services (CRS), a Boston nonprofit. She recalled her fruitful work with the three Catholic priests at the San Rafael parish when she first went to Bolivia as a Peace Corps volunteer. Her initial surprise at finding herself working with Catholics had turned to awareness and appreciation of their commitment and resources.

Joan was pleased and relieved when CRS recognized Mano a Mano as an organization with similar values and commitments. CRS also understood that as a young organization Mano a Mano had neither the financial ability to pay extensive duty nor the reputation to get duty-free status from the Bolivian authorities. CRS agreed to roll Mano a Mano into its Bolivian duty-free status and to pass the supplies on to Centro Médico when they arrived in Cochabamba. In turn, Mano a Mano committed Centro Médico to storing and distributing wheelchairs and other equipment collected by Mano a Mano to Catholic healthcare facilities in Bolivia.

Bolivian customs accepted as duty-free the 32 boxes flown from Mendota Heights to Miami to Cochabamba through Catholic Relief Services. The supplies were transported to Centro Médico, where they were stored and distributed through the year to the medical staff for use with patients. That was Mano a Mano's first big transport of medical supplies—about 2,000 pounds.

After months of searching for transport of a much bigger cargo, Segundo learned that the U.S. Air Force Reserve could, with USAID approval, ship humanitarian cargo on a space-available basis. Mano a Mano received recognition that its cargo would in fact be used for legitimate humanitarian purposes, and for many years the reserves helped move donated medical supplies the 4,600-plus miles from Minneapolis to Cochabamba. By 1996, the end of its third year, Mano a Mano had shipped 70,000 pounds of supplies to Bolivia.

While Mano a Mano was improving its system of collecting and transporting supplies in Mendota Heights, Segundo's brother José was busy seeing that the supplies were well used. As director of Centro Médico, he oversaw the medical and administrative work of its 37-bed hospital and big outpatient clinic on the edge of rapidly expanding Cochabamba. This religiously based, nonprofit clinic was less expensive for users than the private, for-profit hospitals in the area, and so it attracted many people of little means.

A Small Group . . .

José also oversaw the big, open clinic serving many of the Quechua people (the indigenous group including the Velásquez family) moving in great numbers to the city from distant rural areas.

As in most of the developing world, patients in Bolivian clinics and hospitals are expected to pay for the supplies needed for their care. For those recently arrived from the countryside and still looking for work, the inability to buy supplies often deprived them of needed medical assistance. The U.S. supplies from Mano a Mano enabled such patients to receive care at Centro Médico's hospital and clinic.

The passing of health supplies from the United States to Centro Médico was one of the most important partnerships developed by Mano a Mano. José, as the group's director, oversaw the distribution of supplies. The collaboration was solidly grounded in the Velásquez family.

José's involvement with his whole staff in the supply project was as essential as Segundo and Joan's leadership of the dedicated volunteer board and workers in the United States. And Ivo, Segundo's oldest brother, was always there to consult, suggest, and pull in their other siblings when necessary. The intense Velásquez involvement on the ground in Bolivia guaranteed that decisions were based on accurate understanding of local culture and politics. There were no contracts; the respect between the brothers was sufficient security.

The medical supplies sent from the United States enabled Centro Médico to better serve its patients. Its staff stored and distributed the supplies in hospital and clinic. Once their needs were met, staff members provided supplies to other medical facilities that served the very poor. Bolivian volunteers, Velásquez family members, friends, and co-workers—recruited much as in the United States—unloaded supplies and stored them in a second-floor area at the hospital that required much lifting and pulling. Like Joan and Segundo, José transmitted to his staff his focus on detail, resulting in the high level of efficiency that prevails to this day.

Volunteers in Bolivia instituted processes central to the success of Mano a Mano. They formalized the actions resulting from the personal conversations of Segundo and José. The first supplies Segundo carried in his suitcases were basic tools, such as stethoscopes, that José lacked in his clinic. After Mano a Mano found a wide range of medical supplies available, Segundo phoned José to find out which of them would be useful in Bolivia. The informal system was built of continual back-and-forth conversation among Velásquez family members in the United States and Bolivia.

As more supplies were shipped to Cochabamba, José's colleagues took notice. He received requests from other doctors and nurses hoping for similar additions to their meager supplies. The unending need soon pushed the informal system beyond its capacity.

As Mano a Mano identified more and more unused medical supplies in the Twin Cities of St. Paul and Minneapolis, the requests for medical supplies in Cochabamba also increased. It became clear that the supplies sent from Mendota Heights could not meet all the need in José's clinic and the other Bolivian facilities making requests. Furthermore, some of the supplies being sent from the United States were not useful in Cochabamba.

At one point, for example, far too many boxes of tubing than could be used or stored had arrived, and at another, several doctors needed bandages and gauze that they could not procure. Recognizing this, Joan developed procedures to match Mano a Mano collections as precisely as possible to Bolivian expectations for supplies. She created a simple and efficient system of reporting needs and supplies between the two countries that has served the organization well for years.

José's staff and volunteers entertained a concern about the influx of materials that never occurred to the U.S. volunteers. Here's where Mano a Mano's deep organizational position—that all efforts funded by Mano a Mano (USA) for Bolivia be implemented by Bolivians serving Bolivians—came into play. José and Segundo were aware of the need for transparency in bringing mostly unavailable, often valuable items into a country as poor and undeveloped as Bolivia. They grasped the potential for real or perceived corruption as the thousands of pounds of supplies arrived.

With characteristic efficiency, José made detailed lists of every boxed item, presented the list to the officials of whichever facility was receiving the supplies, and unpacked them in front of the officials. A list of the received supplies was posted publicly. No one involved in the distribution of medical supplies ever took any of the donated materials to sell or use themselves.

Clínicas Gloria

Joan's friend Gloria MacRae was about to turn 70 years of age in 1996, when Joan and Segundo were busily growing Mano a Mano. As always, Gloria was intimately involved in Joan's life. They had stayed closely connected through the years. Twice Joan needed Gloria's ear and support and called her in the night. The first was when Joan and David were separating, the second when Joan decided to marry Segundo.

Gloria was always ready to support Joan, just as Joan had always risen to Gloria's needs. From the beginning, Mano a Mano was almost as much Gloria's personal mission as Joan's. As soon as Mano a Mano created promotional materials, Gloria's car was loaded with brochures as well as the donated supplies she was always moving in the trunk of her car.

So when Joan told Chris Ver Ploeg that their mutual friend Gloria was nearing a milestone birthday, Chris insisted they throw a big party in her honor, and Chris wanted it at her house. They called to check with Gloria, and never one to miss a party, she agreed. "But no gifts!" she said.

Joan and Chris technically respected her wishes, but they wanted to do something for her. They enlisted Segundo to help them come up with something special. Segundo's mind immediately went back to a recent decision by the Mano a Mano board of directors to prepare for building a satellite clinic with Centro Médico once the appropriate funding was in hand. During his most recent trip to Bolivia, Segundo and his brother had worried over the many rural villagers who traveled great distances to receive the services provided by José's clinic.

José talked about his wish to come up with enough resources to build a satellite clinic. Segundo was aware that inaccessibility to medical care was a major source of the appalling maternal and child health record of Bolivia's rural areas. He thought of his relatives who still lived in Laguna Sulti, his home village, which had no functioning clinic.

José also told Segundo about his concern for the Quechua families who were ill and must walk many miles to get to the Centro Médico clinic. José had persuaded the hospital's board to reach farther into the countryside by building satellite clinics, though it had little to fund such an effort. Segundo liked the idea and agreed with José that moving forward with a clinic was a logical extension of Mano a Mano's mission to improve the health of rural Bolivians.

Segundo talked with Joan, and the two of them talked to the board of Mano a Mano. The board decided it would support building a satellite clinic—with a big *if*—*if* it could raise the money. During a conversation about possible gifts for Gloria MacRae, Segundo saw an opportunity and brought up the Mano a Mano board's decision to look for funds for a clinic.

"Do you know that with just $3,500 we could enlist the help of the community and build a three-room adobe clinic? And then we've got the medical supplies to equip it." He hit the table for emphasis—once for acquiring the land, a second time for enlisting volunteers, a third for building the clinic, and a fourth for equipping it.

Joan and Chris listened when Segundo had a new idea, especially when he started hitting the table. They had already learned that his ideas about helping Bolivia were good ones. Some of his dreams were impossible for the new Mano a Mano. But this idea made sense as a way to realize the funding of a Bolivian clinic and to honor Gloria, too.

Joan, Chris, and Segundo decided that raising money at the birthday party for Gloria to bring a health clinic into a recently settled barrio in the mountains above Cochabamba was a fitting though somewhat ambitious way to honor one of their most impassioned advocates. Yes, Chris and Joan told Gloria about the party, but they kept secret the plan to ask guests for financial gifts for what they were already thinking of as "Clínica Gloria."

Gloria began making the guest list that Chris and Joan asked of her. She became concerned when it approached a hundred people, but Joan encouraged her to invite everyone she knew. She reminded Gloria that she never went anywhere without making a new friend and that she kept them all. A hundred invitations went out for Gloria's 70th birthday party.

A few days before the event, Joan received a phone call from a local minister, the husband of a woman on the guest list who sang in a church choir with Gloria. He had noticed that the invitation mentioned a plan to fund a clinic in Gloria's name. He was coming to the party with his wife, and he thought Joan should know he was bringing a $5,000 donation from an anonymous person with whom he worked.

When she got off the phone, Joan wept. The $3,000 that she, Segundo, and Chris Ver Ploeg had contributed to start Mano a Mano was long gone. And at that point the organization had never received another gift of more than $25.00.

The party for Gloria was a success. She was thrilled to be the vehicle that moved Mano a Mano into building a clinic in Bolivia. Her friends at the party augmented the $5,000 gift from the anonymous donor with another $6,000. Mano a Mano had $11,000 to build a satellite health clinic.

The phone call from Segundo announcing that Mano a Mano had raised $11,000 delighted José. He said Centro Médico would contribute additional funds and build small brick clinics in two barrios in the

Segundo presents plaque announcing Clínicas Gloria project to Gloria MacRae.

mountains above the city. They would name the clinics Clínica Gloria I and Clínica Gloria II. José was as eager as Segundo to expand services into barrios that had no access to healthcare. Both brothers were sure they could work with villagers in the mountains above the hospital.

The first time Segundo flew to Bolivia after Gloria's party, his mother's long table in her sixth-floor apartment became the workspace for the clinic project. And at this table his brother Ivo moved more intently into the work of Mano a Mano.

Segundo and José's belief that they could pull off the ambitious building project hinged on bringing the considerable gifts of their oldest brother, Ivo, to the clinic project. He had already shown his commitment to Mano a Mano through his heavy involvement in medical supply distribution. And he was a successful carpenter with his own employees. They drew him quickly into the design details of their wish for a satellite clinic.

Ivo brought more than construction expertise to the project. As the oldest son, he had the strongest memories of the family's rural farming life in Candelaria and Laguna Sulti. And he had traveled through the mountains, visiting many villages in his years as a lay leader of Unión Cristiana Evangélica.

Their father, Epifanio, had joined the big, evangelical denomination in the 1980s and subsequently carried nearly every other member of his family into a deep connection with the church. Ivo's faith moved him into a leadership role in UCE. His evangelical work in mountain communities deepened his compassionate appreciation of rural Bolivian life. And as the eldest brother, he brought to the clinic project a maturity and leadership carried lightly and with grace.

Ivo joined the work at Inés's table, and the three brothers carefully and quickly crafted a satisfactory design for a medical clinic. They already had access through Mano a Mano's supply inventory to the equipment necessary for a clinic. They had seen the unfinished clinics dotting the villages around Cochabamba. In their home village of Laguna Sulti such a building stood dilapidated and empty, not used since the government had built it years before. They wondered about that and the other empty clinics scattered across the mountains.

As they brainstormed about how to do a clinic project "right," the brothers decided they must anticipate clinic failure and do all they could to avoid it. They noted that most of the failed clinics were of adobe brick, which weakened quickly and created a level of dust far from hygienic. They also knew that many clinics faltered due to a lack of essential supplies. They suspected some clinics failed from lack of community involvement.

The brothers agreed they wanted to build sturdy, sustainable clinics for the patients prepared to use them. Their work together reminded them all of their joint childhood effort to make 113 tiles daily and help their father in the water-hauling business when they were students.

The Velásquez family had a history of working hard and smoothly as a group, each member finding a suitable role and everyone using his or her best skills. They operated with a solid appreciation of and comfort with the culture of those that would use the clinics they were designing. They had struggled with health issues, unable to afford adequate treatment of Segundo and Blanca's ear problems and Epifanio's muscle weakness. And everyone in the family carried a commitment to give back to the people of their roots.

As the three brothers worked, their sister Blanca came into the dining room. She was by that time a lawyer, and they wanted to consult her about legal issues that might emerge from the government as they moved into construction. She looked closely at some photos they had of a recent visit to one of the barrios that might want a clinic. She saw people who looked very much like herself, her parents, and her brothers and sisters. They were different only in the simplicity of their dress, their obvious poverty, and the starkness of their environment.

She pointed this out to the brothers and said, "Look at these people. They are us. We could be living their life. We must work with them." From then on Blanca was not only the legal advisor of Mano a Mano but also the one who especially nurtured the deep connection of the family with its Quechua ancestry. Though the brothers and sister were deeply involved in their respective professional lives, they resolved to move forward with the Clínicas Gloria project.

After the brothers completed their general plans for the clinics, Segundo returned to the United States to work with Joan on the financial and logistical details of the project. Moving into the clinic construction project while they continued the medical-supply side of Mano a Mano complicated their accounting system—already a challenge for Joan. Now her role as the manager of Mano a Mano in the United States became more demanding of her time and energy.

Ivo continued to prepare for construction of the clinics, identifying people who could take that on. José started a deliberative and collaborative process with the villagers that came to be repeated over the years. First, he went to Primero de Mayo and Molle Molle, barrios

A Small Group . . .

that had contacted him about a need for healthcare in the community.

He met with the resident miners who had been moved from their mining communities to these villages; they were in dire need. He told them he was the director of Centro Médico in the city of Cochabamba. He explained that they might have a clinic with support from Centro Médico and a U.S. organization called Mano a Mano.

José had many conversations with the Molle Molle and Primero de Mayo residents. He asked the junta vecinal to formally agree that it wanted a clinic and that it would provide significant manual labor toward the clinic's construction. Mano a Mano agreed to work with the villagers to build the clinic and to furnish medical supplies. Centro Médico would provide the medical staff.

When both villages decided to proceed, their agreement was sealed with a handshake. In March 1997 Clínica Gloria I was completed in Primero de Mayo. Several months later Clínica Gloria II stood finished in nearby Molle Molle. The shiny brick and red-roofed Clínicas Gloria were a reality.

The Velásquez brothers had designed the Clínicas Gloria at their parents' dining-room table in Cochabamba. Four village residents provided by each junta vecinal worked with master carpenters on Ivo's staff. The two clinics varied slightly in design, as would each of the five clinics built over the next three years. Most of the differences were related to topography. Otherwise the clinics were nearly identical.

The clinics were not big—they measured between 1,800 and 2,200 square feet. Each had a waiting room, examination rooms for a doctor and a nurse, a delivery room, an education room, a kitchen, and a bathroom. Each had two inpatient beds.

As the buildings were completed, the villagers, junta vecinal leaders, *municipio* (similar to a U.S. county, not city) officials, and Mano a Mano workers and staff took part in a festive dedication for each. Everyone enjoyed the music, dancing, and elaborate food, but the most celebrated part of each dedication was touring the new clinic. Villagers walked from space to space, marveling at the modern kitchen and bathroom, happy to see the pleasant patient rooms.

The completion of the first two Mano a Mano clinics was a model of collaboration across organizational and international boundaries. It was finalized with a handshake between José and the barrio leaders in Primero de Mayo and Molle Molle and phone conversations among Joan, Segundo, and José. The continuing relationship between Mano a Mano and Centro Médico required not even a handshake. The bonds among Joan, Segundo, José, Ivo, and Blanca were solid. José incorporated the family's shared goals into his medical career by folding Mano a Mano's commitments into Centro Médico's work.

The U.S. collection and delivery of supplies broadened far beyond the microscopes and gauze that Segundo had carried in his suitcase several years earlier. And by 1996 medical equipment donated to Mano a Mano in the United States had re-equipped Centro Médico's 10 outpatient exam rooms, a waiting room, 32 inpatient hospital rooms, surgical and delivery facilities, x-ray facilities, and a laboratory, in addition to providing it with supplies.

Now José turned to the U.S. Mano a Mano organization with a plan to open an infant/pediatric unit. In response, Mano a Mano immediately began collecting and shipping incubators, bassinets, and cribs to Bolivia.

Centro Médico's board of directors had long been a supporter of José and the partnership with Mano a Mano, but a transfer of its leadership occurred in the midst of the planning for the children's unit and the completion of Clínicas Gloria I and II, raising havoc with the Mano a Mano/Centro Médico partnership.

The new chair of the board emerged as one who did not share the Velásquez tradition of operating with strong personal trust and relationships. Segundo and José had communicated almost daily—whether they were in Cochabamba or St. Paul. Segundo shared his process when working with José and Ivo in Bolivia and with Joan and the board whenever he could. José was in constant connection with Ivo and Blanca.

There were no written contracts between the two organizations. Their working relationship was based on reciprocal family commitment and trust. Through Mano a Mano the U.S. Velásquezes developed financial and organizational resources to meet the health needs of the Bolivian poor. Through Centro Médico, the Bolivian Velásquezes used those resources to the same purpose.

The value differences between the new chair of the board and José were obvious. The new chairman began a move to target Centro Médico services to members of a particular religious denomination instead of all poor patients. And the planned infant/pediatric plan was not on his agenda. Within a year, José left Centro Médico in frustration, going on to direct a big teaching hospital in Cochabamba.

The dissolution of the Centro Médico/Mano a Mano partnership required no legal action, and José's move to a new hospital severed the informal relationship. Mano a Mano had based its partnership on verbal agreements and personal relationships with José and other Centro Médico staff members.

José had also closed the deal to build two clinics in communities of dislocated miners with a handshake. He had envisioned himself a director of Centro Médico for many years, confident he could ensure the healthcare needs of those villagers. But Centro Médico, not the villages, legally owned Clínicas Gloria I and II. Centro Médico did continue to provide doctor and nursing services at the two clinics. But the villagers did not own them, and they had no way to influence decisions about the type of services or the way in which they were delivered.

The end of the Mano a Mano/Centro Médico partnership was a crisis for everyone who had been involved in it. José saw his medical life's work trivialized and cut short. The Mano a Mano board of directors (including Joan and Segundo) was convinced that cross-cultural and international work was best conducted on a personal basis of mutual respect and trust. Now it had to rethink this conviction.

Mano a Mano had by this time energized more than a hundred U.S. volunteers deeply committed to the organization's work in Bolivia. And now that work was in jeopardy. The board of directors knew it could not collaborate with an organization that had moved so dramatically away from its original mission "to increase the capacity of Bolivian healthcare providers to care for their impoverished patients." Centro Médico had shifted its priority from serving the impoverished to serving a particular religious group. In early 1997 the board voted to dissolve its partnership, and Mano a Mano sent no further medical supplies or money to Centro Médico.

Fortunately for Mano a Mano, Ivo and many of the staff members who worked with José before his departure continued to contribute countless volunteer hours to transporting, unpacking and distributing its medical donations. José maintained contact with the many institutions relying on Mano a Mano medical supplies and saw that they continued to receive expected materials.

The Mano a Mano board recognized that the organization would have to rent space in Bolivia for the inventory previously stored at Centro Médico as well as for the U.S. materials readied for transport to Bolivia. The board also began thinking of hiring a part-time employee to manage the reception of supplies in Cochabamba.

Despite the rupture with Centro Médico, Joan and Segundo worked successfully with the board and Mano a Mano volunteers to maintain the movement of medical supplies to Bolivia. Knowing something was amiss in the organization's procedures in Cochabamba, the board carefully processed the breakdown of the partnership.

The board understood and affirmed that familial and personal relationships were central to Mano a Mano's success. It would not have existed without José, Joan, Segundo, Ivo, Blanca, and the Bolivian and U.S. volunteers. Further, no Clínicas Gloria would have existed without José's personal connection with the villagers in Primero de Mayo and Molle Molle. The success of the first two clinics depended on the work of the three brothers in the design and plan for the clinics and on Joan's financial and administrative efforts in the United States.

But Mano a Mano's board also recognized that reliance on personal arrangements had nearly decimated the collection and distribution system for medical supplies needed in Bolivia. And it deeply regretted that Primero de Mayo and Molle Molle villagers would never own or control their clinics because Centro Médico owned them.

The Bolivian Way
While the board was debating the future of Mano a Mano, it also heard from Segundo about the challenges of using donated medical supplies where they were most needed—in the rural areas where there were no clinics. He told other board members the story of Nora, a midwife who for years traveled the 90 miles of rocky dirt roads to Cochabamba, so that she could earn the money to buy medical supplies with which to tend the needs of the villagers of Chullpa K'asa. She had heard about Mano a Mano and asked for supplies for her town.

Nora made good use of the medical supplies that she received from Mano a Mano. In 1997, when she came to pick up supplies, she talked with José about traveling to Chullpa K'asa to explain to its residents what it would mean to have their own medical facility. José agreed to make a trip to the village, commenting that the U.S. Mano a Mano board had already committed to building more clinics. Maybe Chullpa K'asa could be the next project.

The Velásquezes understood that the Quechua villages surrounding Cochabamba City operated within some version of the traditional Inca ayllu system. They remembered the communal *sistema de riego* (irrigation system) of their childhood in Laguna Sulti. When José met with the villagers of Chullpa K'asa, he knew that their Quechua village life was based on the Inca ayllu tradition of communal decision making. And he knew that one village might have several ayllus, or community committees, for various aspects of village life. One might be for schools, another for roads, another for managing sistemas de riego.

Another village might have a formal junta vecinal to oversee several ayllus, and another might have a single ayllu to address all community issues. Understanding how to work with a village's governing structure required an appreciation of the evolution of many traditional ayllus into sindicatos. These unions in turn might relate only to a specific village or to the larger countrywide labor movement.

José and Segundo recognized that a communal process could move efficiently and relatively quickly when desired by the community. They knew that most villages had leaders (elected or based on kinship) with the capacity to commit their villagers to work on community projects. Their juntas vecinales could facilitate a village's decision making as well as its ability to engage the community in the construction of a clinic.[2]

When José traveled to Chullpa K'asa he recognized that the nuances of the ayllu system had enabled Mano a Mano to design its development work around the communal strength of rural villages. The villages had the power and skill to decide upon constructing a clinic, provide the land for, and upon completion, manage it.

Real City Bricks

When the residents of Chullpa K'asa invited José to visit their community, he realized they had heard the rumor of possible village clinics spreading through the high mountains of the region. Many showed up for the meeting, but some members of the community were clearly skeptical about the project. One man rose and said, "You are nothing but *ch'amas* [noisemakers] who promise everything but do nothing!" He spoke angrily about the *políticos* (politicians) who had made promises to the community and were never seen again.

One villager called out the name of a health official who had said, "We will see that a nurse comes regularly to the village to give you your shots." Someone else called out, "And she never came once!" The meeting reverberated with murmurs of too many unfulfilled promises.

José challenged them: "We are serious. We volunteer with Mano a Mano. We heard of your need and have come to work with you." He pointed out that the vehicle they had arrived in held a mold for making the adobes to be used in construction: "We will leave it with you to make the adobes. Once they are made, we will come back and build your new clinic together."

The original speaker said, "You are only using adobe? If we are going to have a clinic, it must be of real city bricks, not mud bricks that make dust and fall apart !"

Undaunted, José responded: "Mano a Mano knows that adobe is not the best kind of brick for a new building, but we have limited resources." He saw clarity and strength in the group before him. He thought the men would be strong supporters of the clinic and said, "All right. I promise you that Mano a Mano will buy you city bricks if you will transport them from Cochabamba."

Mano a Mano's knowledge and determination typically created enough enthusiasm to dissipate such cynicism. In this case, a villager who owned the only truck in the community said he would haul the city bricks if others would pay the cost of the fuel. The crowd answered in a single voice that it wished to join José in the project. Only days later the truck and villagers from Chullpa K'asa drove to Cochabamba, picked up their bricks, and returned home.

When the heavily loaded truck was 200 yards from the clinic site, it stopped, unable to go farther up the hill. The villagers present to greet the truck grabbed their burden cloths, filled them with bricks from the truck, and carried them up to the building site.

Soon the villagers and the master carpenters that Mano a Mano hired began to construct the building. The Chullpa K'asa clinic opened later that year. There was a great celebration at the *inauguración y entrega* (opening and delivery). The skeptic who had equated José with the politicians of empty promises spoke up again. This time he praised the Mano a Mano representatives as the only *dignitarios* (dignitaries) who had come to Chullpa K'asa and kept their promises. "Thanks to them," he declared, "our wives and children will not die."

Clarity and Resolve
While the dissolution of Centro Médico/Mano a Mano collaboration shook the Mano a Mano board of directors, the Chullpa K'asa story reaffirmed its resolve to continue its work in the mountains.

That was not the only village needing a clinic. Joan reminded the board of the numbers behind the realities of rural Bolivian lives. In villages like Chullpa K'asa, mothers, infants, and children died twice as often as Bolivians who lived in cities like Cochabamba. Nearly twice as many rural children died within their first month than did urban Bolivians. The board, many of its members having traveled to rural Bolivian villages, nodded its collective head. Its members had seen the medical challenges before their eyes. And they did not dismiss the solidity of the medical-supply program or the success of the Clínicas Gloria.

The board had also seen documentation of the distribution of supplies far beyond Centro Médico. And though José had new responsibilities at his new job, he and the rest of the Velásquez family, as well the American and Bolivian volunteers, were firmly committed to Mano a Mano's goal of keeping the medical supplies moving to healthcare organizations that served Bolivia's poor.

The loss of the partnership with Centro Médico was disruptive but not disastrous for Mano a Mano. Segundo and Joan led the board to seriously consider sticking with its mission, continuing what worked and modifying what had gotten it into trouble. Thus the board of directors made several major decisions: To continue the medical supplies program with the development of new procedures in Bolivia, to raise funds sufficient to build one or two more clinics a year in rural villages, and to ensure that future clinic development was truly community-

A Small Group . . .

based. This meant that villagers must request help with a project, the partnerships must be cemented by legal documents, and the villages must own and maintain their own clinics.

The Mano a Mano board made a crucial addition to its previous approach in working with rural villages. The organization worked with the Bolivian Velásquez family and volunteers to design new guidelines for decisions about which requesting villages they would collaborate with. The requesting village not only had to initiate a project and commit manual labor to construction but also to work with the government to garner additional resources for the clinic.

Mano a Mano knew that the lack of clinics and schools in the rural areas was due not to a lack of governmental concern but to a lack of money and expertise. Bolivia was one of the poorest countries in Latin America, and its few riches were typically diverted to urban areas. Resources rarely came to the tiny indigenous rural villages with which Mano a Mano typically works.

But Mano a Mano also knew that the federal government, at least theoretically, allocated resources to municipios to address the health and education needs of its villages. Thus, Mano a Mano expected the leaders of villages wanting a clinic to request support from their municipios. That support might come in the form of a salary for one of the clinic staff members, furniture for the offices, connecting the clinic to electricity, or purchasing construction materials.

A framework for the partnership of community, municipio officials, and Mano a Mano developed. The three entities would become long-term partners for improving a village's health (see Appendix A).

The greatest challenge for Mano a Mano was to choose from many requests just which communities it would work with. The Bolivian Mano a Mano staff decided to meet with each village at length to assess its need for a clinic and its level of *ganas* (motivation) to building and maintaining the project. They would also explore a village's potential for working with the official local government. José's continuing report

136

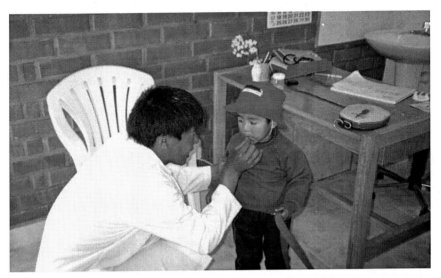

The doctor treats a patient in one of the new village clinics.

of the need he found in the Quechua mountain villages spurred the effort of the U.S. Mano a Mano board to raise money for construction materials and keep sending medical supplies to Cochabamba.

During an assessment meeting with one village, a leader approached both José and German Matías, the master carpenter who came to assess the potential for a clinic. He said, "Dr. José, come with us up this path. You will see why we need a clinic."

José and German Matías followed a small group including a young man holding the hands of two little girls. His wife, Maria, and their baby had died in an unattended birth. Their bodies, carefully wrapped in a heavy wool blanket, were carried to the mountaintop for return to *Pachamama* (Mother Earth). Maria's husband and motherless daughters cried softly as the bodies were laid to rest. José stood beside the blanket-wrapped bodies, thinking, "I must tell Segundo about this.

Healthy children do well in Mano a Mano schools.

7

Serendipity

1997–2000

In 1997 Mano a Mano separated from Centro Médico, losing the space and staff that the hospital had provided for the storage and distribution of the medical supplies from the United States. José had been drawing on family and church members to augment the efforts of Centro Médico staff. Many of the staff members continued as Mano a Mano volunteers even after he left the hospital. Ivo began to pull in family and church connections to expand the cadre of volunteers and so continue the medical-supply program independent of the organization's former partner.

The Mano a Mano board members realized that continuing without Centro Médico meant the need for significantly greater funding. The demands in Bolivia and the United States stretched the capacity of the all-volunteer organizations in both countries. Knowing that Mano a Mano needed help with fundraising, Joan asked Terry Crowley, president of Crowley, White and Associates, which specialized in fundraising for nonprofit organizations, to reprise his role as a volunteer consultant. Crowley had earlier pointed out that since Joan and several Mano a Mano friends were graduates of Macalester College, which was strongly supported by the Weyerhaeuser Family Foundation, the foundation might be interested in a local project headed by a Macalester grad. Indeed, it was the first foundation to make a significant grant to Mano a Mano. Crowley agreed to guide Joan in developing a grant-writing strategy.

Joan invited Terry to a board meeting to discuss the organization's fundraising challenges. The directors voiced various concerns: Segundo noted the unending need for healthcare in Bolivia. Joan spoke of the persistently small individual donations and general lack of interest among local foundations in funding international programs. Deb Kotcher emphasized the limits of the budget in the face of Mano a Mano's broadened aspirations. Chris Ver Ploeg argued incisively for a new fundraising approach. During an impasse, Terry Crowley, who had been sitting quietly, straightened up in his chair and said, "Maybe it's time to go back to the guy who brought $5,000 to Gloria's party."

Thus began a fundraising strategy that moved Mano a Mano to a new financial and organizational level. Chris Ver Ploeg still remembers Terry Crowley's pitch: "You have to get out there, and you should ask for a lot." He suggested an informal gathering including the man who had delivered the anonymous contribution.

The board agreed to pursue Crowley's strategy, and Chris, an adept and comfortable host, offered her home for a dinner, inviting all the members of the Mano a Mano board. Joan called John Slettom, the agent of the anonymous donor contributing $5,000 at Gloria Mac-Rae's birthday party.

Chris remembers the evening well: "The idea was to get to know the donor contact better. After dinner Terry pulled out a piece of paper—a written fundraising agenda. I was mortified. I corralled our guest in the kitchen to say, 'I am so sorry. I didn't think the evening would take on this cast.'

"Slettom answered reassuringly, 'Oh, this is just so normal. It happens all the time. This is just the way it works.'"

Segundo made one of his typically detailed though informal presentations to the board about projects he hoped it would pursue, launching into an enthusiastic description of Mano a Mano. He spoke of its medical-supply program, of the construction of the two clinics emerging from Gloria's birthday party, and of the recent completion of the Chullpa K'asa clinic. Joan sat quietly at his side, occasionally illuminating one of Segundo's points. John Slettom and his wife, Jeanyne, were charmed and intrigued.

Slettom called Joan the next day and asked her to put together a $15,000 proposal for Mano a Mano's effort in the United States. He was acting as the agent of the donor, searching out organizations appropriate to the donor's preference. Joan submitted a short, clear request. After reviewing Joan's proposal with the philanthropist, John told her that the donor would triple the request, spreading it out over three years.

With this $45,000 grant, Mano a Mano found itself in a new situation. It had not only a plan for its work but also a stable, upfront budget to help support it. In close consultation with José and Ivo, the U.S. board hired a Bolivian to oversee the medical-supply effort. The board also hired German Matías, who had worked for Ivo from the time he was building the Velásquez family home, as the master builder of the clinics.

Joan garnered grants from several U.S. foundations, enabling the organization to expand the medical donations program and to build and staff one or two clinics each year. Segundo bought a wall-sized map of Bolivia, mounted it on the wall of the U.S. office, and pointed out the location of each new clinic with a brightly colored pushpin.

Working via Internet and phone with José and Ivo, Joan and Segundo used the new money to upgrade the medical-supply process. They also talked about the transfer of the money they had raised, concluding that it was time for Mano a Mano to become a formal Bolivian NGO (nongovernmental organization).

In 1999 Blanca Velásquez, the lawyer in the family, worked with Segundo and José to complete the complex bureaucratic legal work necessary to creating Mano a Mano Bolivia and its *asamblea* (founding members, ruling body) and board of directors. This policy-making group, including Ivo, José and his wife, Cinthia, and sister Blanca, was to oversee the clinic and medical-supply work in Bolivia. Four former Centro Médico employees of José's also agreed to join the asamblea.

Segundo, as Mano a Mano president, was empowered to add two representatives of U.S. interests. Everyone on the asamblea was a Bolivian, consistent with the Mano a Mano principle that all work in Bolivia should be in response to Bolivian requests and administrated by Bolivians. Mano a Mano Bolivia was created as a parallel, not a subordinate, organization to Mano a Mano USA. This decision reflected the U.S. board's commitment to creating and maintaining a flat, non-hierarchical structure.

A sense of independence was emerging between Mano a Mano Bolivia and Mano a Mano USA. But two matters of fact indicated the need for a partnership of interdependence: The Bolivian program depended on the funds the U.S. organization could raise and the medical supplies it could secure. And Mano a Mano USA depended on the successful completion of programs by the Bolivian board and staff to meet its goals and confirm its legitimacy. Each required the other for its very existence.

The structure of the organizations reinforced a level of dependence from the Bolivian side on U.S. resources. It was in the United States that resources for the expensive and expanding Mano a Mano agenda existed. Joan was the one with the skills, commitment, and time to devote to fundraising. And bicultural, bi-national Segundo was part of both decision-making groups and involved in both programs, and effectively he had veto power over the asamblea.

None of this deterred the asamblea, the Mano a Mano USA board, or the Velásquezes (José, Cinthia, Segundo, Joan, Ivo, Blanca) from working collaboratively on their ambitious agenda in Bolivia.

After completion of the community-owned Campo Via and Lope Mendoza clinics in the late 1990s, that Mano a Mano could work with them to build clinics became common knowledge among the mountain villagers above Cochabamba. The man to talk to was José Velásquez.

*José and Segundo Velásquez
outside Mano a Mano Bolivia's headquarters*

In the middle of one night, José's wife, Cinthia, was the first to awaken to a loud banging at the front door of their house. She was used to late-night requests from José's patients, who knew he would care for them whenever they needed him. But when she opened the door, she was surprised to see a group of dusty men.

They apologized: "Forgive the late visit, Señora. But we are looking for the doctor who builds clinics."

Cinthia went in and awakened her husband. Outside, under the dim streetlight, José saw a cluster of campesinos leaning against a battered truck.

Serendipity

"We've come to ask you to build a clinic in our village. The government sent us a doctor, but he has no place to work. The doctor is a friend of your nephew, who told him that you build clinics. We have land, sand, and ganas to work, but we have no money."

José knew he couldn't turn his back on this request. He said, "We will talk with Mano a Mano in the United States. Come back in the morning. Perhaps our friends there can help us find money for your clinic."

Clinic construction supported by the three-way partnership of Mano a Mano, the local government, and village workers was spreading into more of the rural villages around Cochabamba. And whether villagers walked miles to persuade José to bring a clinic to their community or a doctor had made a life-saving intervention during a complicated birth, Segundo never tired of telling the Mano a Mano story—to the U.S. board, to fellow members of St. Paul's Unity Church–Unitarian, and to the people he met socially.

Segundo always began new connections with polite, almost formal inquiries about family and health. In a short time, however, Segundo was in animated conversation about Bolivia and more specifically about Mano a Mano progress. He frequently ended with, "Well, I'm going down next month [or next winter or next summer]. Why don't you come along?"

More and more people chose to accept the invitation, and the board saw such trips as an excellent way to increase the support of U.S. volunteers, who rarely traveled to Bolivia alone. Segundo's trips had morphed from family reunions, to opportunities to carry medical supplies in his luggage, to collaborations with his brothers to monitor and maintain Mano a Mano programs. He continued to engage in all these activities on every trip. Eventually he added the oversight of group trips to Bolivia.

Every Mano a Mano USA board member at some time joined Segundo on one of his journeys home. His traveling companions often included a dedicated donor or volunteer as well. Gloria MacRae joined one group to attend the inauguración of a clinic she had been instrumental in funding. Typically a group flew to Cochabamba and stayed in a hotel blocks from the Velásquez *apartamento* (apartment building). Settled right in the middle of the beautiful colonial city with its flowering trees and ancient churches, the visitors walked about, seeing the beauties of old and the too frequent squalor of communities full of recently arrived Quechua people looking for work and for food.

Soon Segundo was bringing along volunteers and board members on nearly every trip he made to Bolivia. He walked the visitors through the cultural joys of old Cochabamba and drove them on hair-raising trips up and down narrow mountain roads. They visited at least one of the Mano a Mano clinics in the Cochabamba mountains and valley—Chullpa K'asa, Tablas Monte, Campo Via, or Laguna Sulti, the Velásquez home place.

Each clinic provided basic medical care and health education with an emphasis on maternal and child health. The visitors met villagers who had worked to build their community clinics and often joined them in the inauguración y entrega of a completed clinic.

A Partnership Challenge

Mano a Mano continued to build and open one to two rural clinics a year, using the approach developed with the Chullpa K'asa clinic after separation from Centro Médico. The communities set aside a parcel of land for a clinic, furnished locally available building materials like sand, and contributed the unskilled labor needed for construction of the building. Municipios contributed funds, furnishings, and often, a staff salary.

Following this division of labor and resources was crucial to the successful completion of the project and the sense of pride and ownership it developed on the part of the villagers. This approach continued unchallenged until 2000.

Serendipity

Three months after the Campo Via clinic opened, José learned from the nurse there that she had not yet been paid. He immediately called the municipio's alcalde, who had committed to covering her salary. The alcalde told José not to worry, that the nurse would be paid. But when José contacted the clinic the next week, he learned again that the pay had not arrived.

Whenever José had a major issue within Mano a Mano Bolivia, he talked it over with Segundo, who typically then shared it with Joan. Calling St. Paul, José announced, "The Campo Via nurse has not received her salary. It is important that we hold the government to its commitments. I think we should close the clinic and move the staff and equipment to another community. What do you think?"

At first Joan and Segundo were afraid that might be too extreme. But eventually the three agreed that this was a crucial test of their plan for sustainability. If they tolerated one government official reneging on the commitment to pay staff, they would not be able to hold others to their commitments. But if they shut down the clinic to force the municipio to pay, there were other costs to consider. The villagers would not receive the services they had been promised and had worked so hard for, children and mothers would be unable to maintain their vaccination and nutrition programs, and donors would be disheartened if they found the clinic they had helped fund was no longer serving patients.

Still, José, Joan, and Segundo agreed—they had to close the clinic.

José drove into the mountains to Campo Via. Gathering the villagers at the clinic, he explained that the alcalde had failed to pay the nurse, and he publicly locked the clinic. When the villagers learned the reason for the closing of their clinic, dozens of men jumped into a cattle truck belonging to one of them and drove to the alcalde's office. They demanded that the nurse be paid and refused to leave until they had an agreement.

The loud protest met with success, and the nurse received her salary. When José received news of the payment, he returned and publicly

146

reopened the clinic. Word spread quickly through the mountain villages and the towns with governmental offices: Mano a Mano held all parties to their commitments.

An Anonymous Gift

In 2000, three years after receipt of the $45,000 from the anonymous donor, the Mano a Mano USA board decided it was time to invite John Slettom, the philanthropist's agent, to visit the Cochabamba mountains and valley. Segundo wanted him to see the Mano a Mano projects, especially the new clinics, to which many of the medical supplies from the United States were going. He wanted John to see just what a modest clinic with appropriate supplies and staff could provide to a village. He imagined him coming back in the evening to sit around the big table in the ancianos' apartmento and talk about what he had seen, what he thought about his Bolivian experience.

So Segundo asked John Slettom to join a group of nine others on a trip to Cochabamba. That summer, John accepted the invitation to come with Segundo to see Mano a Mano in action in Bolivia.

John Slettom was fascinated with the lush, flowering trees in the Cochabamba Valley and the never-ending view of the mountains. He examined the details of the storing and distribution of the medical supplies from St. Paul. He reveled in mountain drives with Segundo or Ivo at the wheel of an SUV. And he was especially fascinated by the Quechua villages tucked into the mountains among the flowering potato plants and the tethered llamas and sheep.

John visited several up-and-running Mano a Mano clinics. He saw the new clinic standing in the grove of eucalyptus trees surrounding the site of the old Velásquez home place in Laguna Sulti. He met alcaldes and other government officials who had provided modest funding toward clinic construction. He went high into the mountains to meet villagers who donated land and did all the manual labor involved in the construction of their clinics.

Serendipity

John Slettom joined Segundo and José on a trip to a village that had recently requested a clinic. They were unable to get to the village at the scheduled time because government workers were repairing a three-foot-wide pothole in the middle of a gravel road. They watched as a truck full of mud was quickly dumped and spread over the pothole, making the problem worse. The truck drove off, and the three men went on to see the villagers who had been waiting during their two-hour delay.

John watched José and Segundo describing the Mano a Mano process to the villagers who had asked for help in building a clinic. Segundo translated from Quechua to Spanish to English so Slettom and the others in the group could understand Mano a Mano's role and its expectations for each village. The donor's representative learned that the villagers had to make a request for a clinic and contribute both land and manual labor to the project. Finally, John listened as José told the villagers how to make a formal request for a partnership with Mano a Mano.

After the meeting, John, José, and Segundo drove back toward Cochabamba. They came to the spot where the government workers had dumped the mud on the road. It was already full of deep ruts and again, almost impassable. José and Segundo, in the front seat, talked about how they would have repaired that pothole. They agreed that if the workers had had the appropriate equipment, they would not have taken such an inadequate approach.

John Slettom listened to their talk about the kind of equipment that government workers lacked, and he heard the brothers saying that Mano a Mano had the same problem: unusable roads and thus inaccessibility to otherwise possible clinic sites. Segundo made sure John understood the complexities of Mano a Mano's work. He arranged for him to go to gatherings with José and village leaders to learn why the Mano a Mano model was unique among international development projects.

Segundo explained that the deeply communal culture of the Quec-

148

hua grew out of the ayllu governing structure. This was central to the high level of community participation existing in every Mano a Mano project. Villages were highly organized and had leaders with deep community legitimacy. All of the partners involved in a project signed legally binding agreements. In the process for building each clinic, the village leaders, the municipio officials, and Mano a Mano emerged as formal partners. The model began and ended with the village.

John Slettom was moved by the success produced by such a project model. He was impressed to see José and Segundo in their authoritative and personal negotiating roles with villagers. He was struck by José's active managerial style and with Mano a Mano's remarkable efficiency and frugality. Never had he seen an organization run so effectively, accomplishing so much with so little. John made a strong connection with José, but he left with some concern that all of José's Mano a Mano work was voluntary. He didn't receive a penny for it.

When John returned to the United States, he apparently had no trouble convincing the anonymous donor of the health needs in the villages. He also succeeded in demonstrating that Mano a Mano had the potential to address those needs on a larger scale. In a matter of days after his return to St. Paul, he contacted Joan and asked her to write two grants: one for the construction of 30 more rural clinics, the other for 80.

John Slettom also offered Mano a Mano a $20,000 grant to help develop its plans. Using part of this development grant, Mano a Mano brought José to St. Paul to work with Joan and Segundo in planning a dramatically expanded Mano a Mano clinic-construction program.

Joan remembers those working meetings when the clinic proposal was taking shape: "It was pretty amazing to watch José and Segundo together. They have different styles. Segundo leaps. He's not linear at all. He leaps and leaps, and he's way out there. He knows every step that has to be taken along the way, and it doesn't get missed. He's a very good manager.

Serendipity

"But he also starts with the confidence that he and other people around him will know enough so that they can start even if they don't know exactly how they will get to the end. Or what it will be. Or whether or not they can predict what it will be.

"José will not embark on anything unless he is absolutely sure that he knows every step, knows exactly what the end point is, and knows that he can get there. He will not take the kind of risks that Segundo might.

"That combination was really good, both creative and clear."

Joan did not acknowledge the role she played in integrating the vision of Segundo and the meticulousness of José into a coherent and ambitious project. Her finely detailed $2 million proposal put José in control of everything that was to happen in the recently incorporated Mano a Mano Bolivia organization over the next seven years.

Joan and Segundo agreed with John Slettom's proposal to pay José for his work, and Joan wrote José in as the director of Mano a Mano Bolivia. She incorporated all the plans into a 50-page proposal and sent it off to John.

The proposal described the participatory community-action approach at the core of Mano a Mano's work in rural villages—with one important addition. The budget was based on the assumption that Mano a Mano would fund one staff position from the first day the clinic opened but that a non–Mano a Mano source—the Health Ministry or the municipio—must fund the second staff position. The idea was that if Mano a Mano could operate the clinics without taking on the long-term obligation of funding additional staff, it could build a sustainable network.

John Slettom previewed the proposal that Joan, Segundo, and José had completed and shared it with the anonymous donor. John called Joan to set up a meeting for Segundo, Joan, and José, with the anonymous donor and his spouse just before José was to return to Bolivia. A few days before the meeting, Slettom called with devastating news:

the donor had had a massive stroke. But as his condition stabilized, the donor's wife decided that she and her attorney would meet with the Velásquezes.

The group spent several hours going through the 50-page proposal. Segundo translated for José. Finally they examined the minutely detailed $2 million budget to construct 30 clinics in the Cochabamba region in five years. They went over each item, from personnel to building supplies.

When they came across a budget request for heavy equipment, the donor's wife wondered what that had to do with building clinics. John Slettom told her about the mud holes' delay of their trip to a requesting village. He spoke of his appreciation of the need for heavy equipment in a country so lacking in basic expertise and infrastructure. The capacity to repair roads was a way to provide access to remote villages, the better to serve those most in need.

When the budget discussion ended, John turned to the philanthropist's wife and said, "What do you want to do?"

She paused, looked at the pile of paper before her, pushed it across to her lawyer, and said, "Make it happen."

Making It Happen

The anonymous donor's lawyer did the legal work to make the $2 million project happen. After recovering from tears of surprise and delight, Joan and Segundo began to make it happen organizationally, knowing they were operating at a dramatically higher financial level than ever before, anticipating the complexities of moving that high amount of American dollars to Bolivia over the next seven years.

José went back to Bolivia after the meeting. He talked with Ivo about the implications of broadening the scale of operations tenfold. José and Segundo talked daily, only slowly recognizing that they could not clear up the tangles over the telephone or via the Internet. They requested that the Mano a Mano USA board and Mano a Mano Bolivia

Serendipity

asamblea authorize the primary Mano a Mano Bolivia volunteers to come to Mendota Heights to work with Joan and Segundo.

Authorized, they came: José, who was involved in every aspect of the program, and Aida Suárez, the accountant with tested and sophisticated knowledge about financing a program in Bolivia. It was hard to believe, but all of their previous work had been as volunteers—as had been Joan's and Segundo's. Their commitment ran deep.

For two weeks Segundo, Joan, José, and Aida Suárez sat around the same table in the same Mendota Heights living room that had seen the decision to create Mano a Mano. They talked six, sometimes eight, hours a day, working on the logistics of ramping up for the completion of 30 clinics over the next few years. They followed the approach used in designing the distribution of medical supplies six years earlier, and later, of the community clinic program.

Starting with close attention to the needs of Bolivians as Bolivians defined them, the planners moved through the logistics of meeting those needs. Moving step by step, Segundo and José nailed down the details of the process following the formal request of village leaders and their elected municipio officials for a clinic: a standardized process for the approval to proceed with construction, the physical and transportation logistics required for the building, the staff necessary to complete and manage the project, the formal agreements of all concerned, and finally, the financial resources required to make everything possible.

Surprisingly, the transfer of money between Minnesota and Cochabamba was the most challenging task. From the 1996 construction of its first clinic-building project, Mano a Mano USA had routinely transferred amounts up to $15,000 to Bolivia three to four times a year. The computerized systems in both countries generated the required reports, and the local bank in St. Paul used its standard wiring system to get money to a Cochabamba bank. Three Bolivian Mano a Mano volunteers were authorized to sign for withdrawals. It was simple and it had worked.

But four years later José, Joan, Segundo, and Aida Suárez, in examination of this process in the context of $2 million, came upon one problem after another. As they worked to come up with procedures for transferring the money, José and Aida reminded Joan and Segundo of realities they had not lived with and knew nothing about. While a transfer of funds merited a $30 fee at a U.S. bank, the same transaction in Bolivia could cost hundreds of dollars.

In Minnesota a transfer from savings to checking could occur by phone or computer at no charge. In Bolivia it might take many hours of standing in line and cost hundreds of dollars. Unlike those in the United States, NGOs in Bolivia were treated as businesses and thus were significantly taxed. The Cochabamba banks had none of the U.S. guarantees ensuring the safety of deposited money.

After several days of discussion, Aida, José, Segundo, and Joan concluded that the delays, elaborate bureaucratic processes, and costliness of Bolivian banks could paralyze their project. They also accepted that the security of their newly granted money would be in jeopardy if they were to deposit it in the Bolivian banking system. They recommended to the Mano a Mano USA board and the Bolivian asamblea that the Mano a Mano account in Bolivia be a private one, in the names of José and two non-Velásquez members of the Mano a Mano Bolivia asamblea.

To ensure the security of their money, they kept the bulk of the grant allocation in a U.S. account and transferred relatively small amounts to Mano a Mano Bolivia timed to payments of expenses such as salaries and construction materials.

These agreements cemented a cross-national, cross-cultural relationship that evolved from open sharing and the accommodation of genuine differences of style and values. All agreed that they could make the financial arrangement work.

José and his colleague Aida Suárez returned to Bolivia with challenges both exhilarating and immediate. José left the job at the hospital

Serendipity

he had moved to when Mano a Mano separated from Centro Médico to become the full-time director of Mano a Mano Bolivia. He hired several other Centro Médico employees—an office assistant, a distribution worker, a physician, and a driver. Aida became the full-time accountant.

In 2001, Mano a Mano Bolivia bought a dump truck, a backhoe, and an SUV, and in 2002 it not only purchased a grader and a jeep but also hired an equipment repairperson to take care of all the new equipment. That the increased staff and stuff should be together in its own space soon became obvious. The Velásquezes looked first to what was most inexpensive and familiar, choosing to donate office space and co-locate Mano a Mano with Ivo's carpentry shop in Canata.

Soon Ivo was working as a volunteer from the new office, overseeing the construction staff. After a year of this, the family saw that Ivo's carpentry business and income were suffering from his absorption with Mano a Mano. The Bolivian asamblea and U.S. board agreed with José when he suggested that Ivo be put on the payroll as the full-time construction manager. The staff was complete.

Building a Health Network

Mano a Mano had moved beyond the geographic and administrative constraints of its collaboration with Centro Médico. Its reputation grew as it moved farther and farther into the mountains, building new clinics. José knew that the Bolivian health ministry held significant financial resources that might be leveraged with the funds brought from the United States.

The unique Mano a Mano model had solidified its process of building clinics, and its board and staff knew that the colored pushpins marking completed clinics would multiply many times. They did not know the locations of the next clinics, but there were many requests. They looked forward to seeing at least 30 more pushpins on the map in five years.

The Velásquezes reminded themselves that there were still many old clinics standing empty and crumbling in the mountains. To avoid that fate, they knew they must be deliberate in their work. They cautioned themselves that as Mano a Mano built more clinics, it must never forget its responsibility to see that the clinics were sustained.

Mano a Mano had addressed sustainability broadly in its proposal to the anonymous donor, not limiting its concern merely to healthcare and solid construction. It knew that staffing was crucial. A lovely clinic without doctors and nurses would be of no use.

José had been in touch with the regional offices of the ministry of health through his career and was on good working terms with them. He knew health ministry requirements and how the ministry allocated funds for municipios and regional offices to provide healthcare for villages. He had a thorough understanding of the way public projects were financed in Bolivia and a clear sense of government capacities: A municipio might not have the expertise or funds to build a clinic, but it did have access to regional and federal funds for nurses and doctors.

José proposed that Mano a Mano require the junta vecinal or sindicato of a requesting village to work with Mano a Mano to find a separate source to take on the staffing of the village's clinic. With all agreed, this requirement ultimately made it possible for Mano a Mano to stretch its funding to serve many more communities.

Today 100 percent of clinic salaries are covered by non-Mano a Mano sources from the day a clinic is opened. Segundo and Joan often look back to Campo Via, where the nurse did not receive her salary and José closed the clinic. And they breathe a sigh of gratitude for his good instincts.

Mano a Mano and the ministry of health continued to collaborate successfully to staff the clinics dotting the mountains. But Mano a Mano also understood that the training and nurture of clinic staff were crucial to keeping the doctors and nurses satisfied with their day-to-day lives in remote communities.

Serendipity

Carlos Moises Guevara is typical of the young, energetic physicians who choose to work in villages that are poor and isolated. He said of his experience, "I had just graduated from medical school. I learned about Mano a Mano from a friend of mine, who is a nurse. I asked her to let me know if there was an opening in a Mano a Mano clinic. I heard from her that the clinics are clean and well equipped, that there is no problem getting supplies to use in treating patients, that the personnel in the Cochabamba office are available by phone every day to help with difficult cases. And we doctors [would] receive more training from Dr. Victor Hugo Ortuño, who is very supportive.

"In most clinics in Bolivia, you can't get supplies, the building starts to fall apart, and nobody responds. You are totally on your own. I have found that everything my friend said about Mano a Mano is true. I am very happy to be working in this clinic. I travel to Cochabamba once each month and feel that I am part of the big family that is Mano a Mano."

Dr. Guevara's experience is neither accidental nor unique. The model has worked for him as for others, not effortlessly but systematically and carefully. The sturdy clinics that dot the mountains above the Cochabamba Valley are of red brick, shiny even years after construction. They may be big or small, depending on the size of the community. But each stands out with clean architectural lines, sturdy doors, many windows, and strong metal or tile roofs. There is a big white sign on each building, announcing it is a *Centro de Salud* (health center) with the hand-to-hand symbol beneath it. Below the symbol, the village name and Mano a Mano are inscribed side by side, indicating the key partners in the clinic project.

The partnership between Mano a Mano and a village clinic is intense, especially in the first three years of operation. The Mano a Mano staff knows that without phone connection and public transportation the doctors and nurses are isolated. The only other professionals in a typical village are the teachers, who, while deeply appreciated socially, cannot

156

Centro de Salud at Apote

provide medical consultation. Thus there is a structured system of communication between each clinic and Mano a Mano staff in Cochabamba.

A Mano a Mano medical staff member from Cochabamba contacts clinic staff every day by short-wave radio in the first year after a clinic opens and weekly after that year. A Mano a Mano physician arrives at the clinic every three months to supervise and train clinic personnel. Also the clinic staff is expected to leave the village and come into the Cochabamba office regularly, where Victor Ortuño and other physicians present 12 workshops each year—four each for physicians, nurses, and dentists. Nearly all clinic personnel come to the city at least once a year to attend one of these workshops.

Recently, village clinic personnel coming to Cochabamba had several workshop topics to choose from: traumatology, nutrition, biosecurity, problem pregnancy, and family violence. The continuing education of doctors and nurses—the topics offered change from year to

Serendipity

year—expands their practice skills, benefiting both clinic staff and villagers while mitigating the professional and personal isolation inherent in rural clinic work.

In addition to developing staff, increasing the capacity of a village to promote and sustain the health of its members is central to the Mano a Mano agenda. In the late 1990s, Victor Ortuño first planned and conducted a range of training experiences that he brought directly to remote villages.

Typically Dr. Ortuño arrived in a village with a generator, a television, and a VCR. Villagers noted the electronic equipment with anticipation, undoubtedly informed by medical staff and health promoters (honored members of the village) that there would be health presentations during the day and movies in the evening.

The junta vecinal leaders choose people who are *respetado* (given deference) and who have the most education to be the health promoters. They are expected to work in this capacity as an unpaid community service, just as other villagers are expected to perform manual labor. Reflecting the deep ayllu tradition of communality that undergirds Quechua culture, all members are expected to devote some of their adult years to care of the community. Village health promoters frequently become leaders of the community; others have received scholarships from Mano a Mano to become nurses.

When Dr. Ortuño arrived in a village with his generator, he set his audiovisual equipment up in the clinic. He trained the staff and the health promoters on topics such as inoculations, prenatal care, and his specialty, traumatology. In addition to audiovisual materials, he provided life-size mannequins of children and adults for the participants to practice on. After the training, villagers who had brought burden cloths filled with food joined the health promoters at a central meeting place for a feast of lima beans, country cheese, and boiled kernels of native corn. A movie screen was set up far away from the noise of the generator and high enough so all could see.

158

Dr. Ortuño, who since has left Mano a Mano to receive additional education, recalled putting a health-related movie in the VCR at one of the earliest clinic trainings: "It was dark when the movie ended, and the villagers asked to see it again. They had never watched a movie before, so I showed it again. And I had brought other movies with me as well. Some villagers watched *Star Wars* over and over, far into the night." Now other physicians carry on the Mano a Mano health education work.

In 2003, as Segundo was shepherding an American group of volunteers through Bolivia, he was especially eager to bring the group to the clinic that had celebrated its inauguración less than a year earlier: "Remember the colored pins on the office map of Bolivia that point out our completed clinics? This is one of those clinics. I want you to meet Dr. Luisa Ramirez, the clinic director."

As the SUV turned off the dusty road, the visitors came to a group of women sitting beneath a huge shade tree. The dozens of women were dressed in traditional clothes—wide-brimmed hats, wide skirts, and brightly colored sweaters over their blouses. Many babies snuggled into brightly patterned burden cloths draped around their mothers' shoulders. Smaller children leaned close into their seated mothers, while their older brothers and sisters sat quietly together nearby. Nearly every child wore something on his or her head, some of the girls in tiny replicas of their mothers' wide-brimmed hats and some boys in elaborately patterned stocking caps, others in baseball hats. It was cold, sunny, and windy in the mountains.

Dr. Ramirez greeted the Minnesota group in Spanish, and Segundo translated her greeting into English. The doctor shook hands with the travelers and explained (through Segundo's translation) that this was *Un Dia para Mujeres* (Women's Day) at the clinic. Then she introduced the travelers to the Charamoco mothers, who had been coming to the clinic with their children twice a month for half a year. Dr. Ramirez spoke in Quechua when she told the women that the group was from

Serendipity

Mano a Mano in the United States, the organization that had helped the village build its new clinic.

The doctor explained to the guests that nearly every woman carried a growth chart, that the strings of yarn dangling from them showed the growth and level of malnutrition of each of their children. She then told the Mano a Mano visitors that the goal of the clinic was to reduce the malnutrition that was so prevalent in this village, as it was through most of rural Bolivia. She wanted the malnutrition rate for these children to be zero.

Dr. Ramirez asked the guests to inquire about the women's children's health: "If they have answers, you and I will know that my work here is successful."

She asked the women, "What foods have vitamin A?"

One responded, "Carrots." Several others called out in Quechua that carrots prevent blindness.

The U.S. guests listened to Segundo's translation of the informed answers to more questions about what the mothers fed their children and why they fed them certain things. Dr. Ramirez thanked the women for their comments and invited the guests into the clinic.

Segundo translated the comment of one woman as the guests passed by: "We have learned many things from our doctor!" That the women were fond of their Quechua-speaking physician was obvious.

The guests saw a wide hall running down the center of the clinic with sturdy benches on each side and solid doors opening into examination rooms. There was a table with a scale model of the village that the doctor made. The charming replica of the village included a miniature clinic and school with each surrounding house punctured by colored pushpins representing the number of children and the age of each child living there.

A chart tracking the immunization and growth of dozens of children hung on the wall. Dr. Ramirez pointed out that since the beginning of the year the percentage of children given vaccinations had

160

gone from 7 to 93 percent. Then she looked away from the chart and announced, "We will get to 100 percent by the end of this year."

As he drove away, Segundo commented to his companions that Dr. Ramirez was exceptional and that the procedures she had implemented were the required protocol at all Mano a Mano clinics.

By the end of 2002, Mano a Mano had built and opened 18 rural community clinics—far beyond the 12 projected in the proposal—with funds from its anonymous donor. José's success in negotiating with the health ministry and the municipios to fund staff salaries enabled an accelerated response to community requests, to build nine rather than the projected six clinics per year. Residents of clinic communities were learning that Mano a Mano keeps its promises. With their contribution of hundreds of hours of labor, they saw that they had the ability to improve life for their children. Seeing new possibilities, they began to ask Mano a Mano to join them in meeting other pressing needs.

Successfully building, opening, and co-administering a clinic with Mano a Mano changes a village. Not only do more mothers and babies survive birth and more children grow into adulthood, but also the community redefines its needs. Villagers learn connections between seemingly neutral factors that affect their well-being in ways they've never thought about before. From their new health promoters, for example, they learn that the water they drink affects their health and that their springs, streams, and rivers must be kept clean of the waste that otherwise mingles with these waters. Many villages, now separating their drinking water from their wastewater, are finding that they have fewer infections than in the past.

Several juntas vecinales and sindicatos eventually asked Mano a Mano to work with them to build sanitation facilities for their villages. Providing clean water to augment the health improvement that came with the clinics made good sense. José and his brothers immediately began thinking about ways to respond to these requests.

They worked with the clinic staff of several villages to think through how best to meet the sanitation needs of small communities. They concluded that any facility should be close to a school if one existed in the village. That way it would augment the formal hygiene classes and provide a place to practice what students learned. There should be separate bathroom for males and females, each with showers, toilet stalls, and sinks.

In its effort to provide safe and even warm water for the community, Mano a Mano would pump clean water into a tank on the roof that would have solar panels for heating it. To discourage villagers from washing their clothes in polluted streams, there would be an outdoor tap and laundry tubs. When the first sanitation building was inaugurated, school children stood in line to turn on the faucet and feel the warm water on their cold hands.

By 2012 Mano a Mano and its village partners had built 44 such facilities.

On to Schools

Parents who lived in the villages with functional health clinics and/or sanitation facilities began to look beyond the health concerns and think about their children's education in a new way. Some villages have no schools at all, and their children must walk great distances or miss getting an education altogether. Other villages have broken-down schools that have not seen a teacher in years. Some have schools too small to hold all the children or too dilapidated to protect them from the cold and rain.

To make matters worse, these communities have great difficulty finding teachers willing to live there and teach their children. Those who do arrive often leave for long periods because the living conditions are dreadful. Villagers who have worked side by side with Mano a Mano to build a clinic have learned that they don't have to accept their situation—they can work to change it.

A village that has built a clinic with Mano a Mano knows the model. And many villages decide to move beyond their first effort and ask Mano a Mano to help build a school and some housing for teachers so that they will stay in the community. They know they must make a formal written request. They know they must persuade their municipio officials to contribute some of the resources received from the national government. They know that José or other Mano a Mano staff members will come to their village and work with their leaders to assess their capacity and ganas to provide manual labor for construction and maintenance afterwards.

When a community gets the news that Mano a Mano can fund its school and housing for its teachers, the villagers know that German Matías, the master carpenter, and some of his workers will come to explain the villagers' role in construction. Soon they will see Mano a Mano trucks arrive with bricks and tools. They may see heavy machinery if their road isn't adequate for the needed trucks.

After much negotiation and hard manual labor by the villagers, there will be a celebration—a big white sign raised over the door of a red brick building, announcing the new classrooms and small brick homes for teachers in the village. That there is a building at all is exciting. Often a village has had no classroom at all—the children and teacher, if there was one, attended school outside, weather permitting.

The difference between the teacher housing and the homes of the children is dramatic. The new teachers' houses and classrooms are made of the shiny bricks and red roofs typical of the clinics. The children's homes are of adobe and thatch and are often in need of repair.

Mano a Mano listens to the needs voiced by their clinic partners. It builds sanitation facilities, schools, and housing for teachers. Ivo often says that when Mano a Mano gets to a village and begins working with the villagers, it is hard to leave. He reminds the Mano a Mano USA board and the Bolivian asamblea that this is probably the first time in a hundred years that anyone has come to the villages, made promises, and delivered.

Serendipity

Community workers building the school at Apote

During a visit to one village where Mano a Mano built classrooms and housing for teachers in addition to clinic and sanitation projects, the teachers sought out Mano a Mano staff members. They were delighted with their new homes, happy that they could hang pictures brought from their years in school on solid walls again.

"We will stay here. We're not going anywhere else," they said.

One teacher there told of the shack with rotting wood walls and leaky roof that he had lived in earlier in the village: "When I cooked my soup every day, the steam from the soup would make the bugs in the thatched roof drunk, and they'd fall into my soup. I am so happy to be living in this place where I can eat my soup without bugs falling into it!"

Tito Mamani, a teacher from the village of Jatun K'asa, talked to a U.S. volunteer about his first home there: "I had a single room that was my bedroom, my kitchen, everything. There were rats entering from all sides. During the rainy season when it rained outside, it rained inside. I had to keep moving my things so they didn't get wet."

Things are different since Mano a Mano has helped build housing: "Now we have the best housing in the municipio," said the teacher. "I have worked in other places, and there is nothing like this."

Campo Víbora worked with Mano a Mano to build and operate a clinic and to construct classrooms for a school and housing for teachers. One father described how the villagers' definition of a problem has expanded, how their sense of responsibility has widened, and how they continue to work with Mano a Mano to address new concerns:

"We are responsible [for giving] teachers a place to live. But we can barely afford houses for our own families. Our teachers have been living in little sheds that should be for animals. But we just didn't have any other place for them. So they would come for a week or two and then go back to the city. Who would teach our children? We were so ashamed, but what could we do?

"After we built the clinic with Mano a Mano we asked for help with housing for our teachers. Now we have eight teachers. They stay in our community, and they teach our children."

IV

Sister Organizations

Bolivian residents at the Jusk'u Molle reservoir

8

Beyond Clinics

1997–2005

In its early years Mano a Mano's growth was characterized by tenacity and hope in the face of almost nonexistent financial resources. Then in 2001, it received dramatic infusions of "big money." Over the following four years Mano a Mano USA raised more than $3 million. In 2005 it was anticipating more than $1.5 million before the end of the year.

Recognizing that the unending Bolivian opportunities were straining the capacities of Joan, Segundo, and Becky Monnens, who was hired in 2002 to help with the volunteer program and with grant submissions, the board hired Nate Knatterud-Hubinger in 2005 as a half-time assistant in the U.S. Mano a Mano office and began to search for an executive director. Segundo, Joan, Nate, Nancy White (a board member), and a major donor interviewed seven candidates emerging from a pool of 20 applicants.

The search committee was disappointed that none of the candidates had the unique combination of requirements it needed: an understanding of international development issues, expertise in raising money, a commitment to grassroots community work, and fluency in Spanish. It was about to start the search process again when Joan received an application from Daniel Narr that sounded promising.

Joan phoned Dan immediately and invited him for an interview with the group the next day. He had recently worked for Catholic Charities, a social service organization of the Roman Catholic Archdiocese of Saint Paul and Minneapolis, and learned of Mano a Mano's search for an executive director.

The requirements for the Mano a Mano position intrigued Dan Narr. To him, the position felt like almost a perfect fit. Now in midlife, he had a decade earlier left the business world to enroll in a Protestant seminary. He came away radicalized by a theology that paid special attention to the needs and rights of the poor. Disturbed by the structural inequities perpetuating the extensive poverty in the Philippines, he made several study trips there.

At Catholic Charities, Dan Narr did community organizing and raised money in the corporate division of its development office. The only requirement he lacked for the Mano a Mano job was fluency in Spanish. The search committee was pleased by his strong fit with Mano a Mano's requirements. Drawn by Dan's appreciation of an egalitarian, collaborative style of management, fundraising experience, and his passion for the poor, the board decided that those qualities outweighed his lack of Spanish language skills. Mano a Mano hired him in 2006.

Dan Narr immediately created an egalitarian partnership with the staff. Becky Monnens left to work with a local foundation during the following year. Nate Knatterud-Hubinger, who had started out as part-time operations assistant, moved into full time, gradually taking on a greater role in nearly all the work of the office—the coordination of volunteers, the oversight of medical supplies, communications within the United States and Bolivia, and the organization of trips to Bolivia.

Fluent in Spanish, Nate came to Mano a Mano from development work in Chile and Ecuador and from his international studies at the University of Minnesota. His time in South America had left him vividly aware of the shortcomings of the typical Western model of development that dominated U.S. work internationally. Joan had come to see Nate as the embodiment of the principles that drove the Mano a Mano model (see Appendix A).

Nate Knatterud-Hubinger and Dan Narr soon learned that they shared a preference for collaboration and casualness and a commitment to international development, and that their experiences complemented each other's.

After getting to know Dan, Nate told him he was convinced that Mano a Mano was the closest they would ever find to an international organization in which "the community [rather than the funder] was the driver." Dan saw that Nate's casual and quiet style belied the strong commitment and intellectual clarity he brought to his efforts.

Nate saw and understood the work of Mano a Mano through the lens of Nobel laureate Amartya Sen's approach to development. Sen emphasizes that a certain level of physical and social resources is necessary for the realization of meaningful individual freedoms: "The organizing principle [of development] that places all the different bits and pieces into an integrated whole is the overarching concern with the process of enhancing individual freedoms and the social commitment to bring that about."[1]

Nate recognized that Mano a Mano's commitment to respectful partnerships with Bolivian villagers did, in fact, enhance the health and economic stability of their lives and consequently expanded their freedoms as individuals. Dan shared Nate's appreciation of being part of an organization solidly dedicated to Sen's "social commitment." In addition, both men valued the "homespun," relaxed style of the Mano a Mano organization.

With Dan Narr on staff, the space in the Mendota Heights house became even more limited. That year Joan and Segundo partially moved to a condo in St. Paul. This move provided the level of physical accessibility that Joan's postpolio syndrome required and some psychological space from the demands of the organization for the couple. They continued to use some of the living space in Mendota Heights, but Joan soon did much of her grant writing and evaluation work from an office in their condo.

The staff appreciated the clearer boundaries, as did Joan and Segundo. The two agreed to allow Mano a Mano to "live" in their house for two years—until it could raise funds to purchase a building of its own.

The Definition of Need Expands

When Dan Narr joined the organization in 2006, he learned that the level and complexity of Mano a Mano's outreach had grown proportionately with its increased funding. The organization had distributed nearly 2,000,000 pounds of supplies in Bolivia. It had built 72 clinics. It had completed 22 school projects, and 21 teachers' housing units were in place. Its first water reservoir and road projects had been completed too.

Yet the requests in Bolivia mounted. Government officials and local peasants alike had come to trust the efficiency, respectful collaboration, and integrity that Mano a Mano brought to all its partnerships.

In Bolivia, José Velásquez burnished the image of Mano a Mano as he managed the collaborative clinic and supply projects while responding to the requests for more new clinics, schools, and teacher housing. Ivo was drawn geographically and personally into connections with villagers deeper and deeper into the mountains surrounding Cochabamba. Working with his brothers on his frequent trips in and out of Cochabamba, Segundo was constantly struck by how well things were being done but also, with growing concern, by how much more there was to do.

One of a group of U.S. guests on a trip to Bolivia commented on how much she liked approaching one beautiful mountain after the other, their appearance never seeming to end.

172

Segundo replied, "I used to feel that way about the mountains too. But now I just think of how they don't end and how much the people on each mountain need. It is always there."

In 2005, 59 pushpins on the bulletin board in the Mendota Heights Mano a Mano office represented functioning health clinics in Bolivia. Each clinic had begun operations with an inauguración y entrega. Each village had put on a great fiesta of food, music, and dancing. Often the villagers presented government officials, Mano a Mano staff, and visitors with flower- or balloon-covered wreaths to put around their necks or wear as crowns. All listened to the often long and always heartfelt speeches.

All the parties involved had formally accepted their various responsibilities for the future of the projects. The juntas vecinales or sindicato leaders and the municipios accepted responsibility for operating and maintaining the clinics. The officials of the ministry of health formalized their commitment to pay doctor and nurse salaries. Mano a Mano acknowledged its commitment to provide the clinic with medical supplies and continuing education for staff. A deep sense of accomplishment pervaded Mano a Mano in Bolivia and in the United States.

Segundo came to Bolivia frequently and rarely alone. Sometimes he brought a group from an organization like the Rotary or a church. On other occasions he came with potential donors or foundation representatives, Mano a Mano volunteers, or a Mano a Mano USA board member. He combined engaging with these visitors, hanging out with his big extended family, and working with his siblings on the continuing Mano a Mano effort. It was all of a piece to him.

Segundo got excited every time he told visitors about the clinics' success in saving the lives of mothers and newborns and about the numbers of villagers who worked so many hours to build their own clinics. Despite these accomplishments, he returned to Bolivia from the United States always reminded of the impoverishment of so many of the Bolivian people, especially his fellow Quechua.

Beyond Clinics

Every time he drove into the mountains, Segundo saw mothers and children sitting dangerously close to the highway selling meager piles of vegetables or sweets. He worried that they might be hurt, and he constructed in his head a government program that would build them safe market spots off the highway. He estimated the cost of putting such markets along the highway. He shook off the idea that he could protect the women on the edge of the road as unrealistic and drove on. But he could not avoid the constant stream of people with burden clothes on their backs walking on the side of the highway. They held their empty hands out to the passing cars without losing a step.

When Blanca went along to a village meeting or a project inauguración she took plastic bags of fresh bread and fruit that she had bought in Cochabamba. She asked whichever brother was driving to slow down as she put a bag in each hand held out to her win-

Every village meeting and celebration includes a shared meal.

The plaza in Cochabamba

dow, until there are no more bags to give away. As they drove on, they saw more empty hands. She understood the inadequacy of her generosity.

Blanca, like Segundo, refused to accept the deep poverty all around her. Whenever Segundo walked through the streets around the family apartment building, he saw peasants who had come down from those harsh mountains into Cochabamba. He encountered some of them begging, seemingly homeless and obviously hungry. If there was a child unattended, too little to be left alone, he invariably looked around for the caregiver.

Segundo knew that Quechua mountain people were inextricably tied to the work in their fields. And here they were, in the midst of a strange and big city, with no work. Years of drought, more families on the same or even shrinking areas of land with inadequate water for irrigation made it more and more difficult to feed a mountain house-

Beyond Clinics

hold. A death in the family or a new disability added to the difficulties mounting from broader changes.

For varying reasons, families were pulled one by one to the cities to look for a solution to dwindling incomes. Some tried sending young family members into Punata, Cochabamba, or even to Spain to augment their income. But too often the situation became desperate, and the entire family moved to the city.

When Segundo saw his Quechua *compatriotas* (countrymen or women) begging on the streets near his family's apartment, he gave the coin in his pocket or the fruit he carried from the market to whoever asked. But he knew the fruitlessness of such charity. He asked himself whether Mano a Mano was doing the right things when there were so many people barely surviving. He puzzled about the harsh life of the Quechua families in the mountains and about the urban poor who had lost their connection to the land and sometimes to their families.

Segundo shuddered every time he saw young Quechua men walking the streets in a drugged state or mothers sitting on the sidewalk with a young child's hand outstretched to beg. He found some comfort in Mano a Mano's improving the health of many of his people through the clinics. But he pondered what else Mano a Mano could be doing in the severely underdeveloped country.

Sister Organizations

In response to the family's visceral reaction to the unending needs of their compatriotas, the Velásquezes found themselves growing their organization in ways that no one had anticipated. In 2005 two new organizations emerged to augment the work of Mano a Mano. Mano a Mano Bolivia had started in 1999, coupling José's unique medical gifts and community commitment with the support and generosity of his family. And so it was in 2005 (see Appendix B).

Mano a Mano Apoyo Aéreo (Air Support) emerged from Segundo's aviation expertise and his concern about safe and efficient travel to remote regions. At the same time, Ivo's knowledge of road construction made it possible for Mano a Mano to create Mano a Mano Nuevo Mundo (New World).

All three brothers and several other Velásquezes worked together to expand the presence of Mano a Mano in Bolivia. Ivo became the executive director of Nuevo Mundo and Eugenio Arvidsson, a Swedish pilot who had flown for Misión Sueca Libre, a Lutheran mission in Bolivia, for years, took on the leadership of Apoyo Aéreo. The two organizations evolved simultaneously but through different channels before both emerged in 2005.

Apoyo Aéreo provides emergency transport for patients and income for Mano a Mano.

9

Apoyo Aéreo

2001–2010

Beginning in the early 2000s, Mano a Mano evolved in two new directions, one toward the sky and the other on the ground and in the water. While José necessarily concentrated on the particulars of the increasing scale of Mano a Mano Bolivia, his brothers' aspirations for Mano a Mano broadened.

Ivo was approached by many rural leaders who saw a deep need for road construction. Segundo saw air transport as imperative for Mano a Mano to serve more distant communities. From these two visions, two entities evolved, simultaneously but along different paths to organizational reality (see Appendix B).

Segundo, often thinking of air as a better route to distant places than Bolivian roads, saw an opportunity to solve two problems with one solution: "If Mano a Mano had access to air transportation, we could save time and money when our staff made trips between our base in Cochabamba and distant clinic construction projects. And we could respond to patient emergencies that our clinics couldn't manage."

The brothers decided it was time to take a serious look at putting their organization into the air, and the Mano a Mano process kicked in. As always, starting with the recognition of a need they hoped they could address, Segundo and Joan began to search for funding.

Segundo contacted Dick Wagner, the NWA pilot whose contributions and consultation, continuing from the 1990s, were invaluable to Mano a Mano. Wagner and his wife, Bobbie, had been active in identifying and delivering medical supplies from Milwaukee. They also made financial contributions to Mano a Mano.

Segundo gave Wagner two rationales for Mano a Mano paying Misión Sueca Libre (the Swedish Free Mission) to periodically rent flight hours on its six-passenger Cessna. The air transportation would address both the cost of overland transportation of Mano a Mano staff to faraway construction sites and the need to respond to patient emergencies. Segundo wasn't surprised when Dick Wagner said he was already concerned about the cost for staff transportation. But Segundo didn't expect to find him knowledgeable about the isolated communities due to an earlier philanthropic mission of his own.

Dick Wagner liked the idea of Mano a Mano flight and asked Joan to write a proposal to his family's foundation for flight hours. She requested $10,000, and the Wagner Foundation allocated $13,800. José began planning response-by-air to short-wave-radio requests from distant communities. Segundo and Dick were pleased that they had increased Mano a Mano's productivity and efficiency by freeing staff members from driving back and forth to distant villages.

Once air transportation was available, Mano a Mano Bolivia began to expand its use beyond transporting staff to distant clinic communities. The tribal groups in the tropical Beni—the *departamento* (department, similar to a state in the United States) immediately north but at a much lower elevation than the mountainous Cochabamba—wanted and needed healthcare but were isolated from one another as well as from the outside world by the Amazon Basin and its many rivers and streams. Much of the Beni was accessible only by air. José Velásquez was well aware of the isolation and lack of healthcare—high infant and maternal mortality, unvaccinated children, untreated chronic illness, and appalling dental health. He thought about what Mano a Mano could bring to these indigenous communities with its access to an airplane.

The task of organizing a response to the Beni fell to physician Victor Ortuño, who fully supported Mano a Mano's commitment to partnership. He developed and coordinated what became a fine-tuned jornada partnership that continues to this day. *Jornada* was a play on the two different meanings of the Spanish word—a journey or a day (or two) of hard work. A group of doctors, nurses, and dentists took an airplane journey to the Beni for two days of hard work to care for isolated villagers in a jungle tent hospital.

Mano a Mano's shortwave radio became the communication center. Its medical supplies were also central to the project.

Search and Rescue (SAR, a Bolivian NGO) met arriving emergency patients at the Cochabamba airport and got them to a hospital. The Sisters of Charity, a Catholic religious order, organized the logistics of both the jornadas and the growing emergency transportation in Beni. The nuns watched over patients and whatever family members the plane could hold when they came to Cochabamba. The nuns then arranged for the return home of the patients and their families. Dr. Ortuño worked closely with Nemecio Saavedra, an active Lutheran lay leader who became the main contact for weekend clinics in the Beni.

When Saavedra got a community request for a jornada, he worked with Dr. Ortuño and the Sisters of Charity. They matched the community's needs with the health professionals appropriate for the particular requesting community.

Dr. Ortuño initially wondered how the people who streamed out of the jungle to a jornada would know the tent hospital was there: they may well have no modern form of communication. Nemecio Saavedra knew this countryside well; all the potential patients were indigenous people who often did not speak Spanish. He told Ortuño, "You can't

Apoyo Aéreo

put up a sign announcing a jornada. Most of these folks living in the jungle can't read; many speak no Spanish and don't go far from their settlements. That's where my network kicks in."

Nemecio Saavedra's network was based on his longtime family connections and his shortwave-radio system. When a sindicato leader saw that a jornada was needed in his community, he knew how (or he knew someone who knew how) to reach Nemecio by shortwave radio. Nemecio had built relationships across the Beni by delivering again and again on what he promised.

And Nemecio understood what it meant to the patients to go to Cochabamba on an airplane. They were leaving everything they had ever known and going with people they had never seen before and had no reason to trust. The same was true for the villagers who came to a jornada for the first time. Many believed, with some reason, that city people came into their communities claiming to help but were really there to take their land, their children, and perhaps even their internal organs. They knew this was not the case for Mano a Mano.

"If I die, will you bring me back?" asked Jorge Lazano, a very sick man, as he was carried to a small plane sitting in a clearing beside Rio (River) Beni. The tall Saavedra leaned close to Jorge's ear and whispered, "We will not only get you back home. You will come back alive." In his mind Saavedra added, *Si Dios quiere* [God willing]."

Nemecio Saavedra was and is a religious man, hopeful but realistic in the face of the precarious well-being of the Benianos. The residents of traditional communities in isolated areas like the tropical lowlands of the Beni are especially vulnerable to injury or death from falling out of trees or from trees falling on them.[1]

Injuries from a huge tree that fell on one Beniano—Jorge Suárez—as he was logging in the jungle, brought him to a jornada where villagers were being treated in a tent hospital. Nearly a week after his accident, he still had trouble breathing and he could not walk at all. Having heard that doctors were coming from Cochabamba, his family carried him out of the jungle to the clearing beside the river.

The physicians examined Jorge Suárez and concluded that he needed more help than they could provide during the jornada. They couldn't do major surgery in their rudimentary hospital, so they decided to send him to Cochabamba. Jorge was able to travel in the airplane that Mano a Mano was able to use with the donation from the Wagner Foundation.

The success of the jornadas depended on the ability of Mano a Mano to develop its new air service. The Sisters of Charity were a strategic choice. The order of nuns cared for indigenous Beni children through schools, an orphanage, and community work in the Beni lowlands. Mano a Mano not only supported the sisters in their work with emergency patients but also transported food and clothing for their other projects in the Beni—free of charge. This informal exchange resulted in better care for the children and the enthusiastic support of the nuns when patients arrived in Cochabamba with a medical emergency.

A similar exchange evolved with Nemecio Saavedra, who volunteered and still volunteers to coordinate jornadas in Beni and go on many of the two-dozen jornadas scheduled each year. As a businessman, Nemecio moves back and forth between the Beni and Cochabamba for his work and his volunteering. When there is room on a plane, he has free access to travel with the jornada volunteers. The informal culture of reciprocity and generosity so natural to the Velásquezes consistently moves them and Mano a Mano to share their resources.

A Growing Reputation

With the Wagner Foundation funding, Mano a Mano became a frequent presence in the air between Cochabamba and the Beni. Word got out that Mano a Mano flights were going in and out of Cochabamba on a regular basis. More and more requests came into the office to fly emergency patients. The availability of a rented plane opened up other ways for Mano a Mano to serve as well. Flight hours were a

Apoyo Aéreo

boon to Dr. Ortuño's work. He could fly into previously inaccessible tropical and mountainous communities to train health promoters and supervise clinic staff. Sometimes he set up a tent hospital near the site of a proposed clinic. This helped some villagers see the importance of having such professionals there permanently.

Dick Wagner received Joan's reports of the expanded use of flight hours and, with Segundo's urging, increased the funding for Mano a Mano's rental hours for two years more. As usage of the flight hours expanded, Dick told Segundo it might be time for Mano a Mano to buy a plane: "Let me know if you hear of a good one coming up for sale in Bolivia."

When Segundo learned that the single-engine Cessna owned by the Lutheran Misión Sueca Libre was going up for sale, he called Dick Wagner. Thus began a conversation in Bolivia and the United States about the feasibility and desirability of Mano a Mano buying a plane.

There was quick agreement among the United States and Bolivian decision-making groups that having an accessible airplane would allow Mano a Mano to respond more quickly and efficiently to a range of needs. Segundo and Dick, the aviation experts, determined that the price and capabilities of the Lutheran mission plane met their standards.

The increase in flights for staff travel to clinic construction and weekend clinics and for emergency patient transfer was well documented. Responding to Dick Wagner's concerns, Segundo estimated how much a totally available plane would be used. The Wagner Foundation had funded a small airplane for a mission program in Bolivia, and Dick was familiar with other South American mission programs.

Dick Wagner was appalled that several planes and pilots had been funded by others but few flights were made—and those for dubious purpose. He knew of planes used only to pilot missionaries to what he called "home visits," which occurred rarely, and he wanted to fund a Mano a Mano plane only if it could be justified by a high demand for air transport. He also wanted it to be done efficiently.

Dick Wagner pushed Joan and Segundo to think carefully about the need for an airplane and added a new wrinkle to the conversation. He wanted them to begin thinking of the airplane as a profit center, as a way to generate income for an aviation program serving the rest of the Mano a Mano enterprise.

As Dick considered a major contribution to Mano a Mano, he became intrigued with its organizational structure—at the time, there was only one paid staff member. As usual, he was full of questions: "How do you run this place with you and Joan doing so much of the work? How does money raised in the United States get transferred to Bolivia? How do you guys in the United States make decisions about what happens in Bolivia?"

Segundo took one question at a time: "The U.S. board of Mano a Mano knows we are stretched and has just authorized a search for an executive director." Then Segundo described the efficient money-transfer system they had created years previously, taking into account the idiosyncrasies of both Bolivian and U.S. banking practice.

Speaking about decision making between Mano a Mano Bolivia and the U.S. board of directors, Segundo described the creation of the U.S. board in 1994 and that of the Bolivian asamblea in 1999. He reminded Dick that he, Segundo, was part of both entities and had veto power in Bolivia over funds raised in the United States..

Dick Wagner asked those questions because he was thinking beyond the purchase of one plane. He was starting to identify the conditions he saw as essential to a successful aviation program funded in the United States but implemented in Bolivia. He was satisfied that Mano a Mano had successfully addressed the staff and money-transfer issues.

But he had other concerns: "Segundo, it's great that you have a doctor running the medical program. You need an aviation expert to manage this one. And to protect the assets of the organization, it must be owned by a separate entity."

After Dick Wagner's comment about the leadership of the poten-

Apoyo Aéreo

tial aviation program, Segundo thought about the importance of having José on the ground as the director of Mano a Mano Bolivia. He had the expertise to work out the details of the medical-supply program, and he drove the successful model for community and governmental participation in clinic construction and administration. From the start, Segundo had depended on Ivo to manage the construction process. And Blanca was central to the decision-making when Mano a Mano faced the legal issues that emerged with every new program.

Whenever Mano a Mano had come to a crucial development decision, the Velásquezes seemed to have someone in the family with the level of professional expertise to pull off an ambitious effort. Given Segundo's lifelong career in aviation, he, working with the expert staff in Bolivia, could help make the Mano a Mano aviation program a reality.

Segundo told Dick Wagner he could be involved in the organization through frequent communication. And he would help create a board of directors, which in turn would identify and hire an executive director living in Bolivia. The board chose Eugenio Arvidsson for that position. Dick was pleased that Segundo and Eugenio, whose expertise and leadership he trusted, agreed to take the lead.

Dick Wagner had set three conditions for making the gift of the airplane: the venture must be overseen by someone with significant aviation experience, it must manage the use of flight hours in a way that could generate income for its own sustainability, and it must be a separate legal entity. He then said, "Segundo, I think you should have a lunch with Misión Sueca Libre about buying its six-passenger Cessna. Make them an offer."

A Gift with Conditions and Consequences

Misión Sueca Libre accepted Mano a Mano's offer for the airplane. The gift to Mano a Mano from the Wagner Foundation included the plane, a hangar adjacent to the Cochabamba airport, some spare parts, an experienced technician, and the involvement of two volunteer pilots.

Dick and his wife, Bobbie Wagner, had a personal interest in the aviation program and came to Bolivia to see it. During their visit, Segundo talked with Bobbie in the hangar office while Dick was checking out the new airplane. Coming into the office, Dick saw Bobbie and Segundo deep in conversation.

Laughing, Dick said, "Okay, you two, what are you talking about?" He knew them well enough to know they were dreaming up some improvement to the program.

Segundo responded, "Dick, all the major decisions have been made. All you have to decide is the number of zeroes after the dollar sign."

Dick and Bobbie Wagner returned to Wisconsin to find Joan's work plan and itemized budget in their mailbox. Soon the foundation made a contribution to create what Bobbie called a "decent" lobby for the new organization. After all, Mano a Mano Apoyo Aéreo was supposed to become a moneymaking enterprise. It had to make a good first impression when someone walked in the door. The aviation program started off with a small but professional-looking office of its own.

Segundo, who had been talking with his brother José about broadening Mano a Mano's involvement in air transportation for at least a couple of years, was eager to tell him about the plane and the hangar that came with it. José had agreed that this would be a logical extension of the flights for staff travel and the emergency and jornada trips operating with the Mano a Mano Bolivia shortwave radio. He listened carefully when Segundo mentioned the three conditions of the gift.

To Segundo's surprise, José was bothered about the new aviation project being a separate legal entity. When José realized that the aviation project would not be under Mano a Mano Bolivia, he told Segundo, "We spend the money very carefully, and we get excellent results. Why wouldn't the airplane be under us? What more do you expect from us?"

What made sense to Segundo, Joan, the Mano a Mano USA board, and Dick Wagner was seen by José as an implied criticism of the work

Apoyo Aéreo

done by the Bolivian side of Mano a Mano. Segundo assured José that there was nothing but praise from the United States regarding the frugality, efficiency, and accomplishments of Mano a Mano Bolivia.

Segundo said, "The Wagner Foundation's condition of creating a new entity was an organizational one, not an evaluative one." He told José that the only expectation for everyone concerned was that Mano a Mano Bolivia continue to flourish with its clinic, medical-supply, and education-infrastructure programs.

Segundo came to understand that this notion of a separate entity struck José, and probably Mano a Mano Bolivia's asamblea, as an invasion of Bolivian responsibility and control. It was not the movement to a profit center or the requirement for aviation experience of the leaders that bothered José most. It was the formal organizational separation from Mano a Mano Bolivia—required by Americans—that triggered resentment of historic and continuing "colonial" intrusion.

José had never expressed dissatisfaction that the majority of Mano a Mano Bolivia's funds came from U.S. contributions. But this aviation proposal was different. He thought the quality of his work and his position as director and president of the asamblea was being questioned: this new entity was being proposed by his bicultural brother, Segundo, who seemed too American when, on occasion, he became impatient with Bolivian pace and style.

To Segundo, the aviation project was an exciting opportunity to further Mano a Mano's values and goals. He saw it as another way for Bolivians to serve Bolivians—a mantra of the organization. José saw the situation differently but agreed to come to the United States to work with Joan and Segundo to find a mutually satisfying resolution of their disagreement.

Everyone compromised: José agreed that there would be two separate legal entities, and Joan and Segundo recommended that every Mano a Mano Bolivia asamblea member have a seat on the aviation board. José left for Bolivia with a plan that they all could live with, prepared to present it to the asamblea. But Joan called Bolivia a few weeks later to ask José about the status of the plan only to learn that he had decided not to present it to the asamblea at all.

Despite José's lack of support, the U.S. board of Mano a Mano, including Joan and Segundo, enlisted Blanca to proceed with creating the new aviation organization. Through 2005, she and Segundo worked to address the legalities of the aviation program, planning to name it Mano a Mano Apoyo Aéreo. The inclusion of the words *apoyo aéreo* clearly indicated that the purpose of the organization was air support for the work of Mano a Mano.

Mano a Mano Bolivia staff members used the Mano a Mano Cessna when the distance to a destination exceeded four driving hours. Mano a Mano Bolivia continued to coordinate jornada activities. The goal to move to self-sufficiency through income generation was clarified by a plan to apportion use of the plane so that, eventually, half its flight hours would be dedicated to paid use by other paying NGOs, businesses, and private individuals. During the year awaiting Bolivian bureaucratic approval, Mano a Mano Bolivia ran the aviation program.

Near the end of 2005, the legal issues had mainly been addressed. Blanca needed only the names of board members to complete the creation of Mano a Mano Apoyo Aéreo. Blanca and Segundo asked José for the names of Mano a Mano Bolivia representatives to be listed on the new roster. Because he objected to the creation of a totally separate entity, José decided not to participate on the Apoyo Aéreo board at that time. The legal incorporation of Mano a Mano Apoyo Aéreo was delayed.

Segundo saw the impasse as a cross-cultural situation, that is, that he and his brother were operating from the perspectives of two different cultures. More hierarchical and traditional, José saw the aviation activity as a *patrimonio* (asset of a business or estate) that belonged to Mano a Mano Bolivia and could not be separated from it. Segundo saw himself as less personally invested—continuing the aviation program under Mano a Mano Bolivia for another year was a business decision. For him it was a short-term necessity to work out of that organization during the transition year to incorporation.

At the end of the year, Mano a Mano Apoyo Aéreo still lacked José's support for separate organization. But Mano a Mano USA could not accept the Wagner Foundation funding without separately legalizing the new entity. And Segundo wanted a clear resolution of their difference.

Fortunately, all of the Velásquezes, including José and Segundo, knew that improving the lives of their impoverished Bolivian brothers and sisters was more important than how they incorporated the organization. Blanca agreed, in lieu of her brother José, to become a member of the new aviation board. Because she and Segundo were both members of the Mano a Mano Bolivia asamblea, they could ensure that its needs and programs were well represented.

Finally, a full year after receipt of the gift from the Wagner Foundation, Edwin Lopez, M.D., a Mano a Mano Bolivia board member trusted by all, accepted an invitation to join the Apoyo Aéreo board. With this quiet acknowledgment of the legitimacy of Apoyo Aéreo as a separate Mano a Mano program, the Velásquezes continued their commitment to Mano a Mano's broader work, regardless of who was in charge.

Air-driven Challenges

The addition of Apoyo Aéreo enabled Mano a Mano Bolivia to move staff, materials, and the occasional small animal more efficiently between mountain projects and Mano a Mano headquarters in Cochabamba. In the tropics of the Beni, the aviation program made it possible to further develop the jornadas and to respond to the increasing requests to bring emergency patients to Cochabamba for medical care.

Apoyo Aéreo also brought challenges new to most of the Velásquez-family. Government rules and regulations for the air were more stringent than the more familiar land-based requirements. The precision necessary to aviation required Mano a Mano to modify the negotiated approach to problems that was so comfortable to the organization. Political and bureaucratic realities also had to be addressed.

Mano a Mano Apoyo Aéreo had to learn the intricacies of dealing with the four different government entities involved in any Bolivian aviation activity: Dirección General de Aeronáutica Civil (DGAC) required that all aircraft inspections and maintenance activity be recorded to stringent specification. Administración de Aeropuertos y Servicios Auxiliares a la Navegación Aérea (AASANA) insisted that a detailed flight plan be filed each time an aircraft left the airport. Dirección General de Sustancias Controladas (DGSC) controlled the amount of fuel purchased so as to ensure that it not be diverted to illegal drug activity (aviation fuel is sometimes used to process coca into cocaine). And the Bolivian Air Force controlled drug traffic. The regulations were challenging for an aviation enterprise focused on quick response to life-threatening emergencies.

The government had designated the Cochabamba's Chapare region and areas of the Beni as part of the "red zone" in which most drug traffic occurred. Because of inaccessibility, the Beni people were frequently in need of emergency medical attention and emergency airlift. In fact, the Beni was the destination of 80 percent of Apoyo Aéreo emergency flights. The air force insisted on approving every flight to and within the Beni, regardless of circumstances.

One Friday afternoon a Sister of Charity called Apoyo Aéreo requesting a flight to the Beni to pick up a woman who had been in labor for four days: The patient would die if she didn't get to a hospital. The start of the weekend was a hard time to find an officer to approve an emergency rescue flight. The one with proper authority was off for the weekend. Blanca's son Ivo Daniel called late into the night, searching for the official who could allow Apoyo Aéreo to fly the pregnant patient to Cochabamba. The connection finally made and the schedule

Apoyo Aéreo

approved, Ivo Daniel took off for the Beni the next morning.

When the family brought the suffering pregnant woman to the edge of the jungle, she was lifted into the Cessna, which took off from a dirt airstrip that the community had cleared. The mother-to-be arrived at the Cochabamba hospital just in time for a successful Caesarean delivery. She flew home a week later with a healthy baby in her arms. She named him after the Apoyo Aéreo pilot who saved them both.

Mano a Mano Apoyo Aéreo had to adapt to rigid governmental requirements and limits. It also had to be vigilant in avoiding the Bolivian tendency to solve a problem by agreeing to what might seem trivial illegal activity. Moving things along with a *mordida* (bribe) is an unfortunate but common response to regulatory problems in many poor countries, including Bolivia.

When Mano a Mano first shipped medical supplies to Bolivia, the U.S. board, with the wholehearted support of the organization in Bolivia, made a firm decision regarding mordidas that never, under any circumstance, would Mano a Mano bribe a public official or circumvent government policy in doing its work. It did not anticipate that circumstances 15 years later might include the life-and-death emergencies with which Apoyo Aéreo regularly contended. Nevertheless, Mano a Mano holds to that decision, patiently working its way through bureaucratic roadblocks, refusing to practice mordidas or to allow that practice by others to keep it from doing its work.

The regulations of Dirección General de Sustancias Controladas constrain Apoyo Aéreo's purchase and use of diesel fuel. The fuel must be loaded directly into the aircraft or the tank at the Apoyo Aéreo hangar—not any other container. This limitation plus the monthly requirement for a report on the amount of fuel used and the hours flown enhances the value of aviation fuel, and the staff is more than occasionally asked to sell some of the gas stored in the Apoyo Aéreo tank.

Recently an aviation colleague offered to pay any amount of money for some of Apoyo Aéreo's fuel. This was a tempting offer given

Capt. Ivo Daniel Martínez, son of Blanca

the tight budget of the program. Happily, Ivo Daniel, like all Mano a Mano employees, was trained in the appropriate response to such illegal requests. He denied the offer and reported it to the Apoyo Aéreo board of directors.

Segundo's years in NWA's technical operations department prepared him well to oversee the growth of Apoyo Aéreo. In addition to working as an aviation mechanic himself for seven years, he had managed as many as 200 employees at a time. They were the ones responsible for an NWA plane being ready to fly safely in countries around the world.

Segundo understood the importance of keeping a solid inventory for every part in a Cessna 206 at hand. He accepted the reality that when new parts were required to keep the plane in the air, Apoyo Aéreo probably would not be able to purchase all of them in Bolivia. He

Apoyo Aéreo

didn't want Apoyo Aéreo to fail to save a stranded patient or to cancel a jornada because of the lack of a part. So he worked closely with Ivo Daniel to develop a system addressing the need for replacement parts.

First, Segundo and Ivo Daniel ensured the maintenance of an inventory of frequently needed items like starters, magnetos, hoses, and rivets of many types and sizes. The staff projected the need for these parts based on hours flown. It informed the Mano a Mano USA office when inventory lacked a part not available in Bolivia. The USA office purchased and transported small parts in the luggage of visitors heading to Bolivia and bigger parts in the medical-supply-shipment containers. Apoyo Aéreo carefully developed a Bolivian/American way to run an aviation program.

More Planes for Apoyo Aéreo

In 2007 Dick Wagner and Segundo Velásquez reviewed the extensive use of Mano a Mano Apoyo Aéreo's Cessna and recommended that a second aircraft be purchased—provided funding could be raised. When another longtime donor offered funding, Dick began to scour the country for a good deal on another Cessna 206. He located one for the right price in New Mexico.

Segundo traveled to inspect the aircraft and found it in excellent condition. It had a bigger engine, giving it more power for faster take-offs from the short dirt strips used in the Beni. Purchase of the aircraft doubled the Apoyo Aéreo fleet.

Going over the Apoyo Aéreo statistics in 2010, Joan, Segundo, Ivo Daniel, and Dick Wagner counted 1,416 patients transported for lifesaving medical treatment. They were pleased with this success but quickly moved on to their worries and wishes. Was it safe for their pilots to fly in highly variable weather conditions in a single-engine plane? Wouldn't it be great if they had enough room to accommodate the greater range and number of medical professionals they would like to be able to bring to jornadas? Wouldn't having a twin-engine aircraft draw in more revenue from private flights? In answering these questions, the four concluded that Apoyo Aéreo needed a bigger and faster plane. The U.S. board concurred.

Dick Wagner said, "I'll start looking for the right plane, one that meets the Mano a Mano demands."

The group agreed that a twin-engine plane would best address most of the concerns that the pilots, Dick, and Segundo had identified. After reviewing many options, they decided Dick would search for a twin-engine Piper Navajo Chieftain. Using his extensive network, he soon found in California just what they wanted, for a good price.

Segundo had been talking to the Lored Foundation in St. Paul about Mano a Mano Apoyo Aéreo and the benefits of adding another plane to its fleet. Along with Dan, Joan, and Ivo, who was visiting from Bolivia, Segundo made a presentation to the foundation board about what a new plane could mean to the people of Bolivia. Lored committed to financing part of the cost of a plane, and the Mano a Mano delegation went home elated.

Just as he arrived home, Segundo got a call from the Lored people: "We believe in your cause. We have decided to donate the full amount you need to buy the plane. So you can go ahead and purchase it now." With the money in the bank, Segundo traveled to California to check out the Piper Navajo and returned pleased with its condition and performance.

In the midst of all this activity, Dick Wagner stepped forward to announce: "I'm not giving my plane much use, and there is so much need in Bolivia. I'm going to donate my twin-engine Comanche to Mano a Mano."

When Joan checked out this offer out with Bobbie Wagner, Bobbie said she was surprised that Dick was willing to part with his beloved plane. But they all knew Dick well enough not to argue, and Mano a Mano accepted the offer of a fourth aircraft for its aviation program. Segundo and Dick Wagner discussed the details of getting both planes

Capt. Ivo Daniel Martínez, Cristian López, and chief technician Jóse Luis

to Cochabamba. Dick personally prepared his Comanche for the long ferry flight. When two Apoyo Aéreo pilots arrived in Milwaukee during Thanksgiving weekend, the airplane was ready for the trip to Cochabamba. Dick checked out each of the pilots to make sure they fully understood the operation of the aircraft.

Then, Dick and Bobbie Wagner opened their home to the two young men for the holiday weekend. Dick took them to visit area aviation museums and talked them through the intricacies of the 44-hour flight from Milwaukee to Cochabamba. He sent them on their way confident that his plane was in good hands.

Three weeks later two Apoyo Aéreo pilots traveled to California to pick up the Piper Navajo for its 34-hour ferry flight. Dick was glued to his computer in Milwaukee, following the flight of the Navajo. He imagined the new planes at home in the squeaky clean hangar that Ivo Daniel managed so well.

That evening Bobbie Wagner called Segundo, who had also been tracking the first leg of the flight to Cochabamba. She told him that Dick had died of a heart attack. Stunned to have lost his good friend and benefactor, Segundo flew to Milwaukee for the funeral. The Piper Navajo landed in Bolivia just as Dick's funeral service began.

Several months later Mano a Mano USA held its 17th annual volunteer picnic. More than 80 volunteers sat on folding chairs on the grass in the backyard of the Mendota Heights office and previous home of Joan and Segundo. It was late summer and the grass and leaves on the trees were a vivid green. At such picnics, the volunteers heard about the latest projects in Bolivia, and they wondered what they would learn from Segundo this time. Joan sat at one of the last tables and watched as Segundo talked about the expansion of Mano a Mano's air-transport work with its two new airplanes.

Segundo began to talk more personally about Dick Wagner's death, ending with this sentence: "We can use Dick's airplane and [contributions] to increase Mano a Mano's capacity to serve the poor and the goal that Dick, Bobbie, and the Wagner Foundation have always worked for—to help people help themselves."

Ivo Velásquez, on his cell phone, working with the engineers on a construction site. Segundo is at right.

10

Nuevo Mundo

2004–2012

In 2004 Segundo was talking with his brother Ivo in Blanca's apartment. He said he was nearly overwhelmed by the immensity of need in Bolivia despite Mano a Mano's hard work and tangible success.

Ivo listened, then spoke of recognizing both realities—the impoverishment and the accomplishment: "I remember the poverty of the peasants I visited in the years I worked in the mountains with Unión Cristiana Evangélica. That's why I'm so grateful to do the work of Mano a Mano, with people just like those I visited long ago." He spoke further of his work with Mano a Mano as a way to fulfill his religious responsibility.

The conversation turned to the road projects Ivo had completed for Mano a Mano Bolivia. He mentioned the backhoe and the bulldozer that had made it possible to turn pathways into roads that could carry the trucks loaded with materials for clinic and school construction.

Then, "Remember Dad telling us about how he knew how a road should be laid out when he looked at a mountain? I can see that too," Ivo said. "I think it may be time for Mano a Mano to build new roads from scratch." Then Ivo told Segundo a story about El Palmar.

Nuevo Mundo

A few weeks earlier, Ivo was sitting in his Mano a Mano Bolivia office when the receptionist mentioned that a request to build a road had come from the community of El Palmar. He recalled the community more than 200 miles away that he had encountered on his travels in the semitropical mountains for his church.

After reviewing the request, Ivo decided to vist the El Palmar region to determine whether Mano a Mano could take on the project. Getting to El Palmar and the site of the new road had presented a challenge. He flew in the Mano a Mano aircraft, landing on a natural grass strip on the outskirts of El Palmar. Twelve leaders, including the mayor who had sent in the request, met him there on horseback after traveling for two-and-a-half days by truck, then by horse from the alcalde's office.

One of the leaders dismounted, shook Ivo's hand, and immediately spoke: "Don Ivo, there are no roads in the entire El Palmar region, only paths for horses. Even a motorcycle, a bicycle, is of no use here. We feel like we are living in a corral. The only way we can get our crops to market is in the bellies of our hogs."

Ivo knew that if they had a road to get to the highway they would be able to transport the materials they needed to rehabilitate their school. They could also use the road to get their produce out. With the fertile land and abundant rain, they were growing more than they could eat. But they couldn't transport it to a market other than on their backs or atop a mule. Most of the excess food rotted in the fields or spoiled in their bags carried many miles.

The leader concluded, "We need a road."

"Mano a Mano mainly builds clinics and schools, not roads," Ivo responded. He acknowledged that Mano a Mano had improved roads in the process of building clinics, but that wasn't the same as the major construction this group was asking for.

The El Palmar compañeros repeated their needs and stood to leave.

Ivo shook hands all around and said, "I will talk with the Mano a Mano people in Cochabamba."

When the compañeros left on their horses, Ivo began to dwell on the possibilities . . . There must be a reason for there being nothing but a path. He had been to El Palmar, and he remembered the tortuous path. The terrain was steep and full of boulders and rocks. Perhaps Mano a Mano could widen the path?

The more Ivo puzzled over his memory of the terrain the more he believed he could complete such a road-building project. He would have to review the study made by the engineers in the municipio and walk the site before making a recommendation. He ended up telling Segundo and most of the family, "Mano a Mano must give these villagers a road. It will change their lives."

Later, Blanca heard her brothers talking about the request. As Ivo spoke, she imagined the frustration of successful farmers producing fruits and vegetables they could not get to market. She reminded her brothers of their mother putting a burden cloth on her back twice a week to sell lard at the markets in Punata and Cliza.

"Where would our family be if we had had no way at all to make money? If we had had no roads to the market, no way to deliver our tiles?" Ivo talked about all the communities in the mountains that were isolated, the people who needed a road to improve their lives, adding, "I think Mano a Mano has the right equipment to build the road for El Palmar. The municipio and community will pay for diesel fuel and other expenses. We should take on this project."

The next day Ivo went to José's office to tell his brother about the request from El Palmar. He talked about all the communities in the mountains that were isolated, about those needing a road to improve their lives. And he said, "I think Mano a Mano can build the road for El Palmar. The municipio and community will pay for diesel fuel and other expenses. We should take on this project."

José listened but was skeptical, reminding Ivo that they had hundreds of requests for more clinics and schools. "Do we want to be diverted?" He saw operating and maintaining heavy machinery as costly.

Nuevo Mundo

Building a new road through the mountains was much more complex and less predictable than constructing a brick building.

Consumed by the projects to which Mano a Mano Bolivia was already committed, José was being asked to consider another new venture. His organization was building 12 clinics every year and transferring the clinic model into building more and more schools and homes for teachers. When Ivo mentioned that many villages needed roads as an economic outlet for their produce, José accepted the centrality of the economic isolation of remote villages. He also considered Ivo's argument that communities with good roads could someday make enough money to pay for their own clinics.

Recognizing that Ivo had inherited their father's gift of being able to see a road in a mountain, José agreed reluctantly that Ivo should go ahead with the El Palmar project. He suggested they proceed only after going through the regular review process. Ivo accepted that condition, and the two brothers had an agreement. Ivo contacted the people of El Palmar and the municipio, telling them that Mano a Mano would consider building a road with them as active partners. He arranged to meet with them to discuss engineering design and funding.

Ivo's effort to get to El Palmar was a vivid demonstration of the community's isolation. He flew again to the region, this time to examine in detail a potential route for the road. The municipio engineer had drawn a design, but before signing a project agreement, Ivo wanted to inspect the route for himself. He had to be able to look at the mountain closely to see the road.

Ivo met the alcalde and several other villagers, knowing they would arrive on horseback with an extra horse for him. He followed them across shallow rivers and along a path no wider than the back of the horses that trod ahead of him in single file. He spent two full days riding along the proposed route with these companions.

After Ivo returned to Cochabamba, the municipio engineers completed their detailed study of the route, calculated the hours of work and type of machinery needed, developed a budget, and created a time-line. When their work was complete, Ivo met with the community leaders and the municipio officials to hammer out an agreement. Then he turned to developing the work plan for their first major road project.

Segundo kept the U.S. board and several of Mano a Mano's major funders informed of Mano a Mano's possible expansion into more complex road projects. Several funders had traveled to Bolivia to see the results of their grants. Many had visited rural villages and traveled on dangerous, nearly impassable roads. One remembered being stranded on a road that maintenance personnel were trying to fix without equipment or needed materials.

John Slettom, the anonymous donor's agent, had long recognized the importance of improving rural roads, and he had allowed Mano a Mano to include a minimal itemization for heavy equipment in its budget request. During his quarterly meeting with Segundo and Joan, John said he understood José's reluctance to take on a major road construction project. But he also saw great value in Mano a Mano moving into economic development projects. Mano a Mano should "go ahead and do it," whether through a contract with another group or by creating a new organization.

Segundo and Joan put El Palmar on the U.S. Mano a Mano board's agenda. All its members had traveled to Bolivia and were aware of the conditions of the roads they used in the mountains. Before the meeting Segundo, Joan, and Ivo developed a plan including a tentative budget for El Palmar. The board concluded that Mano a Mano would need significant U.S. financial support to take on this new direction.

Segundo reminded the board of Ivo's willingness to move out of clinic construction to road construction and of José's reluctance to take on bigger development projects. The board knew that when Joan or Segundo presented a potential project, they were coming with a need in Bolivia that they felt called for action. The board analyzed the fit between the need and the capacity of Mano a Mano to take on a new project. If the board concluded that the depth of need matched the potential capacity of Mano a Mano, the organization could move on to budget and fundraising.

The U.S. board had no difficulty in accepting the inherent value of assisting communities in acquiring needed roads. It had just approved the creation of the sister organization Apoyo Aéreo to manage the aviation program. During those discussions, Chris Ver Ploeg had recommended that the board create another sister organization.

As Chris pointed out, Mano a Mano was accumulating bigger and heavier equipment that had little to do with clinics and nothing to do with its medical-supply program. The machinery was kept in a lot near the Mano a Mano Bolivia office when it was not in use on distant projects. With Chris's previous suggestion in mind, the board began its typical deliberation, analyzing Bolivian need and Mano a Mano USA's capacity to respond.

In December 2004, the U.S. board created a Bolivian organization to implement community projects requiring the extensive use of heavy equipment. The board wanted Ivo to build the road to El Palmar, but it also wanted to establish an entity with the capacity to respond to other such requests. Segundo, as board president, enlisted Blanca to complete the Bolivian paperwork necessary to establishing a nonprofit organization. Ivo was named its executive director. Then the brothers enlisted a Bolivian board to oversee Mano a Mano Nuevo Mundo.

The new Mano a Mano entity needed administrative space, and the Velásquez pattern combining work and home life resurfaced. The family apartmento had an empty space on the first floor, where Epifanio, Inés, and Tia Juanita had lived for several years. They had recently moved to an upper floor providing a beautiful view of *Cristo* (a big statue of Jesus) in the distance. The unused space emerged as a no-cost solution to housing the Nuevo Mundo operation. Ivo and his crew were soon ensconced on the first floor of the Velásquez apartamento.

The U.S. board, in authorizing Mano a Mano to seek funding

for road projects, went around and around about the complexities of such an expansion. The directors remembered José's frustration upon Mano a Mano's Apoyo Aéreo expansion. His lack of interest and support remained bothersome. They saw tension around the shared use of road-improving equipment in clinic communities and the construction of the El Palmar road.

Segundo saw it differently. A strictly American situation was one thing: The CEO would say, "Okay, you don't want to do this? We are going to get rid of you and put in someone who can handle this task." The Bolivian approach was another: "Fine," a Bolivian CEO might say. "You are doing a good job with what you are doing, and we want you to continue just as you have. We will find someone who wants to take this on, someone with whom you can collaborate."

Segundo set aside his American proclivity for efficiency and outcome to draw on his Bolivian tendency to maintain relationship. He recalled Blanca's typical response when he called her from the United States to complain about how long it took Mano a Mano staff to respond to a request for a report or other information.

She said, "Yes, Segundo, you are right. That is the pace at which it would be done in Minnesota. But this is Bolivia. That's not how it is done here."

Segundo had learned from Blanca that he must continually balance his propensity for efficiency and results with the more relational and nuanced approach of his Bolivian siblings. Ivo resigned from his position as construction manager for Mano a Mano Bolivia to take responsibility for Mano a Mano Nuevo Mundo.

Water for All

As Ivo settled in as the director of the new organization, he knew villagers needed more than roads to improve their productivity. A year earlier, the village of Ucuchi had held an inauguración for its new school classrooms. During the formal signing of the project, men from the irrigation sindicato approached Ivo with a plea for help in enlarging and repairing the village's water reservoir. They took Ivo and other Mano a Mano staff members to a nearby field that held two side-by-side plots they had planted. The irrigated plot held a mass of bright red strawberries. The other was parched and without a plant in bloom.

Ivo remembered the leader's well-considered words: "Please, Señores, we have worked hard to build the school so our children can have hope for the future. But we are desperate to solve another problem. We have good land but not enough water to keep crops alive. Our young men go to Spain to work because they cannot make enough money here to sustain their families. Now Spain doesn't want Bolivians anymore, so the men are coming home.

"But how will they feed their children? Our water runs away and the plants produce little or die of thirst. We know that a bigger *represa* [water reservoir] would hold enough rainwater for all of our fields. Please help us. You know we have ganas and will work every day if you bring your machines and build with us. Then we can feed our children and sell the rest of our fruit and vegetables in the city."

Now that Mano a Mano was moving beyond clinic and school construction, Ivo suggested to Segundo that Mano a Mano honor Ucuchi's request. The Nuevo Mundo board recommended the project, and the U.S. board approved it. Joan and Segundo secured funding from the St. Paul-based Yackel Foundation, to complete the organization's first irrigation project.

A basic motivation for Mano a Mano's engagement in water projects was the Bolivian protectiveness of the country's water. The internationally famous "water war" of year 2000 had been fought in Cochabamba and won by a broad coalition of indigenous groups including rural *regantes* (irrigators) like the Ucuchi villagers who had showed their crops to Ivo.[1]

In the midst of weeks of unrest, some of the Cochabamba protesters had hung a huge handwritten sign on one of the tallest buildings in

Cochabamba: *"El agua es nuestro, carajo* [The water is ours, damn it]!" The protesters resorted to such language to direct attention to their previously ignored concerns.[2]

As a result of the long, steady protest, Cochabamba's water had returned to being a public resource, not one owned by a for-profit corporation. The water war was the popular response to a quietly signed government contract with the international corporation Bechtel to govern and manage drinking water in Cochabamba. The Bechtel contract had converted water from a communal resource to a product to be bought and sold.

The rural regantes who joined in the protest against privatization did not even live in Cochabamba, and they would not be drinking the contested water. But as rural Quechuas like the farmers of Ucuchi, they understood that for Bolivians to lose control of their water was to lose their way of life. They were determined to join their urban compatri-

Expanding the Ucuchi reservoir

otas to maintain public governance of the usos y costumbres of this precious resource. The water governance practices in the city were certainly different from those of the rural irrigators. But the principle of community rather than corporate control for profit was valued across the rural communities, the Cochabamba region, and eventually the entire country.

An activist irrigator explained the deep connection between the people and their water: "Usos y costumbres imply the communal form of life and communal work that campesinos exercise over their irrigation infrastructure and the water itself . . . also, usos y costumbres are intimately associated with what water means in the campesinos' communities, no?

"They say a lot about Pachamama, the water, and earth . . . It is a type of interdependence between water resources and human beings, no? It is a kind of divinity, a sacred meaning they give it."

A Reservoir for Laguna Sulti

The Velásquezes were hearing about the desperate need for accessible water on many fronts. A year after Ucuchi's project was complete, Joan received a late-night call from Bolivia. Segundo told her about an opportunity to transform the economic well-being of thousands of rural Bolivians.

This time it was not a request from a group of horsemen from the mountains. The appeal originated with Segundo's *Tio* (Uncle) Alberto Velásquez and a playmate from his old village in the Cochabamba Valley. Segundo had missed the 2006 inauguración of Laguna Sulti's Mano a Mano clinic, but he soon heard from staff that his tio wanted to talk to him.

The next time Segundo was in Bolivia, he drove one of the Mano a Mano SUVs parked under the Cochabamba apartment to the new clinic, which stood just to the side of the site once occupied by his family's Laguna Sulti house. Segundo remembered the chronic ear infections he and Blanca suffered as children there. He was grateful that the children of Laguna Sulti no longer needed to go far for medical attention. They could go to a Mano a Mano clinic with a big white sign, in a village no longer empty and decaying. The children of Laguna Sulti could avoid the chronic ear problems he and his sister had.

Staring up at the trees, then back to the earth, Segundo saw his Tio Alberto shambling from a house nearby. He was old and small, and a tiny black cat rubbed against his long pants. Wearing a rumpled hat, Tio Alberto reached out to shake his nephew's hand. He still lived in the dilapidated house of Segundo's paternal grandmother.

Alberto told Segundo he was glad Segundo had come because Primitivo Montaño, the sindicato leader of water in Laguna Sulti, wanted to speak with him. Alberto reminded Segundo that the leader lived just up the road, behind the house where Segundo's mamanchaj had lived for so many years with Tia Juanita.

Segundo said, "That must be my old playmate. We called him Primo then." Then he walked to the adobe house of his old friend and found him at home. After they caught up on the years since their shared childhood, the conversation took a turn.

Primitivo Montaño told Segundo that Laguna Sulti was even poorer than in the past. The drought of the previous year had made it nearly impossible to farm. The sindicato leader reminded Segundo about the hard work that the villagers had donated to build their new clinic with Mano a Mano. They had seen some big trucks then, had heard that Mano a Mano had even bigger ones and that sometimes it built roads.

The sindicato had met and decided to have Segundo's Uncle Alberto Velásquez talk with Mano a Mano about the local sistema de riego. Primitivo said the sindicato needed help with harnessing the water that came so abundantly for a few months a year: "We need to save the water so we have it year round."

Segundo listened, remembering the little channel that ran along side their house, the channel that he had helped Ivo and his father clear of silt. He had noticed that the channel was there still, but that it was almost empty of water. What had been field upon field of corn, potatoes, fava beans, wheat, and fruit when the two friends were boys was now an empty, desert-like expanse.

Primitivo Montaño reminded him of the machines everyone had seen near Cochabamba. He knew that Mano a Mano had used even bigger machines to make the Ucuchi reservoir bigger.

Segundo was surprised that Primitivo knew about Mano a Mano's first reservoir project and went in his mind to what a reservoir could do for his home village. Listening carefully, he nodded, then said he would talk to the Nuevo Mundo board and staff about the possibility.

When Segundo told someone he would go to the board with a project, he likely had made an initial decision to pursue the idea. He shook the hand of Primitivo Montaño and went to the SUV realizing the opportunity before him.

Water was a constant, growing problem for the Bolivians, especially for the campesinos. Segundo remembered how as a five-year-old he had gone with his father in the middle of the night to irrigate their fields. He had carried a candle lantern so his father could see to take advantage of the water running down the stream when most farmers were sleeping. Epifanio had jumped at the opportunity to make use of the water flowing past his fields. Segundo thought, "Yes, Mano a Mano can take on this project. We can build a reservoir in Laguna Sulti."

That evening Segundo was at his mother's table, full of stories of his time with Tio Alberto and Primitivo Montaño. Most of the family—Inés, Epifanio, Ivo, José, Blanca, and several of her children—was there. Inés sat longer than usual during dinner, letting Blanca do the serving for a while.

Intrigued by the stories of Laguna Sulti, Inés remembered when, as Segundo and Ivo's playmate, Primitivo was called Primo. She got the latest news about her brother-in-law Alberto and said, "It sounds like your tio brought an important request to Mano a Mano."

Segundo responded to his mother's comment with the details of his conversation with Primitivo. When he talked about the drying up of the channel near their by-that-time-torn-down adobe house, everyone had a story about its importance to their household for watering both their mother's small garden and their fields. They commiserated about the drastic change in the climate of Bolivia, about how drought was devastating the fields of people who depended almost exclusively on the food they grew to survive. They recalled tales of a wealthy landowner diverting the water from the mountains to their fields at the expense of farmers above and below them.

When Segundo told them about the request from the Laguna Sulti sindicato for help in solving its water problem, they listened carefully. Blanca, not usually the first to speak, reminded the family that these were their people: "They are us. Remember, we could be them. The family was moved by Blanca's passion. This request from Laguna Sulti was especially difficult to ignore: Blanca and Rubén had been born there. The discussion about whether Mano a Mano should work with the Laguna Sulti sindicato to build a reservoir was short. Everyone wanted to bring more Mano a Mano work to the home village. The conversation moved quickly to figuring out how to make it happen.

Van Miguel (Vanchi) Martínez, Blanca's son and a budding engineer, spoke at length with Epifanio, Ivo, and Segundo about technical issues, such as the lay of the land and the equipment necessary to take on such a task. Ivo listed on the back of a piece of paper that he pulled from his shirt pocket the machines they might need, the number of workers, and how much the project might cost financially.

Side conversations emerged. Vanchi and Ivo worried over the distance between the village and the placement of a reservoir.

When Segundo made his regular phone call to Joan from Bolivia, he told her about his trip to Laguna Sulti and his conversation with the family. Joan listened to Segundo's excited description of the day's meetings and took a deep breath. The challenging El Palmar road project and the much smaller Ucuchi reservoir expansion were moving forward on schedule, proving that Nuevo Mundo was up to such tasks.

Joan reminded Segundo that Mano a Mano was expanding with little staff support in the United States. She wondered how much more fundraising work she could handle. They talked more. Segundo described to Joan his conversations in Laguna Sulti, his tio's pride in the community's work to build a clinic, Primitivo Montaño's persuasive plea about the village's need for more water, and his own desire to give back to his family's home place by increasing its self-sufficiency.

"What could be better," he asked, "than starting with our friends and relatives in Laguna Sulti who have asked for this help? They have ganas. They have proven in their work on the clinic that they are willing and capable of providing significant manual labor. And I've talked with Vanchi and Ivo. They know Mano a Mano is capable of building this kind of reservoir with them. It will be the first of its kind in Bolivia—a system where water will flow uphill."

And Ivo had already begun to plan how to distribute water to fields above the reservoir by incorporating piping and a pumping system.

The Cochabamba/Mendota Heights conversation went on into the night, Segundo slowly convincing Joan that the U.S. board would resonate to the idea because it was consistent with the 18-month plan approved for Nuevo Mundo. He mentioned again Blanca's passionate support of the Laguna Sulti reservoir as well as the Nuevo Mundo board's confidence in Ivo's judgment. Segundo added, "Ivo says that he can see a reservoir at the edge of the plateau near Laguna Sulti."

Joan was convinced by Segundo's persuasive justification for building a reservoir with Laguna Sulti. She knew that the St. Paul Rotary was eager to receive a project proposal from Mano a Mano. The Mano a Mano USA board had approved a similar project in developing the 2005–2007 plan with Nuevo Mundo.

Segundo and Joan predicted, correctly as it turned out, that both the St. Paul Rotary and Rotary International would be interested in funding this project. Joan wrote other grants and soon the Wagner Foundation, the Lored Foundation, the International Foundation, and the ERM (for Environmental Resources Management) Foundation augmented the Rotary funding provided for the project.

With the approval of the Bolivian and U.S. Mano a Mano boards of the funding for a reservoir for Laguna Sulti secure, Mano a Mano established a formal agreement with the community: Ivo and the Laguna Sulti leaders and the municipio thought through the pipe and pump details together. Primitivo called a meeting of the community so that its people could learn about the proposed reservoir and decide whether they wanted to work with Mano a Mano Nuevo Mundo to build it.

Well more than a hundred people gathered around Ivo as he and Primitivo Montaño stood in an open space near the clinic. The two childhood friends described the physical details of the proposed agricultural water reservoir. A municipio leader added that the government was in support of the project and would partially fund it. Primitivo reminded the people that to get the water they longed for they would have to labor alongside the Mano a Mano workers. Several people had already signed up. Others called out their willingness to volunteer and approached Primitivo, asking him to put their names on the work schedule.

As Ivo was explaining the kinds of tasks they must complete to honor the community's commitment, he noticed an old woman struggling to reach the group with the help of a walker. He recognized her and called out, "Doña Martína, have you walked the mile from your house to be here?"

"Yes," she answered. "Look around you. See all the dust and scrub where we used to grow good food. You know, Don Ivo, that without water for our fields, we cannot live." More men and women came forward to get on the work schedule.

Primitivo then reminded the crowd of the support they had given for the Mano a Mano/Laguna Sulti clinic partnership and how important their clinic was to them: "Now you have to decide. You need to vote yes or no. Do you want to cooperate with Mano a Mano again? Do you want to help build a reservoir?"

The crowd called out a resounding, unanimous "Sí!"

Before heavy equipment rolled into the Cochabamba Valley, dozens of community members worked to prepare the huge space. Men and women from the 13 small Laguna Sulti communities removed rocks big and small to make way for the equipment. As the project continued, the men shoveled dirt and the women carried rocks in their white aprons. Others dug trenches or fed the workers. Soon the heavy-equipment staff created a huge levy of compacted earth surrounding a 150-acre basin to hold the river water. Within a few months, the shallow, nearly two-mile long reservoir was built. It looked like a big lake.

In January 2007 the project was done, and an inauguración took place. Many of the people who had voted for the project gathered again, around a bright blue tent. They listened attentively to the leaders from the community, the municipio, and Mano a Mano dedicating the reservoir. They applauded the long speeches and hung flowered wreaths around the leaders' necks. The celebratory food was abundant. A group of young men dressed in white performed a traditional, athletic dance.

Representatives of Laguna Sulti, Mano a Mano, and the municipio cut a ribbon at the reservoir port, revealed a small monumental plaque, and embarked on the new water in a small boat flying the Bolivian flag. The ribbon and plaque covering were also red, yellow, and green. Children took turns climbing into three blue-and-yellow plastic paddleboats tied at the edge of the reservoir. Delighted with their new lake, they glided across the water, the distant mountains behind them.

Soon their parents spoke proudly of the reservoir lake, its 150 acres holding 1,500,000 cubic meters of water available to 600 farmers across the 1,300 acres of the valley.

Upon completion of the Laguna Sulti reservoir in 2007, Mano a Mano U.S. had three parallel, well-functioning sister organizations:

Mano a Mano Bolivia emphasizing the construction of clinics and schools, Nuevo Mundo using heavy equipment to build roads and water projects, and Apoyo Aéreo concentrating on air transport to support Mano a Mano programs. Some member of the Velásquez family led all but the air transport program, in which Ivo Daniel was increasingly involved. All of the Mano a Mano "hands" shared the organizational principles of sustainable, community-based development in the context of a Bolivian/U.S. partnership (see Appendixes A and B).

Mano a Mano incrementally built a bicultural organizational family. When American visitors came to Bolivia, they sometimes wondered why both Mano a Mano Bolivia and Nuevo Mundo owned heavy machinery. Bolivians did not question that the machinery at Mano a Mano Bolivia was there (because it always had been there) and that it was useful to the sister organization (that always had managed it).

An American solution with an eye to efficiency and order might have seen the duplication of heavy equipment as potentially inefficient and moved it all to Mano a Mano Nuevo Mundo. But leaving some of the machinery where it was, readily available for clinic and school construction, kept the two organizations in healthy collaboration. This is just one of many ways the sister organizations share resources and accommodate one another.

When Ivo began to direct Nuevo Mundo, Mano a Mano Bolivia found that its clinic construction continued effectively, with the architect taking on Ivo's role as construction manager. Apoyo Aéreo worked closely with the other entities—flying patients, workers, and machine parts—as it continued its emergency rescue and jornada work. Blanca completed the complex Bolivian legal work needed to create the new sister organizations. And whenever Segundo came to Cochabamba, he joined the family around his parents' table. The needs of rural Bolivians and the workings of Mano a Mano were still a frequent topic of conversation.

V

Water Is Life

Ivo and Blanca (second and third from left front), meeting with the alcadesa to discuss a reservoir project at Jusk'u Molle

11

Atajados for Omereque

2005–2010

The Mano a Mano/Omereque collaboration began with one person, Héctor Arce, who had no connection with Mano a Mano when he was pulled into the development of his isolated municipio, Omereque.

Héctor was an agronomist, someone who knew a lot about plants and soil and how best to take care of them. He was Quechua, and he lived and worked in Cochabamba with his wife and family. He grew up in the countryside of the Omereque municipio in the southernmost part of the Cochabamba Departamento.

Héctor's family's farm sat in a narrow valley more than 8,500 feet above sea level, surrounded by foothills, then by mountains more than 16,000 feet high. His farming family struggled with the region's erratic climate and lack of a market for its harvest. He was fortunate that his family and relatives could put together enough money to send him to university to learn more about the science of his family's agricultural life.

In 2005 Héctor Arce sat at his NGO work desk, awaiting a visit from a Señor Mendoza, a vecino of his father, of Omereque. A few days earlier Mendoza had called to say he was coming to Cochabamba to meet with him. Now he wondered what this man who had farmed alongside his father might want of him.

Héctor heard a commotion outside his door. Opening it, he saw Mendoza, as well as several other men he recognized from his childhood and from frequent trips to his family home. Mendoza had brought several other Omerequeños, and each came up to him, shook his hand, and reintroduced himself.

After several minutes of conversation about the news from Omereque, Mendoza moved a few steps in front of the group and spoke: "Don Héctor, we are here because we need a new alcalde. We are worried about things at home. We have had no rain, and we have a disastrous harvest. You can't get anywhere on our roads. You are the only person we can think of who could change things."

Héctor Arce listened, recalling his last visit home, when he had seen the dry fields outside town. His father had told him then that even in a good year it was impossible to get his produce to market. He thanked the group for coming so far to talk to him.

Mendoza reminded him, "We came to you because you are from the *llajta* [your home place] Omereque. Please consider moving home and running for alcalde."

Before saying good-bye, Héctor Arce said he would talk to his wife and his boss about the group's request. His wife was uneasy about moving the children from Cochabamba and the only life they had known. His boss immediately offered him a significant increase in salary. Héctor called his Omerequeños, saying he was grateful for their faith in him but it just wasn't possible for him to leave his job and Cochabamba at that time.

Within a week, the same group of men arrived at Arce's office without notice. Again he heard the group outside his door and opened it to hear them say, "Come to Omereque and run for alcalde."

He knew the frustration and the hope that led these men to come all the way from Omereque a second time. Their ganas triggered his tie to his home place, and on the spot he answered, "Yes, I will come home and run for alcalde." He left Cochabamba, ran for alcalde of Omereque, and won.

When Héctor Arce became the mayor of Omereque, he brought together the 12 members of the junta vecinal. He talked with them about how best to serve the nearly 7,000 residents living in their 67 communities.

Curious about how the municipio had used the money received annually from the departamento and gobierno central, Héctor had looked into how funds were distributed through Omereque. He told his *colegas* (colleagues) that the money was typically divided among many little projects in a fruitless effort to make everybody happy. The junta members recalled that one village was delighted to get its soccer field graded and another was grateful for a public water faucet.

Alcalde Arce listened, then told them he had brought them together to consider a fundamentally different approach to governing. He suggested that they stop spreading their limited money over many individual projects in the 67 towns and villages in the municipio. He acknowledged that these small projects were wanted and appreciated by the communities that received them. But he suggested they made no significant impact on the poverty flowing from Omereque's lack of water for their fields and accessible markets for their produce.

Alcalde Arce persuaded his council to work with him to pool its resources and choose one or maybe two projects that could make a difference to the whole municipio or at least to a big part of it. He and his colegas talked with one another and with their constituents. After many conversations across Omereque, the alcalde and the council decided that the first thing they wanted to do was to improve the roads in Omereque so as to break through their isolation in the mountains. Once they had better roads, they could plan a better sistema de riego.

Early in his first term as alcalde, Héctor Arce went to the monthly asambleas of the alcaldes of the entire Cochabamba Departamento.

There he met people who faced the same kind of economic development challenges that Omereque had decided to address. He heard about an organization called Mano a Mano that had helped several alcaldes with structural projects in their communities.

Always on the lookout for new partnerships, Héctor Arce talked to his fellow alcaldes, learning that the person to talk with at Mano a Mano was a fellow Quechua—Ivo Velásquez. Ivo was the director of Mano a Mano Nuevo Mundo, just finishing construction of a road at El Palmar. Arce met with Ivo, who saw much ganas in the alcalde. Ivo agreed to visit Omereque to find out whether Nuevo Mundo could work with the alcalde and his compañeros to build a road.

First a Road

Ivo drove south following Ruta National 5 (National Highway 5). When he arrived in Omereque, he met with Alcalde Arce and his 12 council members, hearing the details of the road they were so eager to have. Ivo told the group he needed to see the area where the road would go before he could make a decision.

The alcalde arranged to have a truck take Ivo, the council members, and himself to the place where the road would start. As they rode into the countryside, Ivo explained that he must inspect the area—the rock construction and terrain—to determine whether building a road there was feasible.

The truck pulled up in front of a path completely overgrown with thick bush. Ivo, eager to make an inspection, tried to push through the thickness. He went back to the truck to say that not even a horse could get through that thicket. He asked the men to cut the brush so he could do an inspection. He told the alcalde that he was sorry and climbed into the truck.

The men took Ivo back to his SUV to drive the 150 miles back to Cochabamba. He told his workmates that Omereque was not yet ready for a road.

Three months later, Alcalde Arce called Ivo to ask him to return. They were ready for him to inspect the road site. Ivo returned to Omereque and went with Arce and his council members to the site, where Ivo found that the community members had not only cleared all the brush but also opened up the area by preparing a wide, smooth walking path. Ivo was impressed with their work and asked them why they hadn't done it earlier—for themselves. They said no one had ever challenged them before.

The people who did the work proudly led Ivo to the path and brought him a horse to do the inspection. He mounted the horse and traveled across the smooth new path, examining the mountainous terrain all the way to Omereque. He met with the Omereque council and the alcalde. Ivo said he thought the path could become a sturdy road and that Mano a Mano could work with them to build it.

When Ivo started talking about the organization's model of collaborative partnerships, Héctor Arce interrupted him. Having learned about Mano a Mano from his alcalde colegas, he already had commitments in hand. The council had already consolidated the local resources and secured a significant amount of money for a road from the municipio. And in true Bolivian ayllu fashion, the alcalde had talked to the town and village sindicatos about their willingness to assign community members to such tasks. They were ready.

After several more visits to Omereque, Ivo, the municipio engineers, and Mano a Mano Nuevo Mundo's engineers together developed a work plan and budget. With Mano a Mano contributing the use of its road-building equipment and expertise, Omereque could finance the remaining project cost. They would not ask for funds from the United States.

In 2006 Nuevo Mundo moved heavy equipment to Omereque over the 150 miles from Cochabamba. A bulldozer, a road grader, an excavator, and several dump trucks arrived at the spot where the first of several roads was to begin. It took 180 days to cut deep into the mountainside to build a nine-mile road to the Omereque town of Chucupial. In the next year the group worked another 170 days to build 13 miles of road to Kumuthago-Kaiñal.

Alcalde Arce described the efforts of the hardworking villagers and Mano a Mano staff on the road-building projects: "Dozen of villagers, using picks, shovels, machetes, and axes, cleared trees and brush. Behind them the surveyor marked the roadbed. Then came the bulldozer, carving its way into the hillside. Then the excavator, the dump trucks, and the road grader came. It reminded me of an ant colony with its highly organized structure, each focused on its task, determined to follow its path. Now that the farmers have a road, they can plant more crops because we can transport what their families don't eat and sell it in the faraway markets."

Atajados: Small Ponds for Many

The Omereque council saw its plan to open the region with new roads carried out more quickly than it could have imagined. But it never lost sight of its other big plan—to improve the sistema de riego and relieve the annual drought that ruined the fields of the area's many farmers.

In 2006 the council had thought of building a big reservoir like the one Nuevo Mundo built in Ucuchi. But two years later, working with Mano a Mano engineers, the council accepted that there was no basin on which to build a reservoir big enough for all its needs.

The topography of the Omereque region was especially difficult to develop because of the unique narrowness of its valleys. Farms did not butt up to each other: one farmer might have a farm on one side of a mountain, and the closest neighbor might be well on the other side.

Nuevo Mundo worked with the alcalde and community leaders to find an alternative strategy to bring sufficient water to the farmers nestled in the foothills and natural terraces of the mountains. They had to devise a sistema focusing on smaller bodies of water that could serve the farms a bigger, channeled reservoir could not reach.

The farmers and Nuevo Mundo engineers together designed atajados that could save the rain when it fell so as to be available for the inevitable dry times. Sometimes it was necessary to build a separate atajado for a single family. Where the land was flat and wide enough, three or four farms could share a pond.

By October 20, 2010, Nuevo Mundo and Omereque had built 148 atajados. They were not tiny: each was 177 feet wide, 131 feet long, and 13 feet deep. They were mounded on the sides with dirt, and each contained a cement device to trap undesirable material. The result was water for the fields.

The atajados were designed to reduce erosion, a serious problem in the mountains. A valve system released water into a channel from the atajado to the fields. Everyone who farmed in the area received access to atajado water. Just as everyone had hoped, the rains that came in the wet months collected in the atajados. And when the rainy season ended, a farmer could open his channel and water the fields.

One Omereque farmer told Ivo, "I used to produce two sacks of my beautiful onions. I was always proud of my onions, but before the atajado, all I could ever get was two sacks. I had only one season to grow them in. Now with water all the time, I get 50 sacks a year."

Now he can also get his onions to market. Nuevo Mundo had to build many small roads to get machinery to the atajado construction sites. This gave each farmer or small group of farmers their own access to the main road. Multiplied by the plentiful water, the extra produce of the entire region now travels to distant communities for sale.

A Three-way Collaboration

The Omereque/Mano a Mano collaboration resulted in 148 atajados and more than 105 miles of new roads. But Omereque's partnership with Mano a Mano did not end after its collaboration with Nuevo Mundo. And both of the other Mano a Mano sister organizations now have a deep presence in Omereque.

Atajados for Omereque

Mano a Mano Bolivia has worked with several of the 67 outlying communities to build a typical clinic for the area and to add a new wing for the hospital in the city of Omereque. The organiation provided funding, furniture, and medical supplies for these facilities as well as training and support for clinic staff. Omereque now has 24 new classrooms as well as 16 housing units for its teachers. Apoyo Aéreo flies staff, equipment, and materials for construction and road projects undertaken in Omereque by Neuevo Mundo. The Mano a Mano sister organizations share vehicles and staff as needed.

The three brothers—Ivo, Segundo, and José—have worked together to build a continuing connection with this mountainous region 150 miles from their home base in Cochabamba.

By 2010, Héctor Arce was president of the Cochabamba-area governing body that he came to as a new member in 2005. Another energetic Quechua leader succeeded him as alcalde in Omereque. Alcalde Marcelino Solis is continuing Héctor's work to increase Omereque's agricultural economic capacity. He recently hosted a visit from the president of Bolivia, Evo Morales, for the inauguración of a sistema de riego.

It is said that one day in 2011, Bolivian president Evo Morales was flying over the Omereque region in a small plane and spotted the water gleaming from the 148 atajados below. Relations between the United States and Bolivia were less than congenial at the time, and he was surprised when the official flying with him said that Omereque had built them with the U.S./Bolivian organization called Mano a Mano. President Morales acknowledged that people thought he didn't support U.S programs in Bolivia. But after seeing the extent and obvious success of the atajado project in Omereque, he said he would encourage his alcaldes to bring forth projects like that one—and that his government would support them.

Years earlier Mano a Mano had decided to use its Bolivian expertise, its U.S. resources, and its shared ganas for the development of poor and rural Bolivian communities. It recognized early that such an ambitious goal could be met only through partnership with Bolivian communities and their governments. Evidence of the fruit of that hope lies on Omereque's website. It is full of videos of Bolivians like Alcaldes Arce and Solis and photos of Omereque's celebrations of new roads and irrigation projects. Mano a Mano is mentioned on the website as an institutional partner. The site states that the organization "by agreement, undertakes improvement and construction of roads and irrigation systems."

The Mano a Mano model of community requests, formal agreements, governmental contribution, and community participation is profoundly realized in Omereque. And such collaboration is evident across Bolivia, from Chari Chari in Omereque to Jusk'u Molle in Punata, to Jironkota in Tapacari, and beyond.

Determining how to cross the flooded road in an SUV

12

Four Men on a Mountain

2010–2013

Few Mano a Mano ventures were as dramatically initiated as when the El Palmar horsemen came to Ivo with their request for a road. More often, community representatives came to the office with a project request. In 2011, when the Velásquezes prepared for a trek to the Pachaj K'ocha reservoir, they knew they would talk with the leaders of four different villages about a water project.

Early on a Sunday morning, Segundo and Ivo sat at the apartment's patio table awaiting two U.S. volunteers to drive with them to the Pachaj K'ocha reservoir to determine whether Mano a Mano would collaborate on a water project there.

Bob Lundgren and Margi Singher were stalwart volunteers who had come to see Mano a Mano in action. After a tour of Cochabamba the afternoon before, the two joined Segundo, Ivo, and two of Blanca's sons to learn about Ivo's work with Mano a Mano Nuevo Mundo. Entering the big office on the first floor of the apartment, they were surprised to see the same kind of plasticized posters and maps they had become familiar with in the Minnesota office they spent so much time in.

Bob and Margi heard the stories of the Nuevo Mundo projects completed since its inception six years earlier. Ivo described the completed reservoirs and smaller atajados and showed them maps of some of the hundreds of miles of roads that Nuevo Mundo had built. Carefully examining the vivid photos of villagers contributing their labor, the two volunteers noted the hard work of the men and women carrying rocks and sand. The posters of elaborate celebrations with villagers, government officials, and Mano a Mano staff cutting ribbons and signing formal documents showed them the collaborative nature of the organization's work. The evening ended with a reminder from Segundo that they would be leaving for the mountains early in the morning.

Seated with the Velásquezes the next morning while finishing their traditional breakfast of Blanca's homemade *salteñas* (sweet, meat-filled pastries, a family favorite), Bob Lundgren and Margi Singher spoke of their experience at the Nuevo Mundo office the night before. They said it gave them a sense of how well the Mano a Mano development model worked, even with highly technical and expensive projects.

As they spoke, Blanca came into the patio with two pairs of tall black rubber boots in her arms. The night before she had asked the two volunteers for their shoe sizes. She handed the tallest and biggest pair to Bob and the smaller pair to Margi. Pleased, Blanca announced, "They fit."

Getting up from the table while reaching for one more salteña, Segundo told their guests that it was time to go down to the SUV: "We have an important meeting at a mountaintop reservoir called Pachaj K'ocha—you could translate it as 'sacred pond.'"

Walking down the stairs, the group came upon Blanca entering the small elevator with a huge yellow bag carrying two liters of Coca Cola and orange soda, bags of food, and several raincoats. They met her as she left the elevator on the first floor; all went outside through the brown metal door.

Israel Martínez, one of Blanca's boys, drove up from the basement garage in the SUV, parked, and got out. Loading packages of food, blankets, and the yellow bag into the back of the SUV, he helped Blanca as she climbed into a small jump seat in the back. Ivo got into the driver's seat, and Bob sat beside him.

Segundo and Margi settled into the back seat as they passed out of the somewhat commercial neighborhood through a residential area with some of Cochabamba's legendary flowering trees overhanging the boulevards. Soon they were on a main highway driving east, out of the city.

Blanca asked Ivo to slow down so they could give small plastic bags of food to people walking in the rain, hands outstretched toward the SUV. It was the rainy season, and as they moved out and above the Cochabamba Valley, the gentle rainfall came and went. Ivo turned off the main highway and drove up, down, and over mountain after mountain. The group was silent, frequently passing water that met the road and nearly stopped the SUV. As the car went higher, the riders saw big patches of white, yellow, and pink flowers.

"Potatoes," Segundo said.

Every few miles the visitors saw groups of men and women working together in the fields on either side of the road. The women wore white scarves or wide-brimmed hats, wide skirts to their knees, blouses, sashes, aprons with wide shoulder straps, and sweaters layered one upon the other. Some of the men wore wool hats with earflaps, others wore baseball caps, and a few were bareheaded. Their pants were short or long, and they wore a variety of shirts, scarves, and layered sweaters. It was cold in the rain.

Each group added to a pile of dug potatoes, and few looked up as the SUV passed. There was almost no flat land. The view stretched from the potato farmers up the sides of the mountains. The mosaic pattern of cultivated land was more obvious the higher they went. Then, at a certain altitude, the cultivation ended and the mountaintops emerged.

The group passed an occasional walled farmhouse with a tile roof.

Here and there the travelers saw a solitary cow, llama, or sheep tethered by a rope tied to a single leg. Dogs sat on the side of the road, watching expectantly. Every few miles someone stood alone on a precipice looking out at the rocky, seemingly empty fields around him.

Margi asked, "Are they shepherds?"

Segundo said they were, but their herds were typically one or maybe a few llamas, goats, or sheep. Pointing to a solitary woman wrapped in her burden cloth, he said, "She may well be watching her family's single goat or sheep or llama—her household's only source of milk or even meat."

The woman didn't move as the rain increased dramatically.

Ivo peered through the windshield, then stopped abruptly as the road suddenly disappeared into the water. He got out of the car and walked ahead. He returned to the SUV, then doubled back and found a narrower and rockier road.

The riders saw a slender man, water dripping off his wide-brimmed, canvas hat. He wore a pink backpack over a long-sleeved shirt and high boots, much like those Blanca had given the volunteers. Speaking Quechua, the man talked with Ivo and pointed to a path that looked too narrow for the SUV. He turned to walk straight up the mountain.

Ivo took the recommended path, which barely accommodated the vehicle. It was getting hard to see the dirt road, but he persisted. Coming to a man in a striped stocking hat standing on the edge of the road, Ivo rolled down the window and listened to his directions, accompanied by more pointing.

Ivo turned left at the next opening. Mist now joined the hard rain, and two more times Ivo encountered men who explained to him how to navigate the water covering the road. The SUV finally stopped at the edge of a big levee overlooking a reservoir with a few small islands in the distance. The water stretched into the clouds. Four men stood in a circle as a huge cascade of water overflowed the reservoir with a roar, spilling down the valley for miles.

This Is Pachaj K'ocha!

As the SUV came to rest, Segundo announced: "This is Pachaj K'ocha!"

The men they had encountered coming up the mountain were already there, some dressed in ponchos, sombreros, and elaborately stitched shawls in addition to the layered shirts and sweaters. They were waiting for Ivo, Blanca, and Segundo, who got out of the car and walked toward the men with outstretched hands. The greeting from one to another was a traditional Quechua series of welcoming gestures, somewhat different when exchanged with Blanca.

Then each of the Quechua men spoke seriously and at some length. The Velásquezes, in American windbreakers and hiking boots, listened as intently as the men spoke, learning that their families had worked for thousands of years building an elaborate irrigation system through the area. The system had been destroyed over the centuries of war and disjointed political leadership.

Since the redistribution of land during the Bolivian National Revolution of the 1950s (also referred to as the agrarian revolution), their grandfathers and fathers had struggled to divert some of the precious water to their fields. They had dug a trench for that purpose, but it had disrupted the soil and caused a landslide that washed away part of the mountain and cut off the channel from a mountain spring.

Nearly a century earlier the patrón of a hacienda located farther down the mountain had usurped the Pachaj K'ocha reservoir from the campesinos living nearby. He forbade their access to this water. Forced to find other water or abandon their land, the campesinos identified springs and snowmelt at a higher elevation. They dug a channel about three-and-a-half kilometers long, following the curve and slope of the mountain so as to guide the water toward their fields.

Toward the end of their digging, however, the campesinos encountered solid rock. Unable to penetrate it, they finally gave up. If they had been able to complete the channel, the water would have continued its flow. Instead, it pooled where the rock stopped it, then overflowed and undermined the channel. A kilometer section of the mountain slid to the valley, completely cutting off the channel.

Having heard about the reservoirs and atajados that Mano a Mano Nuevo Mundo built with other communities, the men had asked for this meeting. They had heard a rumor that Ivo Velásquez could look at a mountain and see a road. They hoped he could look at their mountain and reservoir and see a way to channel the water toward their fields. They wanted Nuevo Mundo's help.

The wind and rain whipped about the Quechua conversation in an increasing fog. Ivo, who had been taking notes in a small pad, glanced at his watch. He unzipped his jacket, stuck the pad in his shirt pocket, and began to say good-bye. After sharing the traditional Quechua handshake all around, the four men turned back down the mountain path. The Velásquezes joined Margi Singher and Bob Lundgren in the dry, warm SUV. Unable to understand Quechua and somewhat taken aback by the thinness of the air at 15,000 feet, the two had retreated earlier to the car.

Ivo drove the group down the tortuous paths-turning-to-roads with little conversation. Margi and Bob understood enough Spanish to know that Ivo wanted them all to watch for a broken-down *autobus de la escuela* (school bus).

Ivo was driving fast, seeming to ignore the huge puddles, sharp turns, and deep crevices at the edge of the road. Segundo called out at the sight of a rickety school bus parked in a bend in the road, and Ivo pulled up to a brown adobe structure with a basketball hoop and a cement playground in a flat spot between mountains. An overhang on the school building protected several people standing with the four men from the top of the mountain. They had walked down steep paths and arrived on foot well before the Velásquezes did in their SUV.

The one in a wool stocking cap spread out a colorful burden cloth where he laid fava beans and *queso de campo* (fresh cheese). Blanca brought the yellow bag of food and drink from the SUV to add to the villagers' gifts. All reached for the food, which they ate with their fingers.

The Quechua conversation continued as Bob and Margi sampled Bolivian lima beans—much bigger than expected and delicious. Ivo, full, looked at his watch and began the handshakes again. As the Mano a Mano group got in the SUV, Segundo explained to the visitors that this was the beginning of a complicated partnership.

The drive from the Pachaj K'ocha Reservoir back to Cochabamba felt much shorter than the drive to get there. Segundo explained to Margi and Bob that this meeting was typical of the way Ivo assessed the possibilities of a new Mano a Mano project. Soon Segundo was speaking to Ivo so intently that he stopped translating for the couple.

When Margi asked Segundo to tell her what was going on, he said, "When Ivo and I saw all that water flowing to the tropics, I asked, 'How about we catch all that water in the channel we are already building? How can we get this excess water into a channel?'

"And then we began to think of taking it to an even bigger reservoir that the departamento had built with German funds . . . Then there would be water for everybody."

The conversation between the brothers continued, Ivo paying close attention to Segundo's response, for he was the one who would have to go home to the United States and work with Joan to raise Mano a Mano's portion of the funding. Continuing to talk about the immensity of water flowing from Pachaj K'ocha, the brothers tried to calculate just how many cubic meters of water could be harnessed.

Once back to the apartment, the travelers made their way to the Nuevo Mundo office, where they found Vanchi and another of Nuevo Mundo's engineers—just the ones they needed to help figure out how much water they were talking about. Together the two uncles and their nephew, switching from Quechua to Spanish and back, concluded that potentially 40,000,000 cubic meters of water could be channeled toward the Cochabamba Valley each year. Only a few generations back,

235

the valley had been the "bread basket" of Bolivia. Now, for lack of water, much of the valley lay idle, producing only during the increasingly shorter rainy season.

Ivo knew that the Pachaj K'ocha was important to many more communities than the four villages represented in the mountaintop conversation. Seven other communities on that side of the mountain plus more than 10,000 residents of the valley below lacked sufficient water.

The nearby valley towns of the Sancayani area in the municipio of Tiraque had already enlisted Mano a Mano in addressing its water deficiency. Nuevo Mundo and the many villagers involved were constructing two reservoirs: Sallamani Grande to serve five communities and Sallamani Chico to reach three more. The reservoirs would regulate the flow of water, capturing it during the heavy rainy season and releasing it for irrigation during the dry months. This procedure would occur seven times during the seasonal rains and snowmelt, filling and emptying the reservoirs to make best use of the water.

With the villagers' help, Nuevo Mundo secured commitment from the local governments to partner on the reservoir project and provide the balance of needed funding. Ivo and Segundo were beginning to see this major effort as part of an even greater irrigation system that might also include excess water from Pachaj K'ocha.

The immensity of the overflow of Pachaj K'ocha put any decision regarding the need of four mountain villages into a larger context. Ivo and his siblings did not minimize the needs of the men they had met that afternoon. But they were aware that such a large amount of water could meet the needs of thousands of farmers, all the way to the outskirts of Cochabamba City.

They decided that Blanca's son Vanchi, a family member of the next generation and another Mano a Mano engineer, would be part of this potentially huge undertaking. They suggested he go to a scheduled meeting with the men they had met that day and others from the villages and towns up and down the mountain and from the valley below.

Vanchi said he needed to rest up for the next day. Blanca looked at her watch in the growing dark. The group had been intensely involved in Mano a Mano work all day. No one had been to church; no one had relaxed on this traditional day of rest. As Blanca moved toward the door to the apartment hallway, she looked back and said, "It is Sunday, you know. But it is not Sunday for the Velásquezes."

The Water Is Ours

Ivo had asked Vanchi to represent Mano a Mano Nuevo Mundo at the Monday meeting that would include many more villages than the four of the previous day's conversation near the reservoir. When Vanchi returned to the office Monday evening, he told his Tio Segundo and Tio Ivo that Quechua communities up and down the mountain were interested in this project. They knew that Nuevo Mundo was already laying a roadbed/platform near Sancayani for the construction of a channel.

The roadbed/platform passed near the overflowing Pachaj K'ocha outlet. Some communities wanted to take advantage of the roadbed by building a bigger closed channel, one with access windows so they could maintain and clean it. With windows, the channel could capture runoff from the 17,000-foot mountain and collect enough water to fill the Sancayani reservoirs and another that a German NGO had built in the region.

There were so many different sources of water—snowmelt, rain during the rainy season, big and small reservoirs, and runoff—that such a channel could become dangerous. One community's project might cause flooding in another's.

Mano a Mano had called the meeting to find out whether the groups could work together, could combine their efforts in constructing one channel that would bring water to everyone.

In describing the conversation at the meeting, Vanchi said, "Some

Four Men on a Mountain

in Sancayani, those who live on the mountain, are kind of jealous about the water. They are afraid that other communities want to take all of it." Vanchi identified an issue likely to consume the various Quechua communities, government officials, the German NGO, and Mano a Mano for months and probably years to come. With too much water for some and too little for others, there were many competing agendas for its use. Vanchi was in the midst of a classic Bolivian struggle.

Vanchi had been a teenager when the water war of 2000 exploded in Cochabamba. His meetings with villagers from the mountain of Pachaj K'ocha to the Cochabamba Valley were teaching him again of the passion behind the protest "El agua es nuestro."

Nuevo Mundo and Vanchi knew in 2011 that the Sancayani usos y costumbres for water differed from one village to the next because of altitude, history, and crop characteristics. But they also shared an appreciation for the intrinsic value of water and the necessarily communal nature of their care of it. As a result, they were willing to attend village meetings with Nuevo Mundo to talk about getting and sharing the water around them. They also sat with other sindicato leaders from the mountain and the valley to figure out whether a single channel could meet the needs of everyone.

As Ivo, Vanchi, and Segundo continued to work with Sancayani and the surrounding villages, they also worked with their Pachaj K'ocha compatriotas. And they learned much more about the German NGO that had been working for years to provide water in the Punata region.

In 2012, a year and a half later, the goal of pulling together dozens of communities to use cooperatively the 40 million cubic meters of water from Pachaj K'ocha was at hand. A technical plan to create an extensive irrigation system was evolving. Mano a Mano was working with the government officials toward an agreement about the process. U.S. foundations and Bolivian municipios had committed much of the funding. The *gobernador* (governor) of Cochabamba was on board, as were the alcaldes of the many towns and some of the community councils. The German NGO was in basic agreement, too. But many communities still struggled.

Segundo understood the villagers when he heard in one meeting after another, "This is Pachaj K'ocha, our natural resource, and we do not want it to go to Punata."

In meeting after meeting, Vanchi and Ivo explained the technicalities of ensuring that water went to each community as it made its way to the valley. Segundo and Vanchi reminded the villagers that at that point none of them was getting the water—100 percent of the overflow water was going to the tropics.

Segundo was tenacious and, more aptly, patient. He accepted how hard it was to convince people that Mano a Mano Nuevo Mundo was not like the Punata hacendado of a century earlier, who had taken the land around Pachaj K'ocha and diverted all the water to his fields. Mano a Mano's commitment to its model of community and government collaboration was being put to the test.

Nuevo Mundo continued work on the irrigation system, building a channel big enough to handle immense amounts of water. Smaller reservoirs and channels were constructed while Nuevo Mundo worked to convince all the villages to join in an effort that would benefit them and many other Bolivians. The Velásquezes recognized that it would take patience to undo years of exploitation by the hacendados and the resulting lack of trust in the Quechua people. They did what they could, worked as hard as they could, and prepared to accept whatever came of their work, invoking Ivo's mantra: "Si Dios quiere."

A student of the history of the water war reminded them of what happened to the governance of water after the conflict of 2000. Irrigation activists worked with the federal government, and in 2004 the congress passed law No. 2878, for "Promotion and Assistance of the Irrigation Sector." This resulted in two federal agencies and the continuing participation of irrigation sindicatos. Shortly after the 2005 election, the proudly indigenous president of Bolivia, Evo Morales,

Village leaders look at the Pachaj K'ocha/Sancayani reservoir with Segundo.

created a federal ministry of water. The 2000 water wars stopped the government's movement to a private market system of water control, and the communal control of water was institutionalized.

So, at least in recent times, Bolivians were coming together across many entities to maintain the community control of water for the benefit of all. Due to more than a year of tenacity and patience on the part of Mano a Mano and the Sancayani communities, communal sharing became a possibility. Bringing the Pachaj K'ocha water from the top of the mountain to the valley below was an ambitious dream to be accomplished si Dios quiere.

What came to be called the Sancayani project was a complex collaboration of the technical expertise and equipment of Mano a Mano, the municipio, and many vilage communities. One after another, they committed to the project, offering their manual labor to the effort. The cooperation was enough that those who signed up as regantes have received the water they hoped for. Sancayani is a success.

Early in the Sancayani project more than 300 young and old women and men joined a "work day" to help build the levy for the Sallamani Chico reservoir. Working conditions were challenging for staff and villagers alike. Much of the work had to be done at a high altitude—well over 13,000 feet. A Mano a Mano staff member reporting on the conditions said, "At an elevation of more than 13,000 feet, there is constant fog, mud, and subfreezing temperatures."

Dozens of women in traditional dress bent over with their sturdy hoes in a long row, breaking up the tough clay. Men stretched out along the levy, firmly packing the dirt, in readiness for the next phase of the process. Such workdays were repeated as construction of the reservoirs continued. Finally, on a cold, blustery day in March 2012, the participants joined in dedicating the completed Sancayani reservoirs. The typical Mano a Mano enthusiasm prevailed in a cheerful celebration abundant in speeches, flowers, music, and food.

Tomas Rojas, a leader of the Sancayani sistema de riego group, spoke of how much better his life would be as a potato farmer, with more than the one short growing season he was used to: "With all this new water, I will have one full or maybe even two good crops a year."

Tomas Rojas's realized expectation of the Sancayani project has been repeated many times among the farmers in Cochabamba Departamento. Success in Ucuchi in 2005 led to a creative response in the Omereque mountains in 2010 that ushered in an entirely different sistema de riego. With 32,000 hours of community manual labor, the Choquechampi reservoir was completed in 2010. And in 2012, a reservoir bigger than three football fields was completed in Jusk'u Molle. Every water project has resulted in increased water and productivity from now well-irrigated fields. The 2013 enlargement of an existing reservoir in Pasorapa increased its original capacity eightfold.

Mano a Mano Nuevo Mundo is now known in Cochabamba Departamento for its collaborative development, for its ability to work well with and for communities affected by the drought.

VI

Twenty Years

13

In Good Hands

2010–2013

As the sister organizations in Bolivia thrived, Ivo, José, and Blanca were supported by the dozens of Mano a Mano employees and, perhaps more importantly, by one another. But Joan and Segundo were the only U.S. Velásquezes deeply tied to Mano a Mano. Segundo's three U.S. siblings—Rubén, Margui, and César—were supportive of the organization but lived distinctly separate lives.

Rubén was a chemist for 3M corporation in Texas, Margui worked at a hotel in Washington, D.C., and César directed a mental health program in California. César, the U.S. representative to the asamblea for Mano a Mano Bolivia, had the Mano a Mano blood that Blanca sees in the Bolivian family, but his distance from both Minnesota and Cochabamba and the demands of his professional and family life limited his involvement.

As Joan and Segundo moved toward Mano a Mano's 20th year, they accepted that no other family members in the United States would be devoting their lives to the work in Bolivia.

Happily, Joan had honed her gift of attracting friends and collaborators outside of her immediate circle to create family-like communities and commitments. Segundo acquired the same expansiveness, and the two had gathered intensely loyal U.S. companions for the Mano a Mano journey.

"Chief scrounger" and networker Gloria MacRae, packer of supplies and equipment Mark Petzoldt, driver and messenger Jerry Sauter, editor and craft-seller Margi Singher, and photographer Michael McClure were just a few of the hundreds of volunteers who had signed on to Mano a Mano, staying as close as the members of a huge extended family. Such volunteers, like the founders, were still very much a part of Mano a Mano.

Five of the original incorporators were still on the board. Joan and Segundo, of course, as well as Chris Ver Ploeg, Deb Kotcher, and John Foxen, were constant and committed. Early additions to the governing group, like Nancy White and Terry Crowley, also remained on the board. Most of the board members had served more than 15 years, and many planned continuing involvement. All operated intimately and creatively, as Mano a Mano continued to evolve. Whenever Blanca visited the United States, she reiterated her conviction that the board, as well as the corps of loyal volunteers, had more than a little of the Mano a Mano blood in its veins.

The Mano a Mano USA board pushed and pulled with Joan and Segundo to continue the systematic planning and development it had overseen for years. The board's appreciation of the need in Bolivia was equaled only by its determination to make realistic decisions as to how Mano a Mano could best respond.

Operating with an eye to the challenges in Minnesota to raise money to support Bolivian projects, the board also consciously acted to support U.S. staff members. Segundo, with Joan at his side, tended to concentrate on the need of the rural Bolivians. He operated as if all those around would respond with the same total commitment that he and Joan brought to their work. The intensity of involvement varied among individuals in the U.S. operation, but everyone knew that together they could work through their varying styles and passions as the Mano a Mano vision and scale of work expanded.

The U.S board, including Joan and Segundo, adapted to the growing pains of a rapidly expanding entity. Segundo was busy coordinating the Mano a Mano sister organizations in Bolivia and fine-tuning their relationship to the U.S. organization. Joan, Nate, and Dan were spending more time raising money and negotiating the more complex organizational interactions.

For a long time, Joan had not attended the Saturday morning medical-supply work of the volunteers. But when she got a call from Mark Petzoldt as to whether he should just stop clearing his calendar for that time, she realized something was amiss. For years Mark had arrived early every Saturday at the Mendota Heights facility, ready to lead volunteers in packing and transporting medical supplies.

That Mano a Mano's emphasis on the collection and transport of medical supplies to Bolivia was diminishing became clear. The program had always been dependent on U.S. volunteers. The need for the supplies never lessened, but Segundo's role in supporting the volunteers had decreased as he was pulled into the organization of the Bolivian programs and the creation of Mano a Mano Nuevo Mundo and Mano a Mano Apoyo Aéreo. Nate Knatterud-Hubinger earlier had picked up some of the volunteer management from Segundo, but his writing of grant proposals and reports with Joan left no one in the U.S. office to overlook and nourish volunteer activities. No one had time to give the U.S. side of the medical-supply program sufficient attention.

In 2012, the board decided to search for a Spanish-speaking person with international experience, who could, among other responsibilities, coordinate the volunteer program.

When Dana Dallavalle emerged from the search for a volunteer coordinator, Mano a Mano was still operating from the Mendota Heights house. She was the enthusiastic choice of all: an effervescent young woman with U.S. experience working with Amnesty International,

In Good Hands

with Vietnamese and Burmese refugees in Chicago, and with Burmese refugees in Denver. She had studied international development and nonprofit administration in graduate school and tested her knowledge as a Peace Corps volunteer in Panama.

Assigned to a poor community with no defined task, Dana, like Joan in Bolivia many years earlier, had learned to find out what people wanted and create her own role to help fill their needs. The passion and grasp of animal health that became the basis of her work in Panama was evident in her devotion to the small, well-behaved dog she soon brought to work at Mano a Mano.

Dana Dallavalle described her work as a Peace Corp volunteer in this way: "I did whatever the community wanted. It turned out to be a lot of animal health and education. No matter how much I denied it, everyone thought I was a veterinarian. When there was a problem, they would call or come with their pets. I would help them or contact a vet by phone for advice."

The excellent fit between Dana Dallavalle and Mano a Mano was evident in discussion of her first six months with the organization: "That's how I came to understand poverty and how deep the causes are. What I love about Mano a Mano is the whole model. I have never seen anything like that on the ground. I honestly do not know anything that comes close to the way it maximizes its dollars [or] works with government. In Panama I also saw the divides that come when international organizations come in and say you need this or that and this is how we are going to do it."

Dana learned about the ganas of Mano a Mano volunteers early in her new job, when she met the group of longtime volunteers who came into the office every other Friday to do what needed to be done. She was to help the group prepare for a Mother's Day fundraising event. When the volunteers realized they couldn't finish the task before the end of the day, each gathered up materials to finish the work at home.

Dana grasped the importance of the innumerable volunteers to

Mano a Mano's success, understanding that they completed most of the time-consuming tasks that made the medical-supply program work. Some, like the Friday group, were always at the ready to donate detailed and time-consuming effort. And she knew most of the volunteers were there because of their personal connections with Joan or Segundo. Almost all had been to Bolivia, where it was easy to catch at least a slight case of Mano a Mano fever.

Nate saw all these efforts as ways to pull volunteers into the reality of the needs in Bolivia and the work of Mano a Mano in addressing them. He coordinated trips to Bolivia and saw to it that many of the students and interns went there as part of their learning experience. As he said, "Pretty much everyone who goes with us to Bolivia becomes a strong supporter of Mano a Mano."

Joan, Segundo, and the rest of the U.S. board saw the successful expansion of the U.S. office as necessary to the sustainability of Mano a Mano. All were relieved to see Dana fitting smoothly into the flat organizational style of the U.S. office. She quickly learned and expanded the volunteer program while also drawing from her Spanish fluency and cultural sensitivity to form relationships with the staff in Bolivia.

Dan Narr, Nate Knatterud-Hubinger, and Dana Dallavalle worked well together, continuing the dance of Mano a Mano in the world. They recognized the centrality of the Velásquez family members as founders, board members, and volunteers. Joan and Segundo were more than full-time, unpaid members of the staff and members of the board, active leaders of the enterprise. Dan shared that leadership in the far-from-linear organizational structure. He built on the expertise and flexibility of staff and founders alike, balancing his leadership with that of a strong, working board and the organization's founders, with whom he worked every day.

Anyone who saw Mano a Mano as the exclusive passion of the five Velásquezes was missing the presence of Dan, Dana, and Nate; their compassion and tenacity were deep. All three had been to Bolivia—Dan and Nate repeatedly—and they easily empathized with the Bolivian campesinos facing huge challenges in the Cochabamba area. None of the three was immune to Segundo's energy—he often worked 80 hours a week in and out of the St. Paul office.

Dan, Dana, and Nate connected frequently with Joan, whom Dan described as "the scribe of Segundo's intimacy with the needs and strengths of Bolivia." They caught more than a little bit of the Velásquez passion and commitment. Their ganas lay in their own experience and values, which told them that what they are doing was important—Mano a Mano was doing something unique in Latin America. The energy and creativity emanating from the St. Paul office showed that though they did not carry the Velásquez name, they were very much a part of the Mano a Mano family.

In Bolivia Mano a Mano was also deeply tied to the Velásquez family, but in its new breadth, more and more nonfamily members were involved in the organization. Recognizing the risk of tying Mano a Mano exclusively to the current generation of Velásquez family members, its leaders formed a plan.

Each sister organization employed Bolivian professionals who were prepared to move into leadership roles. José Velásquez mentored several management-level staffers at Mano a Mano Bolivia. Four Nuevo Mundo engineers managed major projects under Ivo's direction. Apoyo Aéreo had four Bolivian pilots sharing administrative tasks.

Nate acknowledged that when he needed to communicate with someone in Bolivia, he typically contacted one of the Velásquezes. But he knew they were not the only ones he could work with. There were others who could step in. The Bolivian organizations clearly were moving into a family/employee hybrid that made them less "Velásquez determined." The inevitable transition to new leadership was to be incremental and varied.

Nate Knatterud-Hubinger frequently heard people asking, "What will happen when José or Segundo or Ivo or Blanca is gone?" He responded with a Segundo-style combination of optimism and practicality: "In Bolivia it's working well right now, so let's not break it. There are enough fires to put out elsewhere. Sometimes you lose some of the important things by doing something that seems urgent."

The Bolivian side of Mano a Mano continued its partnerships in rural Bolivia, responding to the evolving health and economic needs of the region. The planning and fundraising supporting these partnerships continued in St. Paul. The incremental resolution of the family/employee transition did not impede the work.

Leaving Mendota Heights

When Dana Dallavalle came to Mano a Mano, the U.S. office was still crammed into the house in Mendota Heights. From the time of the 1994 incorporation, the house had been Mano a Mano's only home in the United States. Even after Joan and Segundo partially moved into a condo in St. Paul in 2006, the U.S. offices remained in their house above the Mississippi River.

There had been talk of the couple selling the house and Mano a Mano buying a new building. But the financial downturn of 2008 hit Mano a Mano's budget hard enough to make buying a new space impossible. The office foursome—Dan, Nate, Joan, and Segundo—slowly shepherded Mano a Mano out of the recession.

In 2012 Joan and Segundo decided it was time to sell their house. Six years was long enough, they said, for them to carry responsibility for Mano a Mano's space needs. Despite the delight Dan Narr took in the deer that came from the surrounding woods to his window, he was well aware that the house was far from ideal. It simply did not have the right space in which to manage the growing programs in Bolivia. The mere processing and storing of medical supplies was nearly beyond control.

Joan, who developed the agenda for Mano a Mano's board meetings, listed moving out of the house as an item for discussion. She reminded her colleagues that it had been six years since the cost-saving

In Good Hands

decision to have Mano a Mano continue operating from their house after Dan was hired. Deb Kotcher, the treasurer, said the organization was by then positioned to raise the funds to buy a new building. Chris Ver Ploeg added that it was about time they stop taking advantage of Joan and Segundo's generosity.

The U.S. board authorized the fundraising for and purchase of a new Mano a Mano building. Dan and Segundo started looking. After touring many buildings they found a space big enough to meet the storage needs for all the medical supplies and provide offices for the staff and room to expand. It was located in an industrial center equally accessible to Minneapolis and St. Paul.

After long, firm, and frugal negotiation Mano a Mano owned its first piece of real estate in the United States. In the bitter cold of January 2013, Segundo, the Mano a Mano staff, and countless volunteers spent a week transporting thousands of packed boxes and pieces of palletized equipment that had been stored in a rented warehouse in a nearby suburb. They also moved staff files and furniture from the Mendota Heights house and into the organization's new building at 925 Pierce Butler Route in St. Paul.

Dana Dallavalle was especially delighted with the move. She knew the main reason she had been hired: to make better use of existing volunteers and figure out ways to attract new ones, including younger people. She would now have generous and congenial space to support the existing volunteers and to work with Nate in building a new cadre of corporate and academic volunteers.

The office on Pierce Butler was set up intentionally to accommodate teams of corporate employees and students who want a way to learn and volunteer. Dana concentrated on the corporate volunteers, and Nate and Joan worked with the University of Minnesota on research and data analysis, an increasing element of Mano a Mano's grant writing and fundraising. Nate took on more and more of the academic connections and mentoring of students and interns.

By the summer of 2013, Mano a Mano's first year in the new space, there was enough room to add five summer interns to the staff. The first five comprised a diverse group of students from Grinnell College, the University of Minnesota, Johns Hopkins University, and DePaul University. They came with expertise in graphic design, data management, graph composition, global studies, and grants management. Most had academic and language experience that fit well with Mano a Mano. Two of the five were related to the Mano a Mano U.S. office: Nate's sister Emma Knatterud-Johnson and Joan and Segundo's nephew Julio Velásquez from Bolivia. Mano a Mano was open to all who wanted to be part of the family.

Joan and Segundo saw the move of Mano a Mano out of the Mendota Heights house as part of a bigger plan—like that in Bolivia—to accommodate the reality that Mano a Mano would ultimately cease to be a family enterprise. Now in both the United States and Bolivia, nearly every part of the Mano a Mano organization would have its own home, independent of Velásquez family members.

Joan and Segundo were encouraged about Mano a Mano's continuity, flexibility, resources, and leadership as they watched the move from their old house into the new building. Then a much more personal problem reemerged. Joan's body was telling them that it needed rest.

Slowly, out of respect for Joan's wishes, and gracefully because of everyone's flexibility and gifts, others lifted a portion of the Mano a Mano work from her. Nate assumed more grant writing, and Dana increased her involvement with volunteers. The U.S. organization rested in Dan's hands, while Segundo continued his involvement in all things Mano a Mano everywhere. He spent and spends 80 hours a week on Mano a Mano work in and out of the office. Joan continued to work at home with staff members and volunteers coming frequently for supervision and consultation—much as was the case with Ramsey County staff members when she first retired. She continued to take major responsibility for Mano a Mano written materials.

In Good Hands

Given the strong board, Dan Narr's leadership, and the multicultural and intellectual gifts of Nate Knatterud-Hubinger and Dana Dallavalle, the Velásquezes knew that Mano a Mano USA would flourish. Joan and Segundo's concerns about the future of Mano a Mano USA's capacity had been addressed as far ahead as they could see.

The deep grounding of the organization in the leadership of Joan and Segundo and its cadre of seasoned volunteers enabled Mano a Mano to adjust quickly and effectively to the departure of Dana Dallavalle in the summer of 2014 and of Dan Narr in the spring of 2015. While disappointed at losing these colleagues, Joan and Segundo drew immediately on the strengths within.

Nate effectively took on the most critical responsibilities previously covered by Dan. Longtime volunteer and donor couple Karen Abraham and Ray Wiedmeyer filled Dana's position, committing to do so for two years. The newly hired office manager—Carmen Paredes Dockry, born and raised in Bolivia—is fully fluent in Spanish and English. According to Joan, "Carmen's presence enhances Mano a Mano's functioning as a bicultural organization."

Joan and Segundo continued to perform their historic roles with new energy. Joan said with obvious pleasure and some relief, "Again we have an excellent team of people who work easily together."

The board had changed the name of the U.S. organization from Mano a Mano Medical Resources to Mano a Mano International Partners—clarifying its role as a partner, not only with the sister organizations but also with the people and governments of Bolivia. While fundraising remained a challenge, the collection and shipping of medical supplies, the research leading to and evaluation of Mano a Mano projects, and the oversight of volunteers and trips to Bolivia were in good hands.

Joan and Segundo were just as confident about the future of the sister organizations in Bolivia. Each has capable, well-trained managers committed to Mano a Mano. Some are family members, others not.

Nate Knatterud-Hubinger welcomed the new office manager—Carmen Paredes Dockry—to the Mano a Mano headquarters in St. Paul.

Beyond the Brothers

When asked about the future of Mano a Mano in Bolivia, Blanca immediately replied, "Mano a Mano's Bolivian future lies with my boys. We now have a second generation that we are moving on to. Four of my five children—Ben Samuel, Van Miguel (Vanchi), Ivo Daniel, and Israel—are very involved."

At the time, Vanchi was already an engineer with Nuevo Mundo; Ivo Daniel was a pilot with Apoyo Aéreo. Ben was studying communications, and Israel was in medical school. They seemed to be gaining the expertise and ganas to help sustain Mano a Mano in the future. They constantly moved in and out of the many Mano a Mano organizations and programs. The "boys," as Segundo lovingly called them, were then still in their twenties.

Blanca saw her boys as Mano a Mano's future. But the Velásquez and Mano a Mano families saw Blanca, younger than her brothers by ten years or more, emerging into leadership. Now that her boys were grown, she was devoting most of her life to Mano a Mano. Recently married to an American internationalist from Belgium but still living in Cochabamba, Blanca has quietly increased her involvement and influence from a position of relative objectivity. Her brothers have always instinctively turned to her for help or advice.

They remember her role in the 2010 crisis that threatened Mano a Mano's ability to bring in supplies from the United States. New Bolivian requirements made it nearly impossible to bring duty-free cargo into the country. Blanca's legal expertise, her connection with the government, and her calm tenacity gained the enterprise the government's approval. After a yearlong delay, the medical supplies became available to the clinics and hospitals needing them.

Blanca's mediation skills emerged during family differences—she assertively steered her "brothers of steel" toward effective compromise. She was the quiet architect, lawyer, and mediator during the creation of each of the sister organizations. The brothers looked back at Blanca's involvement and realized that their growth and success had occurred with Blanca at the center. They saw her as powerful and diplomatic as their mother, Inés, who deftly held together the siblings and their powerful father, Epifanio.

Blanca was the compassionate soul of Mano a Mano, keeping the Bolivian poor at the center of all its discussions. Asked about her family's role in the development of the organization, she spoke of the religious nature of the enterprise: "I have only one God, the one I find in my faith." She insisted that she was not idolatrous, but: "I often feel that I am part of a family that has another God, one called Mano a Mano."

All of the Mano a Mano Velásquezes are religious. Ivo, José, Blanca, and their mother Ines are as active in their Cristiana Evangélica churches in Cochabamba as Segundo and Joan, in their Unitarian-Universalist church in St. Paul. Each of their congregations emphasizes the importance of active compassion in the face of injustice. Like Blanca, all would say that one of the main ways they live out their faith is through Mano a Mano.

A consistent advocate, Blanca pushes her brothers for a positive answer to the unending requests from villages farther and farther away from Cochabamba. She is an important Bolivian link with Mano a Mano USA, working with Segundo and those in the U.S. office to schedule travels to Cochabamba, then overseeing the trips when the groups arrive. She and varying combinations of her sons typically follow the U.S. groups through their week in the Cochabamba Valley with unflagging energy. You might find her frying chicken at 3 AM to bring to a village meeting. And she still finds the quiet time to hammer out yet another complexity in the government rules and regulations continuing to require her expertise.

Blanca knows that the commitment that drives her three brothers and her has resulted in a deep devotion of their lives to work with rural Bolivians. Her mother, Inés, even at age 95 works as diligently for Mano a Mano as when she was selling lard at the Cliza and Punata markets to secure food for the family. No one can begin to count the traditional Quechua meals that Inés had cooked for U.S. volunteer visitors or how many thousands of blue strings she has tied to the bookmarks that Mano a Mano gives as gifts to U.S. volunteers. Blanca sees all of the family as deeply dedicated to Mano a Mano, perhaps even more than to their respective churches. She said, "It is said that Mano a Mano is our religion. The blood we have running through us is Mano a Mano. *Todo Mano a Mano* [Everything is Mano a Mano.]"

Blanca spends hours talking to Segundo, whether he is in Cochabamba or St. Paul, and to Ivo and José—mediating the big decisions and small details of Mano a Mano's work. She is close to her three older brothers. She sees each of them as strong, like hard steel. She wishes they had more flexibility. But she accepts their different personalities and says that the good thing about them is that they inevitably do what is best for the people Mano a Mano serves.

The depth of Blanca's brothers' skills and energy is central to Mano a Mano's success, but Blanca tends to minimize her own strength and ganas. Her brothers and the U.S. board, however, recognize her centrality to the success of the organization. In 2012, Dan Narr prevailed

Blanca speaking with residents of Sancayani

upon her to take charge of the latest sister organization—Mano a Mano Internacional. This nonprofit is Mano a Mano USA's formal presence in Bolivia. That Mano a Mano International turned to Blanca, a Boliviana and a family member, to take on this delicate international, cross-cultural task was no accident.

After nearly 20 years as an unpaid volunteer, Blanca became the salaried executive director of Mano a Mano Internacional, responsible for legal and administrative matters related to each of the Bolivian and U.S. Mano a Mano organizations.

Blanca sustains the transcontinental connection through her close ties with Segundo and even more intimately with Joan. Asked where she goes for support in the midst of Mano a Mano internal and external politics, Blanca replied, "*Llamo a Joanie* [I call Joanie]." She counts on Joan, just as the Velásquezes have come to count on Blanca, for intelligent and compassionate calm. The two women have the Mano a Mano blood in their veins, and they keep the organization bubbling but not boiling over.

A woman selecting harvested potatoes at Sancayani

14

The Work Continues

When Blanca Velásquez became the executive director of Mano a Mano Internacional in 2013, she joined the family's conversations about one of Mano a Mano's long-term goals—to provide a permanent and stable place for Nuevo Mundo's roads and water work. Joan, at the same time and with the support of the U.S. board, was determined to raise enough money to get the Bolivian sister organizations settled into independent and stable physical places—in other words, to cut further the ties between personal Velásquez property and Mano a Mano.

Several years earlier, Mano a Mano USA had acquired a property in El Abra on the outskirts of Cochabamba. Nate and Joan succeeded in raising enough money to construct a new building for the Nuevo Mundo operation and to move its equipment from a lot owned by the Velásquez family. Ivo broke ground.

As Ivo was organizing the move to El Abra, he was excited that he would be able to operate out of space commensurate with the long list of projects he was committed to. He had already decided that Nuevo Mundo needed a building in which mechanics could repair and maintain the heavy equipment. But Segundo wondered what opportunity might be hidden in the situation at hand. He arranged a time to meet with Ivo and Blanca to review the plans for the property. He wanted to be sure they made the best possible use of the new space.

Ever vigilant as to the needs of their compatriotas, the three siblings talked about ways they might develop the El Abra space to respond to concerns that had been nagging at them.

Ivo shared his worry about the lack of people power for Nuevo Mundo projects. Most of the workers available lacked the skills needed to complete his long list of construction projects. He elaborated on his consistent difficulty in finding Bolivian workers with the expertise needed to work on NM's major infrastructure projects. He feared he would soon have to delay an anticipated road or water project because he could not find workers with the skills required. NM might well have community and governmental cooperation, the equipment, and even the money for a road or water project and still be hampered by a lack of workers who knew how to handle heavy equipment. The huge machines were in short supply in Bolivia, and experienced workers were scarce.

After listening to Ivo's worries, Segundo reminded Blanca and Ivo about a recent report from interns at the University of Minnesota's Hubert H. Humphrey School of Public Affairs. The three of them had helped the students complete interviews with many of the campesinos benefiting from the water projects they created with Mano a Mano.

The campesinos were uniformly thrilled with their newly stable supply of water. The size and quality of their produce had dramatically increased. They were full of ideas and questions emerging from their experience of living with the infusion of sufficient water. They bemoaned the changes in their climate, citing the greater and greater dryness over the recent decades and the deterioration of their soil. This is why they had so desperately needed their new sistema. But now that they had the water, they were frustrated by the limits of their capacity to use it effectively.

Spurred by the interns' report, Segundo, Blanca, and Boris Rodriguez, a Nuevo Mundo engineer, had recently visited several of the villages, talking personally to many campesinos. The campesinos spoke of the abundant potatoes they had eaten as children, potatoes they had stopped planting due to a lack of water. Others said they wanted to learn to plant vegetables that they had never raised, so their children could grow up healthy. And others talked of returning to the old custom of planting native corns. They were eager to reclaim the lost agricultural practices that their ancestors had used when rain was plentiful and their families were well fed.

The campesinos knew that the continuing drought and depletion of their soil had seriously limited productivity. Now that water was available, they wanted to learn more about the crop diversity and the strong erosion-control practices of years past. They knew their ancianos had many ways to use the water available to them, but they had forgotten those practices and didn't know how to recapture them.

The campesinos had specific concerns: "How can we best use our new water to raise old and new types of vegetables? How do we protect our crops from the harsh cold winds that sweep across our fields? How can we heal our land?"

They also presented a new worry, one flowing from the health education they absorbed from their clinics: "How can we clean our water so that our children don't get sick?"

Segundo immediately saw the connection between their and Mano a Mano's concerns: "What we are seeing here is an opportunity to address what we call capacity building—not only for construction workers but also for the campesinos."

Blanca was excited about the possibilities they could consider. She reminded them that Mano a Mano had a long history of listening to what rural Bolivians said they needed.

Segundo added, "Why not use our space to include training in both equipment operation and agriculture?"

The Work Continues

Segundo spoke of their 15 years of experience in responding to the training needs of nurses, health promoters, and physicians at rural clinics and in the Mano a Mano Bolivia office in Cochabamba. He said, "We know how to give our compatriotas what they want to improve their lives. Now we can build on our health-education experience and expand our view of education and training."

All agreed. The three began to talk about how best to proceed with what they began to call the "Center for Ecological Agriculture." Meshing the long-deferred wish for Nuevo Mundo machine shops with the newly understood need for training farmers and equipment operators was characteristic of Mano a Mano's continuing balancing act: it honored the organization's commitment to initiate, maintain, and perfect the many Bolivian projects as it simultaneously listened and, when possible, responded to new requests from their compatriotas.

Segundo phoned Joan that evening about the conversation that had ended with three excited Velásquezes eager to address training needs. She became an immediate champion of the combined effort. As Blanca's responsibilities included the piloting of new projects, Segundo, Joan, and Dan Narr agreed she would naturally take the lead on the farmer-training initiative. Nuevo Mundo had been training its mechanics in a gravel parking lot. Now Ivo could look forward to doing that in a clean, new building.

When Segundo and Joan met with the U.S. board, they explained that the El Abra property would be the perfect spot for a capacity-building project for campesinos. Segundo explained, "We are going in to build the Nuevo Mundo repair-and-maintenance center here as well as a storage area for NM equipment. Those buildings take only half of the space. While we are constructing them, why not incorporate some training space for campesinos?"

Joan said, "Think of the capacity it will engender!"

Considering the clear need for farmer training and the land available in El Abra, the board supported the idea on the condition of devel-

264

oping new funding. Joan commented on how much the project realized the Mano a Mano mission "to create partnerships with impoverished communities that improve health and increase economic well-being." The U.S. office immediately began developing a fundraising strategy leaning toward foundations and individuals who had been generous during the evolution of Nuevo Mundo.

In anticipation of funding from the United States, Ivo, Segundo, and Blanca sat down to finalize their plan for the incorporation of farmer and worker training on the El Abra land. They had in hand a map of the property with the layout of the planned building as they debated how best to address so many new activities and agendas in the limited space.

As the three grew weary of their conversation, Segundo said, "You see there [pointing to a spot in the layout and hitting the table with the side of his hand] is where Ivo will be with the Nuevo Mundo repair shop, right next to the parking area for heavy equipment and dump trucks [hitting the table again], which is next to the agricultural training center building [hitting the table again]."

He ended by pounding on an empty space outside the building. With a final bang of his hand, he added, "And right there I think we should have experimental fields and ponds for the villagers who want to learn new methods."

Blanca interrupted her brother, "Yes, Segundo, that makes sense. But remember, the campesinos who want to learn new techniques live far away from Cochabamba." She had agreed to lead the agricultural training program and was already anchoring her thoughts in her Bolivian compatriotas.

Segundo picked up the familiar reality check he so often gets from Blanca and Joan: Mano a Mano must always start with the agenda and reality of the Bolivian people it partners with. When Blanca asked, "And where will all these villagers sleep?" Segundo hit a spot on the plan alongside the education building, announcing with a flourish,

The Work Continues

"And the *residencia* [residence or dormitory] will be in this building."

And so it was. With careful planning and extreme frugality Mano a Mano constructed two buildings, one for the Nuevo Muendo repair shop where its mechanics would be trained and another for agricultural training, with a residencia on the side. Mano a Mano Internacional raised the funds to construct the training facilities now standing on the outskirts of Cochabamba. After Blanca agreed to oversee the farmer-training enterprise as part of Mano a Mano Internacional, she named the El Abra demonstration center Centro de Entrenamiento Agroecológico (Center for Ecological Agriculture, or CEA).

Segundo traveled frequently to Bolivia as this project began to take shape. He often phoned Joan to describe the gradual transformation of five acres of hard, dry ground into a lovely urban farm with demonstration ponds, plantings of fruit and vegetables, and animal pens. Joan had not been in Cochabamba in years because its altitude was too great for the capacity of her lungs. He told her he would send pictures online but went on to say that the training facility had the shiny brick walls and red roof characteristic of the Mano a Mano structures across the road and across the countryside. It was a stable and safe place to do Mano a Mano's work.

Segundo's voice showed his excitement: "There is an operating shop where our machines can be repaired and new heavy-equipment operators can be trained. The CEA is everything we had hoped for. It is full of ideas for how the campesinos can apply what they learn, in sparse but comfortable educational rooms. There is a special place for simple tools like sand filters, to make water potable. There are gardens, where they have started to plant fruit trees and are experimenting with new plants. There is a plan to help farmers extend their growing season with community or family greenhouses. And there are two sample ponds where campesinos can learn new ways to collect rain and runoff water."

Joan could see the project in her mind's eye, and she said, "Now tell me all about the residencia." And Segundo told her in detail about

266

the big, open rooms that can house up to 30 villagers coming from the mountains to Cochabamba.

"How wonderful!" Joan responded. She noted that such follow-through regarding the campesinos' search for agricultural skills was exactly what they meant when they talked about capacity building. And she expressed her relief that more of the Bolivian Mano a Mano work was situated in stable and functional space.

Greenhouses

Several months after the CEA garden had been planted, Segundo got a call from Blanca, telling him about the latest group of villagers to arrive there unannounced. The men had come from Jironkota, a community that had partnered with Mano a Mano in 2012 to build a clinic. The men had heard a rumor in the mountains: "In Cochabamba Mano a Mano is teaching campesinos about making plants grow in new ways."

The men in the group certainly welcomed the stable water available for their fields since the municipio had helped them build their irrigation system. But now they were having trouble getting their vegetables to survive the cold climate. They knew Mano a Mano was a long way away, and they had no transportation to get there. So they had walked until they hitched a ride on top of a potato truck that happened to be headed for Cochabamba.

The CEA was not expecting the new trainees when the men arrived, but they had quickly made it known they were from Jironkota, old partners of Mano a Mano. Blanca said later, "Of course, we accepted them without benefit of preparation."

Blanca soon reached agronomist Camila Yavira on her cellphone. Camila came to the CEA and took the men through the first phase of the training curriculum. They toured the garden and ponds and viewed the low-tech tools built since the CEA had opened. They were intrigued by a biodigestor that converted manure to methane gas (the

The Work Continues

residue to return to the soil), by the biosand filters for water and the greenhouses.

The agronomist helped the farmers identify their most pressing need. They told her that the cold winds on their side of the mountain killed their young vegetable plants. They wanted to build a greenhouse.

Blanca settled them into the residencia, and the next day they worked with CEA volunteers teaching them to build greenhouses. They were familiar with the process of making and using adobe brick. They had used adobes to build their own houses. It took them just a day to learn how to build the smaller (three-by-five-meter) adobe structure and add proper materials for the roof. The campesinos returned to their village eager for the delivery of materials needed to complete two greenhouses that would prolong their growing season.

A few months later, Segundo, Joan, and Blanca went back and forth on email and by phone, planning a trip for a group from Unity Church–Unitarian in St. Paul to visit Mano a Mano's work in Bolivia. A visit to a specific program in Bolivia was always a part of such a trip. The three decided that the Jironkota greenhouse project would be an ideal way to introduce the Unity visitors to a classic Mano a Mano partnership.

Twelve members of Unity Church-Unitarian joined Mano a Mano in Bolivia in March 2014, to become an integral part of Jironkota's greenhouse project. They piled into two SUVs to follow a dump truck carrying hardware and roofing materials for the greenhouses. After a long drive into the mountains, the volunteers worked alongside the Jironkota villagers for two days, putting the greenhouses together. The visitors slept in the Jironkota clinic.

In June 2014 Segundo was "skyping" with Blanca to plan another Bolivian trip, this time for U.S. teachers interested in a cross-cultural teaching experience. To his surprise, one of the Jironkota leaders appeared in Blanca's office. Hearing Segundo's voice over the computer, he asked Blanca to speak with him. After their greeting, he said, "Don

Segundo, our vegetables survived the cold in the greenhouses, and they are ready to be picked. But we are waiting for you to return so you can see them for yourself. Then you can go back to the United States and tell all the travelers who worked with us that the greenhouses are a success."

Segundo returned to Bolivia in June and drove to Jironkota to share in the harvest. And while he was at the CEA in El Abra, Camila Yavaria, the agronomist, showed him a list of 70 more requests from the area surrounding Jironkota for Mano a Mano to partner with villagers in building greenhouses for their crops.

A Gala

The volunteers helping to build the Jironkata greenhouse in March returned in time to attend Mano a Mano's Annual (fundraising) Gala, which celebrated the organization's 20th anniversary that year.

A young woman with a lovely Inca profile greeted incoming guests, offering each a handsome nametag directing them to their seats. More than a few guests recognized her as the grown-up version of the little Peruvian adoptee who had brought Joan and Segundo together with her mothers Deb Bushway and Deb Kotcher nearly 20 years earlier. Some knew the story of her singing "Twinkle, Twinkle Little Star" during the meeting that arrived at the naming and incorporation of Mano a Mano. Others recognized her brother, Paco, who had followed her into her family from another part of the southern hemisphere.

Chris Ver Ploeg and Nancy White sat together, as elegant as Gloria MacRae, who gazed happily at the crowd. She thought of the time in 2000 she had flown to Cochabamba for the dedication of one of the earliest clinics for which she had helped raise funds. Few of those greeting her could forget that her 70th birthday party had jumpstarted Mano a Mano's clinic program. Deb Kotcher looked over the guest list with Isabel and gathered up checks from those who hadn't prepaid for their tickets to the gala. She smiled as she saw Paco embracing a family friend.

Segundo, uncharacteristically dressed in a suit, moved from table to table, welcoming guests with a robust hug or handshake. He stopped often to bring two or three people together to share a potentially mutual Mano a Mano interest. This often reticent man bubbled with energy as he talked about Mano a Mano's work in Bolivia.

Dana Dallavalle, along with Nate Knatterud-Hubinger and Dan Narr, moved at the edge of the chattering crowd, attending to the details that would make the gala a success. Joan sat at a front table talking with each in a long line of waiting guests. Dressed in a soft pink suit and a pair of ballet slippers, she listened to each person talking to her as if he or she were the most important person she'd ever encountered.

Segundo returned to his seat beside Joan as Dan approached the microphone. Dan greeted everyone and introduced Ivo Velásquez, who had traded his Bolivian work clothes for a nicely fitting suit. Every year a key Bolivian leaves his or her Mano a Mano work to attend this event. Each is a vivid reminder of the deep ties behind this international collaboration.

After introducing Ivo, Dan presented Segundo, who accompanied Joan to the microphone, his hand under her elbow. Segundo spoke quietly and passionately about Bolivia and its unending need. He reminded the diners that there were still thousands of isolated villages without clinics, acres and acres of land too parched to produce anything, and more and more people eager to work with Mano a Mano to improve their lives. Joan and Segundo sat down.

Dan returned to the podium to remind members of the audience that their contributions are the seed money enabling the Bolivian people to improve their lives through partnerships with Mano a Mano.

The mood shifted when Dan called in an auctioneer, who enthusiastically presented items for bidding—a trip to the Bahamas, a Bolivian dinner for eight with Joan and Segundo, a week at a cabin in the north woods. Chris Ver Ploeg's bid started the auction. Many of the people Mano a Mano had connected with seemed eager to share their wealth.

Few of Mano a Mano "family" members attending at the gala could afford to make the bids going well into the thousands of dollars that some auction items merited. Most of Mano a Mano's board members, volunteers, and staff members have more dedication than money. They enjoyed the gala. They knew they were part of the passionate work of Mano a Mano in Bolivia and the United States. They appreciated the generosity of the gala guests who bid enthusiastically for the more expensive items.

Dana was pleased with the successful gala; she came away with a better understanding of the organization's place in the struggle to increase the funding base for the Bolivian projects. Each gala demonstrates Mano a Mano's continual crossing of cultural, language, national, and economic differences. Mano a Mano enables volunteers and affluent philanthropists in Minnesota to connect with the farmers in the mountains and valleys around and beyond Cochabamba. It reaches back and forth between the United States and Bolivia to support development done by Bolivians on their own terms.

'I Knew You Would Not Forget Us'
There is an unsettling incongruity between the almost lavish U.S. Mano a Mano galas and the realities of the Bolivians who collaborate with Mano a Mano. Ivo and the other Velásquez family members who grace the gala each year are on but a brief hiatus from their homeland. They are Bolivians working with Bolivians.

Ivo, sitting back in his chair at a table at the edge of one recent gala, watched the auction, wondering what Eloy Montaño would think of the event. Montaño is one of Ivo's favorite community leaders, one who carries the entrepreneurial tendencies so familiar among the Velásquez family. Having just read the transcript of an interview that volunteers Andrea Bond and Charles Skrief conducted with Montaño, Ivo told Segundo how much this man reminded him of their father, Epifanio, who had recently died at age 91. The family had mourned in the apar-

The Work Continues

tamento his son built for him, his body laid out on the long dining table he had built to his size.

Eloy Montaño was from Sancayani, in the dry, cold highlands above Cochabamba. Eloy had more education than Epifanio's three months' worth, but he showed the same dedication to his family's education and the same entrepreneurial spirit. Eloy remembered his long trek to neighboring Tiraque, the closest village with a school. He told the Mano a Mano interviewers: "Every day, when I was a child, I walked two hours each way to learn to read and write."

Eloy Montaño also spoke of working in the fields, driving his oxen, and irrigating the soil: "Sometimes when it was cold, rainy, and windy, we worked in the dark, capturing winter rain to survive, with only a candle for light."

By the time of the interview a husband and father of five children, Eloy grew potatoes on land he had tilled all his life. Borrowing money from the community sindicato to augment the savings he eked from farming, he bought a truck. With a vehicle to transport his potatoes to market, he increased his income a bit and developed a small business carrying potatoes and cargo for his vecinos.

After paying back his loan from the sindicato, Eloy Montaño continued to augment his farming so as to pay for his children's education: "I don't want my children to suffer like I did. I want them to be professionals." He was proud of his oldest daughter, a student at the university. But potato farming was becoming less stable as the drought increased.

In 2010 Montaño came to Mano a Mano with his vecinos. They had heard that Ivo Velásquez knew how to build reservoirs. They told him that their years of struggle with picks and shovels to manage the erratic water were no match for the boulders and landslides they encountered: "Now we are often without water and our potato crops are lost."

They asked Ivo to work with them. Nuevo Mundo joined the villagers of Sancayani in their quest for water. Dan and Segundo pulled the

272

Caterpillar Foundation into the effort. With pride, Eloy Montaño described the manual labor that the villagers provided: "We carried sand for cement, laid stones for the reservoir wall with the Mano a Mano engineers, and distributed rock to make the muddy roads passable for the big equipment. We did it for the first reservoir and now for the second one, too. *Somos como familia. Todos trabajamos por igual.* [We are like family. We work as one.]"

Now more than 2 million cubic meters of water serving more than 5,000 people flows through the two reservoirs in Montaño's community. Asked what the new stable water supply means to him and his vecinos, Eloy answered, "With more water, we have enough crops left to sell and more income. More income means better health for my children and my wife and better education for my children."

When the interviewers asked Eloy about his hopes for Sancayani, he responded, "We need to learn how to grow vegetables and better strains of potatoes. We need to become experts about our irrigation system. And I want my children to learn how to use the Internet."

Eloy Montaño was working on his father's fields the weekend he was interviewed. He explained that there were no men to hire because so many have gone to Argentina or Cochabamba for work. That day he had hired two women and two girls to help. He doesn't allow his oldest daughter to work in the field: "She must study . . ."

Segundo laughed as he said to his brother, "Doesn't that sound just like Dad? Remember how he excused the younger ones from making tiles so they could study?"

As Segundo was about to rejoin Blanca, he asked Ivo whether any heavy Mano a Mano equipment would be passing near Laguna Sulti soon. When Ivo said a convoy on the way to Punata would go by the next week, Segundo told him about visiting his Tio Alberto on his latest trip to Bolivia: "I ran into Primitivo Montaño, the *bomba* [pump] manager at the reservoir we built there." Segundo reminded Ivo of the tall young man wearing a red T-shirt and baseball cap that day.

The Work Continues

Ivo Daniel, Tio Alberto, and Segundo at his former Laguna Sulti home

Segundo had learned that the villagers were grateful for the newly abundant water on the sistema de riego schedule that Primitivo monitors, that their harvests are much bigger now. The young man had smiled hopefully as he looked down and said, "We hope that Ivo can return and help us build *un parque pequeño* [a little park] with trees and *bancos* [benches] around the reservoir. It is the only place other than the fields that isn't parched from the drought. It would be good if people could rest and have a day in the country after working in their fields."

Segundo said he had promised Primitivo to ask Ivo about the park. Ivo responded that he was sure Laguna Sulti's parque could be put on the list of approved projects. Segundo saw Blanca looking toward him and added, "And by the way, Ivo, how are the airstrips coming?"

274

The brothers spoke intently about the airstrips that Nuevo Mundo was building for the Apoyo Aéreo planes. They agreed that landing strips must be built—and maintained—free of animals or debris or erosion from wind or rain. The grass or gravel landing runways must be safe. A pilot must be sure these safety issues have been addressed before he lands. This is not a public airport but a community-built one. It has no one available to communicate with the pilot about whether it is empty and safe for landing.

Segundo asked Ivo whether community leaders were selecting a villager to oversee the safety of the runway. Ivo said the airstrip assessment training program for the designated villagers was in the beginning stage. Villagers at each airstrip would learn how to measure ground density and communicate with the pilot via shortwave radio about the status of the runway. Nuevo Mundo, Apoyo Aéreo, and the villages were working together to make emergency and jornada flights safe and reliable.

As Segundo walked back to Blanca, his mind was full of all the things he knew needed to be done in Bolivia. Every time he went home or talked with one of his siblings about their projects—old, new, or hoped for—he was overwhelmed by the things that need to be done, by how many of his compatriotas looked to Mano a Mano with hopes for a better life. He never quite shook off the memory of the women from El Palmar who came up to him as he was leaving the inauguración of her village's first road, looked him in the eye, and confidently confessed, "I knew you would not forget us."

Inés approaching the Candelaria hacienda

Afterword

Hacienda Revisited

The next time Segundo traveled to Bolivia, Ivo suggested he go to Laguna Sulti to meet with Primitivo Montaño, the bomba manager, to pin down details for the parque he had requested. Nuevo Mundo was about to move some heavy equipment along the road running by their old Laguna Sulti home. Ivo could have the workers stop for a day to build a small parque. But he needed to know more about what Primitivo had in mind.

Blanca overheard her brothers' conversation and asked Segundo whether she and her mother could go along. Inés was worried about a longtime Laguna Sulti friend she hadn't seen for years—the woman was ill, and Inés hoped to visit her.

Early the next morning Segundo, Inés, and Blanca drove out of the city toward Laguna Sulti, reminiscing about the years they had lived in the Cochabamba Valley. Segundo told Blanca about his memories of the hacienda where he had lived as a child. Then he said, "Let's stop there. It's right on the way to Laguna Sulti. Mom would love that."

Leaving the main highway, they turned into San Benito, a little town with a sign on its biggest building claiming it to be *La Capital de Durazno* (The Capital of Peaches). As they made their way to the Centro, Inés murmured in Quechua, "Your father used to come here every three days to pick up supplies." Blanca and Segundo assumed she was speaking of the time they had lived on the nearby hacienda.

Getting out of the car, the little group walked slowly through a square of flowering trees and twittering birds. The señora held her daughter's hand as they walked slowly through the park. She was dressed much as on earlier visits to San Benito—in a dark skirt and leggings, a blouse as white as her now long braids. Inés looked quizzically at the statue standing in the middle of the square, a stone image of a strong hand holding a peach appearing strangely fresh and soft. The three walked back to the car, the señora giving her son directions to the hacienda.

Segundo followed a dirt road running through uncultivated soil studded with kilns twice as high as the adjoining adobe homes. A mound of scrap lumber sat near every kiln for the firing of the adobe and red bricks piled near the road. Segundo and Blanca chatted about a kiln owned by their paternal grandfather, then reminisced about the air-dried tiles comprising the family's first enterprise.

Several women wearing white, wide-brimmed hats approached the car as it moved slowly through the community of brick makers. Segundo realized the women saw the three of them as potential customers, there to buy bricks. After they chatted a moment, he drove off in the big tan SUV; he didn't want to raise their hopes for a sale.

Beyond the brick-making community, the terrain was filled with plots of corn. Here and there a small building, not big enough for more than one person, stood amidst the growing corn. Each was for the person responsible for the safety of the plot.

Segundo reminded his mother, "I was just a small boy when I was sent to just such a building to watch for problems when Dad was farming in Laguna Sulti."

Inés nodded in agreement.

Water seemed to be everywhere in the broad valley. The brick-making women talked about never having seen so much rain. Inés almost continually commented as to how Segundo might negotiate the water running here and there over the road. She brightened as they passed over a small bridge, to find open fields as far as the eye could see: "This is where the property starts."

There was nothing but open land for several miles; then Inés called out, "This is it."

A clump of buildings was visible far out on the horizon. As they drove closer, Inés spoke of the outlying buildings, how they had been for the animals, and how the patrona didn't like meat much, so they didn't serve it often. She slipped into the details of the past, pointing here and there for Blanca to see. Inés reminded Blanca that she had been very young when the family left Laguna Sulti.

As they drove closer to the hacienda, Inés pointed to the remains of a towerlike structure with holes still evident in its crumbling adobe walls. She said that was where they kept the doves that she retrieved to prepare for the patrona. Having heard this story many times before, Blanca and Segundo nodded.

Where the road turned from the outbuildings toward the hacienda, rushing water covered it. The señora instructed Segundo about the safety of crossing. Finally another SUV drove past them through the water. Segundo followed. He parked the car in the road, which ended at the village.

As Inés got out of the car, she focused on the buildings beyond a small park. She told Segundo and Blanca she was sad to see the place so different, so deteriorated: "You see, I lived here for 18 years."

Inés took her daughter's hand as they walked away from the several buildings that made up the little community. Segundo explained to Blanca that when he was little there had been a village here, much like this rather ramshackle set of buildings. But then it was for the people who worked at the hacienda: "There were hundreds of cattle and, of course, farming, in this valley, all the way to the mountains you see around us. Now the hacienda buildings are used as a school, with offices for its teachers and administrators and a dormitory for students. The pongueaje of the past are gone."

Segundo looked back at the overflowing water that had nearly deterred them from the hacienda. He told Blanca that their father, who had worked these fields, said that when the patrón was in charge, it was a very different place. The system worked better then. The patrón made sure everything was looked after. He saw to it that the rivers were kept clean and protected, that they didn't flood like the overflowing stream they had just driven through.

He added, "The patrón was so powerful that he could force the people to do all that work. But after the 1952 revolution, everybody was independent and it didn't matter anymore."

As they walked through the little park toward the buildings, Inés reminded them that the hacienda was called Candelaria when she lived there. And Segundo described the house that dominated his early childhood: "There were three patios: The first for the patrón, the second where our parents lived, and the third where we lived when I was born. The house was very Spanish."

Pointing to a big, modern building attached to the older structure, he said, "This is an addition that the community built to the main house, which is part of the school."

A big man approached the three as they talked in the small park, moving toward the old building, a small church close on one side. He introduced himself as Epifanio, the same name as Inés's husband and Segundo and Blanca's father. After much conversation about birthplaces and old relationships, they agreed they were somehow related.

The new relative pulled a heavy bunch of keys from his pocket and asked Inés whether she would like to see the church and the old hacienda building. She smiled acquiescence, and they all walked slowly toward the small bell tower of the stone church.

The bell tower at Candelaria

Segundo lay his hand on the stone wall of the tower, quietly saying, "My dad helped build this. I remember."

Epifanio unlocked the church door as Inés stood quietly by, still holding Blanca's hand. The little group stood in the doorway, looking into the dark church.

Inés murmured, "This is where I was married. The patrona told your dad to go to San Benito and get a license, and then we had a big celebration."

The church was small, with paper decorations draped across the space. All agreed it must be in use, as such decoration was a thing of the present—it would not have been there when Inés was a young woman.

She walked slowly to the front and stood next to Blanca a long time, whispering stories to her daughter of what used to be.

Meanwhile the new Epifanio spoke of the recent renovation of the park and the addition to the original hacienda to make it into a school. He asked Segundo whether the señora would like to go into the school. She nodded, and they all walked out. They passed by the bell tower that was the work of her husband (and Segundo and Blanca's father) and through a door into what Segundo had described as the first patio.

Just as Inés and her children came through the door, a bell rang, and a group of chattering teenagers engulfed them. School had ended for the day. It was hard to get a sense of the place amidst the commotion. But the patio soon emptied.

Inés in the Candelaria church

Part of the old hacienda in 2013

    The birds chirping in the park outside the courtyard gently broke the sudden silence. The courtyard stood much as when Inés's mother brought her there as a girl. An olive tree, easily spanning 30 to 40 feet, spread from one end of the courtyard to the other.

    The addition to the hacienda stood off to one side. It seemed to be a dormitory, as clothes were hanging from windows and young people leaned over its windowsills. It would not have been so casual and youth-filled a scene in the señora's time. But the touch of modernity did not distract from the charm of the orderly but idiosyncratic buildings surrounding the courtyard. It was a calm and contained space.

    Inés and her two children were still standing in the first patio beneath the olive tree, talking of the past, when four men approached. One of the men, taller and younger than the others, introduced himself as the principal of the school, the others as teachers. After they all shook hands, the principal spoke directly to Inés. Then Inés told them about her life in the hacienda, Segundo translating his mother's Quechua words to her listeners' Spanish.

Hacienda Revisited

The conversation turned to the family's history in the nearby village of Laguna Sulti and its recent involvement in the area through Mano a Mano. Then, as Inés turned to walk farther into the hacienda, Blanca handed to each man one of the glossy Mano a Mano calendars she typically carries with her.

Inés took Segundo and Blanca through an opening in the courtyard to show them where she and Epifanio lived and where Ivo, Cati, and Segundo were born—the little house along the outside wall of the first patio and the inside wall of the second, right next to the rooms Inés said were storerooms. The second patio, smaller than the first, opened to the third, which housed animals and the other people who worked for the patrona. This is where the patrona had built for the Velásquezes additional housing, the space now empty but for a restroom in one corner.

Segundo used his cellphone to take a photo of his mother in front of his birthplace. Then Inés announced that she was ready to leave. The three walked slowly from the third to the second to the first patio, there finding the principal and teachers talking over the Mano a Mano calendar. They had newly learned that Mano a Mano helped build schools in rural areas. The principal was eager to talk with Blanca and Segundo about adding classrooms to this school.

The siblings slipped easily into their Mano a Mano roles to describe the process the principal must follow in making such a request. Then Segundo's cellphone rang.

"Quick," he said, laughing. "We have to go outside." He took his mother's arm and began walking to the gate. Passing through it, he called back to the principal, "Call the phone number in the calendar, and ask for Dr. José Velásquez!"

The phone call was from Ivo, who was calling from Mano a Mano's single-engine plane to bring the Velásquez trio to the park outside the hacienda. Blanca led her mother to sit on a bench near the church tower. Segundo stood nearby, peering intently at the sky. He told his

Blanca and Inés visiting the hacienda

mother her grandson Ivo Daniel was up in the sky and wanted to buzz his *abuela* (grandmother). He was flying his namesake Tio Ivo to a meeting in the Beni.

After several minutes, Segundo ran to his mother and pointed to an airplane tipping its wings as it flew toward them, then up.

With her hand warding the sun from her eyes, Inés saw the plane, smiled, and said, "So that's Ivo Daniel up there?" She had moved quickly from past to present in watching one of her grandsons, a licensed pilot for Mano a Mano, fly his uncle, her son, to do the family's work.

Segundo told Inés that after Ivo was done with the meeting about building an airstrip for Mano a Mano, Ivo Daniel would pick up a patient at another airstrip to fly to a hospital in Cochabamba.

Segundo and Blanca, with mother in hand, walked back to the SUV to take Inés to her sick friend and meet with Primitivo about the proposed parque in Laguna Sulti.

Appendix A

The Mano a Mano Model

1. Community leaders come to a Mano a Mano office in Bolivia or to a member of the staff and make a specific request for a clinic, school, road, water, or other project.
2. The request is put on a list from which Mano a Mano chooses projects based on need, viability, and available funding.
3. Every partner has a clear role:
   - Mana a Mano USA raises seed money.
   - The Mano a Mano counterpart in Bolivia develops the necessary partnership and implements the project.
   - The community provides land, an average of 4,000 hours of manual labor, and 2 to 5 percent of the funding.
   - Local governments provide 20 to 50 percent of the funding.
4. The community and municipality retain control and ownership of the project after its completion.
5. Sustainability—through a strong sense of community ownership, housing for clinic staff, continuing education, airstrip management programs, agricultural experiments and training, and so forth—is built into every project.

Appendix B

Mano a Mano Sister Organizations

- Mano a Mano International Partners, founded in 1994 as Mano a Mano Medical Resources, also referred to as Mano a Mano USA:

    For setting the organization's vision and mission and for fundraising, supply collection and transport, research and evaluation, volunteer coordination, and travel

- Mano a Mano Bolivia, founded in 1999:

    For building infrastructure for health and education and co-administering a network of community medical centers

- Mano a Mano Nuevo Mundo (New World), founded in 2005:

    For increasing food security and economic development—by building water reservoirs and roads

- Mano a Mano Apoyo Aéreo (Air Support), founded in 2005:

    For emergency air rescue and the support of Mano a Mano programs

- Mano a Mano Internacional, founded in 2012:

    For clearance of medical cargo through customs, hosting of foreign travelers, seeking donations from within Bolivia, and piloting new initiatives

Notes

Chapter 1

1. Here and following: Benjamin Kohl and Linda Farthing in *Impasse in Bolivia: Neoliberal Hegemony and Popular Resistance* (New York: Zed, 2006) present the low-income Bolivia of the 1980s and thus a political context for the years during which the Velásquez family moved from its rural indigenous home into urban social entrepreneurship. The frequently changing government responded to neoliberal policies that emphasized both democratic participation and free markets structured to benefit private and corporate interests over the public good. Bolivia instituted "privatization, the strengthening of local and national democratic structures, and the devolution of central responsibilities to regional communities through administrative decentralization" (p. 13).

   The neoliberal devolution of resources and political power to the local level reinforced the communal nature of the Quechua and other Andean communities grounded in the ayllu tradition. Already operating as effective, locally controlled communities, they were ready to make good use of resources. These Andean indigenous communities grew into a powerful political resistance to neoliberal policies. The movement led to the election of Evo Morales, Bolivia's first indigenous president, in 2005.

   See also Michael E. Mosley, Ch. 3, "The Inca Model of Statecraft," in Mosley, *The Incas and Their Ancestors: The Archaeology of Peru* (New York: Thames and Hudson, 1992), 49–53.

Notes

Chapter 2

1. Tom Perreault, "Custom and Contradiction: Rural Water Governance and the Politics of *Usos y Costumbres* in Bolivia's Irrigators' Movement," *Annals of the Association of American Geographers* 98 (4):834–54.

2. Union Cristiana Evangélica is a Protestant denomination representing a small but noticeable minority in Cochabamba, an oddity in the very Catholic country of Bolivia. Estimates of evangelicals in Bolivia range between 10 and 20 percent of the population. They are unique in their rejection of alcohol and coca and known for their uprightness and industriousness.

   Andrew Canessa, an expert on evangelicalism in Bolivia reports in "Contesting Hybridity: Evangelistas and Katoristas in Highland Bolivia," *Journal of Latin American Studies* 32 (2000): 115-44: "One of the curious things about evangelistas in Bolivia is that they are not always liked but they are widely respected as honest, upstanding, and industrious" (p. 142). He goes on to say that their practices provided evangelistas with a sense of moral superiority noted by others. Thus many evangelistas transcended, even ignored, the prejudice that many indigenous people experienced in the urban environment.

3. Graham Tipple, "The Place of Home-based Enterprises in the Informal Sector: Evidence from Cochabamba, New Delhi, Surabaya and Pretoria," *Urban Studies* 42 (4):618.

4. When Ines brought the chicken to the racecar driver, she emulated Jared Diamond's suggestion of "compensation" as an effective strategy in resolving conflict. Diamond devotes an entire chapter (pp. 79–118) in *The World Since Yesterday: What Can We Learn from Traditional Societies?* (New York: Penguin, 2012) to the informal and ceremonial strategies he discovered. He cites the death of a child in an automobile accident in Papua, New Guinea, as an example of compensatory resolution of the conflict between the family of a dead child and the driver of the truck that killed him. He acknowledges that while there is no real compensation possible for the death of a child, there are ways to acknowledge harm and allow people to move on.

   Diamond would see Inés's offer of a chicken to the driver as a hopeful and personal approach that, while not resolving the accusation, allowed Segundo to stay on in his role as helper, then quietly move on. Such informal, respectful attention to conflict resolution is a Velásquez family skill that Segundo and Inés's other children acquired and used effectively as they moved into adulthood.

Notes

Chapter 4
1. Saul Alinsky, *Reveille for Radicals* (New York: Vintage, 1989), 54.
2. Benjamin Kohl and Linda Farthing, *Impasse in Bolivia*, 53.

Chapter 6
1. *See* http://www.brainyquote.com/quotes/quotes/m/margaretme100502. html (accessed Nov. 9, 2015).
2. Michael E. Mosley, "The Inca Model of Statecraft," 49–53.

Chapter 8
1. Amartyra Sen, *Development as Freedom* (New York: Anchor, 1999), 297-98.

Chapter 9
1. Jared Diamond, *The World Until Yesterday*, 277.

Chapter 10
1. Democracy Now! *The Cochabamba Water Wars: Marcela Olivera Reflects on the Tenth Anniversary of the Popular Uprising against Bechtel and the Privatization of the City's Water Supply,* April 19, 2010. *See* www.democracynow.org/2010/4/19/the_cochabamba_water_wars_marcella_olivera (accessed June 25, 2015).
2. Here and following, Tom Perreault, "Custom and Contradiction," 840.

Glossary

Spanish and Quechua words and phrases are translated upon their first appearance in the text. The translations of those appearing more than once in the text are listed below.

Adobes	Mud bricks used in construction
Alcalde/Alcaldesa	Male/female mayor
Ancianos	Elders
Apartamento	Apartment building
Apoyo aéreo	Air support
Asamblea	Founding members, ruling body
Atajados	Farm ponds
Ayllu	An Andean system of collective decision-making
Barrio	Neighborhood
Blusa bordada	Embroidered blouse
Campo	Countryside
Campesino/a	Male peasant/female peasant
Capataz	Overseer
Centro de Salud	Health center

292

Glossary

Chicha	Alcoholic beverage made from fermented corn
Cocina	Kitchen
Compañero/a	Male/female companion
Compatriotas	Country men or women
Colegas	Colleagues
Departamento	Department: similar to a state in the United States
El agua es nuestro.	The water is ours.
La familia	The family
Ganas	Motivation
Gobierno	Government
Gringo/a	Anglo/a from North America
Hacienda	Large land holding
Hacendada/o	Female/male owner of hacienda
Herencia	Inheritance
Inauguración y entrega	Opening and delivery
Jornada	Workday or journey for work at weekend clinic
Junta vecinal	Community council
Leche	Milk
Mamanchaj	Greater mother, grandmother
Mano a mano	Hand to hand
Madrina	Godmother
Mordida	Bribe
Municipio	Similar to U.S. county, not a city
Nuevo Mundo	New World
Pachamama	Mother Earth
Parque	Park
Parroquia	Parish
Patrón	Male landowner
Patrona	Female landowner

Glossary

Pollera	Traditional skirts
Pongueaje	Indentured servant
Puesto	Open marketplace/ stand of specific seller
Regantes	Irrigators
Salteñas	Sweet, meat-filled pastries
Sindicato	Community union based on occupation
Si Dios quiere . . .	God willing . . .
Sistema de riego	Irrigation system
Tia/o	Aunt/uncle
Trabajadores, trabajador/a	Workers, male/female worker
Usos y costumbres	Customary practices
Vecinos	Neighbors

Index

Page numbers in *italics* refer to photographs.

Entries for Joan and Segundo Velásquez and others appearing on many pages are limited to key references.

Abraham, Karen, 254

Apoyo Aéreo, see Mano a Mano Apoyo Aéreo

Arce, Héctor, 219–23, 226

Arvidsson, Eugenio, 177, 186

Bolivia: Health Ministry, 150, 155; revolution of 1952, 19, 233

Bond, Andrea, 271

Bump, Don (Rev.), 86

Bushway, Deb, 108–111, 269; see also Kotcher, Deb

Bushway, Isabel, 108, 269

Canata, 30, 154

Candelaria, see Hacienda Candelaria

Caterpillar Foundation, 273

Catholic Relief Services (CRS), 118–19

Centro de Entrenamiento Agro-ecológico (Center for Ecological Agriculture or CEA), see Mano a Mano International

Centro Médico (clinic), 97, 101, 109, 119, 123, 128–31, 135

Chullpa K'asa, see Medical clinics

Cochabamba, *175*; ix, 7, 29, 56, 63, 93, 207, 241

Crowley, Terry (Crowley, White & Associates), 139, 246

Dallavalle, Dana, 247–54, 270–71

Index

Dockry, Carmen Paredes, *255*; 254

Education, *164*; 162–65, 172; school, Ucuchi, 205

El Palmar, *see* Road construction

Foxen, Ann (White) (Mrs. John), 103, 110, 113

Foxen, John (Dr.), 110, 113, 246

German NGO, 238–39

Gillette Children's Hospital, St. Paul, 44

Grants, 62, 141, 147, 149, 151, 180, 213, 252

Great Depression, 1930s, 39

Green, Ellen, x

Grillo, César, 16

Guevara, Carlos Moises (Dr.), 156

Guevara, Che, 65

Hills, MN, 41

Hacienda Candelaria, *281–83*, 7, 22, 280–83; *see also* Laguna Sulti

Irusta, Acensia, *12*; 9–18, 21, 25, 29, 82

Irusta, Juanita, *see* Montaño, Juanita

Jusk'u Molle, *see* Sanitation facilities/reservoirs

Knatterud–Hubinger, Nate, *255*; 169–71, 247, 249–54, 270

Knatterud–Johnson, Emma, 253

Kotcher, Deb, 107–111, 140, 246, 252, 269; *see also* Bushway, Deb

Laguna Sulti, 9, 22, 25, 28, 67, 214, 277, 279, 281, 285; *see also* Medical clinics; Sanitation facilities/reservoirs

Lazano, Jorge, 182

Lopez, Edwin, 190

Lored Foundation, St. Paul, 195

López, Cristian, *196*

Luis, Jóse, *196*

Lundgren, Bob, 229–31, 234–35

Macalester College, St. Paul, 51

MacRae, Gloria, *125*; 53, 72, 86, 110, 122–25, 140, 145, 246, 269

Mamani, Tito, 164

Mano a Mano Apoyo Aéreo, *178*; ix, 176–77, 179, 187–95, 204, 215, 226, 247, 250, 275

Mano a Mano (Bolivia), 141–43, 146, 150–54, 177, 185, 189; *see also* Education; Mano a Mano Apoyo Aéreo; Mano a Mano Nuevo Mundo; Mano a Mano Internacional; Medical clinics; Sanitation facilities

Mano a Mano (USA), ix, x, 111, 142, 185, 186; board of directors, 116, 144, 247; interns, 253, 262; Medical Resources, 111, 117, 254; money transfers, 152; office, 251–52; partnerships, 117; schools, *138*; volunteers, 113–14, 131, 197, 229; *see also* Mano a Mano Apoyo Aéreo; Grants

Mano a Mano Internacional, 258; CEA training center, 263–67; El Abra property, 261–66; greenhouses, 267–69

Mano a Mano International, 254, 258, logo, *244*

Mano a Mano Nuevo Mundo, 177, 199, 204, 212, 222, 225, 229, 234, 237, 247, 261 Martin, Mary, x, *300*

Martínez, Ben Samuel, 255

Martínez, Blanca (Velásquez), *24, 95, 218, 258, 285*; 82, 97, 108, 127, 130, 142, 174, 186, 189, 211, 215, 255–59, 261–65; marriage, 255

Martínez, Israel, 230, 255

Martínez, Ivo Daniel, *193, 196, 274*; 191, 193–94, 215, 255, 284–85

Martínez, Van Miguel (Vanchi), 211, 235–40, 255

Matías, German, 137, 141, 163

McClure, Michael, 246

Medical clinics, 172; Beni, 180–83; Campo Via, 143, 146, 161; Campo Vibora, 165; Chullpa K'asa, 132–35, 141; Clinica Gloria, 125, 128, 129; Jironkota, 267; Laguna Sulti, 145, 147, 209, 213; Lope Mendoza, 143; Omereque, 226; staff training/ workshops, 155–58; Tablas Monte, 145

Misión Sueca Libra, *see* Swedish Free Mission

Moe, John H. (Dr.), 45–47

Molle Molle, 127

Monnens, Becky, 169–70

Montaño, Eloy, 271–273

Montaño, Primitivo (Primo), 209–210, 212, 273–74, 277, 285

Montaño, Juanita (Irusta) (Mrs. Juandelo), 9, 13, 25, 29, 82, 90, 92

Morales, Evo (Pres., Bolivia), 226, 227, 239

Narr, Daniel, 170–72, 247, 249–54, 257, 270

Nelson, Dianne, *see* Van Goor, Dianne

Nuevo Mundo, *see* Mano a Mano Nuevo Mundo

Nord, Mary Ann, x

Omereque, 219–27, 241

Ortuño, Victor Hugo (Dr.), 156–59, 181–84

Paz, Edgar, 65

Petzoldt, Mark, 113–14, 246

Primero de Mayo, 127

Punata, ix, 239

Quechua, ix, 18–19, 30, 148, 159

Ramirez, Luisa (Dr.), 159–60

Reservoirs, *see* Sanitation facilities/ reservoirs

Road construction, *228*; 27, 177, 179, 199–205, 225, 227; El Palmar, 199, 229, 275; Omereque, 222–24

Rock County Welfare Board, 50

Rodriguez, Boris, 263

Rojas, Tomas, 241

Rotary International, 212

Index

Saavedra, Nemecio, 181–183
St. Mary's Hospital, 45
St. Paul Rotary, 212
Sancayani, *frontispiece, 260*; 236, 240, 272–73
Sanitation facilities/reservoirs, *168*; 161–62, 172; Jusk'u Molle, 168, 218, 241; Laguna Sulti, 208, 210–14; Pachaj K'ocha, *240*; 229–31, 233, 235–36, 238–40; Sallamani Chico, 236, 241; Sallamani Grande, 236; Sancayani project, 240; Ucuchi, *207*; 206–207, 212
Sauter, Jerry, 112, 246
Scholten, Margaret (Swanson) (Mrs. Mike), 39–40
Scholten, Mike, 40
Singher, Margi, 229–32, 234–35, 246
Sisters of Charity, 181, 183, 191
Skrief, Charles, 271
Slettom, Jeanyne (Mrs. John), 142
Slettom, John, 140–41, 147–51, 203
Smith, Fred, viii
Solis, Marcelino, 226
Suárez, Aida, 152–54
Suárez, Jorge, 182–83
Swanson, Arnold, *38*; 39–47, 51
Swanson cousins, *41*
Swanson, Joan, *see* Velásquez, Joan
Swanson, Margaret, *see* Scholten, Margaret
Swanson, Stella (Scholten) (Mrs. Arnold), *38*; 40–47, 50-52, 621; marriage, 1936, 40
Swedish Free Mission (Misión Sueca Libra), 180, 184, 186

U.S. Agency for International Development (USAID), 117, 119
U.S. Alliance for Progress, 62
Unity Church–Unitarian, 114, 144
Urey, Alonzo, 10
Urey, Elena (Patrona), 8, 14–16, 18, 21, 28, 67
Urey, Luciano, 10, 15; death, 13
Urey, Rosendo (Patrón), 10–12; death, 12
Uyuni, 11, 55

Valley Springs, SD, 39
Van Goor, Dianne (Nelson), 43, 48–51
Velásquez, Alberto, *274*; 208–210
Velásquez, Blanca, *see* Martinez, Blanca
Velásquez, Catalina (Cati), *24*; 8, 18, 67, 73–74, 77, 81, 284; death, 84
Velásquez, César, *24, 78*; 77–78, 81, 83, 86, 245
Velásquez,, Cinthia (Mrs. José), 142–43
Velásquez, Epifanio, *6, 24*; 7–9, 17–23, 25–34, 67, 76, 82, 89, 126, 271; apartment building, 93, 96 ; death, 271; tile making, 32; water sales, 33
Velásquez, Inés (Irusta) (Mrs. Epifanio), *6, 24, 35, 95, 276, 282, 285*; ix, 7–9, 12–14, 17–23, 37, 67, 76, 89, 210, 256–57, 277–84; market stand, 34; marriage, 17

Velásquez, Ivo, *24, 198, 218*; 8, 18, 27, 67, 82–83, 92, 96, 120, 126, 130, 142, 151, 154, 163, 172, 186, 205, 215, 222, 245, 250, 270–71, 284; *see also* Mano a Mano Apoyo Aéreo

Velásquez, Joan (Swanson White) (Mrs. Segundo) (1941–), *2, 49, 58, 78, 80, 88, 102*; 3, 245; daycare center, 61; education, 51–52; marriage, 51, 53, 85; Peace Corps, 53–56, 59, 68; polio, 40–49; postpolio syndrome, 85, 99; social worker, 53, 77, 87

Velásquez, José (Dr.), *24, 143*; 21, 67, 82, 97, 110, 119, 130, 139, 142, 151, 161, 172, 186, 250, 284; *see also* Centro Médico

Velásquez, Julio, 253

Velásquez, Margarita (Margui), *24*; 25, 82, 86, 88, 90, 245

Velásquez, Rubén, *24*; 82, 86, 211, 245

Velásquez, Segundo, (1951–) *24, 69, 80, 106, 125, 143, 198, 240, 274*; 3, 18, 25, 28, 36–37, 59, 62, 245, 284; aviation training/work, 75, 77, 85, 91, 97, 115; education, 70, 74, 98; marriage, 85; move to St. Paul, 66

Ver Ploeg, Chris, 111–12, 122, 140, 204, 246, 252, 269–70

Vigil, Marilyn, x

Wagner, Bobbie (Mrs. Dick), 116, 180, 187, 195–97

Wagner, Dick, 115–16, 180, 184–87, 194–97; death, 197; Foundation, 180, 183, 185, 186, 188, 190, 197

Weyerhaeuser Family Foundation, 140

White, Ann, *see* Foxen, Ann

White, Dan, 78

White, David, 51–56, 59–65, 68, 71–73

White, Emily, 72

White, John, 78

White, Mary, 73–74, 77, 86

White, Nancy (White), 113, 169, 246, 269

White, Roy, 113

Wiedmeyer, Ray, 254

Yackel Foundation, 206

Yavira, Camila, 267–69

Author Mary Martin, above taking notes in Bolivia, otherwise makes her home in Minneapolis.